Julie Newton.
November 2004

The Power of the Tale

The Power of the Tale

Using Narratives for Organisational Success

Julie Allan, Gerard Fairtlough and
Barbara Heinzen

JOHN WILEY & SONS, LTD

Published in 2002 by John Wiley & Sons, Ltd,
Baffins Lane, Chichester,
West Sussex PO19 1UD, England

National 01243 779777
International (+44) 1243 779777
e-mail (for orders and customer service enquiries):
cs-books@wiley.co.uk
Visit our Home Page on http://www.wiley.co.uk
or http://www.wiley.com

Other Wiley Editorial Offices

John Wiley & Sons, Inc., 605 Third Avenue,
New York, NY 10158-0012, USA

WILEY-VCH Verlag GmbH, Pappelallee 3,
D-69469 Weinheim, Germany

John Wiley & Sons Australia Ltd, 33 Park Road, Milton,
Queensland 4064, Australia

John Wiley & Sons (Asia) Pte Ltd, 2 Clementi Loop #02-01,
Jin Xing Distripark, Singapore 129809

John Wiley & Sons (Canada) Ltd, 22 Worcester Road,
Rexdale, Ontario M9W 1L1, Canada

British Library Cataloguing in Publication Data

A catalogue record for this book is available from the British Library

ISBN 0-470-84227-X

Typeset in 12/14pt Goudy by Footnote Graphics, Warminster, Wiltshire.
Printed and bound in Great Britain by T.J. International Ltd, Padstow, Cornwall.
This book is printed on acid-free paper responsibly manufactured from sustainable forestry, in which at
least two trees are planted for each one used for paper production.

Dedication

We dedicate this book to the memory of Don Michael, a much loved friend and mentor to Gerard Fairtlough and Barbara Heinzen.

Contents

Acknowledgements

As part of her programme on complexity and organisational learning at the London School of Economics, Eve Mitleton-Kelly brought to London a dazzling series of complexity stars to present their work. She also introduced two of us to each other. Gerard and Julie went on to run workshops for the complexity programme and to develop the complexity game, educating people about complexity ideas while they were enjoying themselves.

A different pair of us (Gerard and Barbara) greatly benefited from working with Julia Rowntree at LIFT in her pioneering work in the LIFT Business/Arts Forum. This developed managers' skills and abilities through the theatre, again while enjoying themselves. Julia also contributed to and reviewed Chapter 7 of this book. And it was exciting to work with Rose Fenton, Lucy Neal and Tony Fegan at LIFT. We thank all these people for their inspiration and friendship.

Julie Allan would like to thank the many generous people whose imaginations, stories and support are reflected in the existence of this book. First, the members of Kardia, her professional development peer group. Everybody should have one. Then Petruska Clarkson, as an honoured representative of all those who have lent her the spirit of Cheiron. Sue Hollingsworth, Ashley Ramsden and Bernard Kelly, for their talent and generosity, and as representatives of the wide-ranging and wonderful company of story-tellers by whom we are surrounded. Pat Beatson, Gillie Bolton, Adi Forman, Deirdre Haslam, Geoff Merchant, Noreen Howard and Guy Lubitsh for words or deeds of wisdom and encouragement.

Julie also thanks Mr and Mrs John Allan for, among other things, food, shelter and space away from distractions. And Richard Molland, without whom she'd be impossible.

Barbara and Gerard thank Arie de Geus, who has been a great support to us while writing this book. His wisdom and his championing of the learning organisation has taught us a great deal. Napier Collyns was a generous source of good counsel on authorship. And we remember with the greatest affection our friend, the brave and far-sighted Don Michael, who sadly died while we were writing the book. Others who have helped us include Lisa Fairtlough, Mike Walker and Bill Colquhoun.

We were fortunate to have Diane Taylor as our editor. As a senior editor at John Wiley and Sons, she has a superb set of books to her credit. We thank her and her colleagues at Wiley for publishing our book and telling us how to improve it.

We are grateful to Linzi Mason for her dedicated editorial support.

The authors may be contacted via their website at:
www.wileyeurope.com/go/allan

Icons

Two icons are used in this book:

indicates that the work of the author cited in the text is discussed at greater length in Chapter 9.

indicates that Chapter 10 has a practical exercise relevant to the situation described in the text.

1

Stories in Action

People learn from stories in a different way from the way they learn from generalities. When I'm writing I often start out with abstractions and academic jargon, and purge it. The red pencil goes through page after page, while I try to make sure that the stories and examples remain to carry the kernel of the ideas, and in the process the ideas become more nuanced, less cut and dried.

Mary Catherine Bateson (Personal Communication)

In this chapter we show why story-telling has such a strong influence in organisations, how it works, what different kinds of stories there are, and discuss the various ways of creating stories. We also give an outline of the rest of the book.

The collection of stories known as *The Thousand and One Nights*, or *The Arabian Entertainments*, includes tales from India and Persia as well as from Arabia. The collection is framed by a story of stories that tells of Scheherazade, the daughter of King Shahriyar's vizier.

The king had a horrible habit of marrying a woman, spending one night with her and then having her killed the next morning. Scheherazade managed to escape this fate by telling the king stories, always stopping at a vital point and promising to continue the next night. The king was so keen to learn what happened next that he slept with her night after night. In this way, Scheherazade saved her life each night for 1001 nights. By then, the king was so captivated by her cleverness and courage that he gave up his wife-killing habits. They lived happily ever after – in Scheherazade's case, as happily as she could as the wife of a brute like King Shahriyar!

The Thousand and One Nights is a fantasy that has gripped the imaginations of generations all over the world. It has inspired many re-tellings, including Rimsky-Korsakov's musical version. Some of the individual tales are well known in themselves, such as that of Sinbad's adventures. Its depiction of a woman's sustained bravery, resourcefulness and creativity is powerful. Also, it has power as a story about stories.

Although, thank goodness, most story-telling is not a matter of life and death, *The Thousand and One Nights* symbolises the role of the story in human affairs. Among family and friends, in entertainment of all kinds, in politics and in many other spheres of society, the story is relevant. This book is about the equally vital role of stories in organisations of all types – business, government and non-governmental.

In *Hamlet,* Shakespeare showed how the story of a murder, told in a play within the play, could be used to discover a real murderer. Hamlet suspected that his father been killed by Claudius, who by doing so was able to become King of Denmark in Hamlet's father's place. Hamlet arranged for a troupe of players to enact a murder scene. Preparing for the play Hamlet said: 'The play's the thing, wherein I'll catch the conscience of the king'. Claudius's emotional reaction to the play convinced Hamlet that his suspicions were right.

Before human beings learned how to read and write, story-telling was the medium of collective memory. The stereotypical scene is of the tribe around the fire, listening to Homeric epics or Norse sagas. The rhythmic poetry, the evocative language, the communal setting and the skills of the venerable teller burn the tale into the minds of the younger listeners. Well, something like that, anyway. No doubt this stereotype is only partly accurate, since in pre-literate societies story-telling probably appeared in many more situations than just the fireside gathering. During routine tasks, mothers would sing and tell stories to their children. Hunting, collecting things in the forest and early agriculture would be taught through stories as well as by example.

Aesop's fables, Christian parables, innumerable rhymes and songs – these are more examples of the power of the tale. Story-telling works because the human brain finds it user-friendly. Young children, who are of course pre-literate humans, learn through stories, whether these are classic fairy-tales or new tales.

Bruno Bettelheim's view of fairy-tales was that they help a child to make coherent sense of his feelings and thoughts about the world, so as to develop the inner resources needed to cope. Examples are *The Three Feathers*, which starts with the king contemplating his death, Hansel and Gretel's dangerous journey, and the many other stories in which challenges are met and problems overcome. Bettelheim suggests that these tales help children to deal well with the difficulties intrinsic to human existence. While Bettelheim's concern was primarily with children's development, many of the themes are applicable to the adult who has the capacity to address the metaphorical and symbolic transmission of wisdom. As Bettelheim writes in *The Uses of Enchantment* (1991, p. 26):

> Some fairy and folk stories evolved out of myths; others were incorporated into them. Both forms embodied the cumulative experience of a society as men wished to recall past wisdom for themselves and transmit it to future generations. These tales are the purveyors of deep insights that have sustained mankind through the long vicissitudes of its existence. . . .

Resistance to Story-Telling

Despite the advantages of story-telling, listed above, there is often resistance to the use of stories, for the following reasons:

- The tradition in organisations is 'the drier the better'. Arguments must appear to be fact-based and objective. Bias must be concealed. Quantification is highly regarded, even for things that are actually pretty hard to quantify, like intellectual capital or emotional intelligence.
- Time is limited and people's energies are mostly absorbed by their day-to-day tasks. So attempts to enhance an organisation's learning capacity often meet with fatigue. 'Please, no more flip-charts', is a frequent response. Story-telling gets lumped in with other, more ponderous approaches, when in fact it is simple, flexible and friendly.
- An organisation that knows how to improve current activities may not also be good at more radical learning. Success in shorter-term learning may inhibit 'thinking out of the box', which is necessary for long term learning.

- Narratives usually engage the emotions, which can make story-telling seem frightening.
- Knowledge is often considered to be one vast database, and once you have the means to access this, your knowledge is complete. We believe this is a very limited way of looking at knowledge. Much of what makes up knowledge is constructed by the interaction between the knower and the world.

Because of resistances like these, conscious attempts to tell stories in organisations may be dismissed as 'the latest managment fad', even by those who themselves love telling gossipy tales in the pub after work. A story-teller may be told she is trying to be clever. Listeners may be told they are naive to spend their time listening to stories.

Our book will provide guidance for using stories to overcome these barriers and to achieve a wider set of goals. Using stories will:

- expand the range of perspectives on an issue, beyond the pseudo-factual perspective usually employed. This produces a richer picture and creates negotiated and shared meaning as part of learning;
- grab people's attention, quickly and economically. Narratives work better than other ways of stimulating learning, because they are a central part of human intelligence;
- work on the imagination, in order to generate creativity in an organisation;
- surface suppressed emotions which are dangerous in organisation life. Story-telling is a safe way to do this;
- tap into powerful areas of cognitive capacity in the brain. Organisations operate in an increasingly complex world. Attempts to make sense of such a world by using fact-based, cause-and-effect logic often fail because of the vast number of interactions and feedback loops that have to be taken into account.

When stories are used confidently and consistently, cynicism dies away. An example we give in Chapter 2 shows how growing confidence in the use of story-telling helped a management team to think constructively about a future that was teeming with opportunities and threats. Another example, given in Chapter 3, shows how a bold and skilful story-teller was able to get a difficult change programme back on track. At IBM, the knowledge management programme became increasingly dedicated to story-telling, as a team led by Dave Snowden developed a range of story-telling aids and techniques (described in Chapter 9). These techniques are now being widely applied by that company. Box 1.1 gives an example of story-telling in a society that suppresses the flow of information. These examples show that the cynics are wrong – story-telling really is effective.

The aims of this book are to show why stories are so important in organisations, to show individual readers how they can benefit from story-telling as a regular practice, and to help readers develop their own story-telling skills.

BOX 1.1   Radio Trottoir

In the mid-1980s, a group of academics met in London to discuss a phenomenon they had noticed in Francophone Africa: 'Radio Trottoir', or sidewalk radio. Radio Trottoir was something that had become increasingly important in politics and had been created out of two strong features of African society: a highly controlled press and a long tradition of story-telling. Because people could not get accurate news about political developments from the media, gossip took the place of published news. In order to make an item of gossip credible the speaker needed to trace the source of his information, which might be something like, 'My wife's cousin is the driver to the Minister of Finance and he heard that. . .' Sometimes the news on Radio Trottoir was completely accurate; at other times it was rumour stimulated to achieve a particular purpose; at other times it was simply wrong. No one ever knew which was the case. However, equally, no one could afford to ignore the news on Radio Trottoir. The academics even reported that government officials had been known to circulate counter-rumours whenever some item on Radio Trottoir was giving them particular trouble.

How Story-Telling Works its Magic

Although there are several ingredients in the magic spell, first and foremost stories work because they are memorable. Most people find it difficult to remember a list of more than seven items; but tell a well-made story and your listeners will be able to recount the tale effortlessly, with twenty or more events. Stories are memorable because their structure is like life. In a story, events unfold much as they do when you live through them. We all know how films, plays and books can grip the imagination. They seem real. Human memory seems to treat a story as if it were real life.

Should you doubt the magic effect of stories, think of this. You hear a story at a party. It is such a good story that you ignore the surrounding chatter, you leave your glass of wine untouched and you stop thinking about the attractive stranger standing next to you. The next evening you go to another party and, without premeditation, you launch into the story you heard the night before, creating the same rapt circle of listeners, with the same intent expressions on their faces. Why were you able you perform this feat? Because you were able to remember the story effortlessly and could therefore tell it in an exciting way. And it won't only be you who tells the tale. Before long you will hear the same story told by someone else. Good stories spread quickly. As human beings, we all need to make sense of what is happening around us, helping us to survive in changing conditions, and no doubt we have mental equipment devoted to sensemaking. Sensemaking, or construing, could be seen as telling ourselves stories. Listening to our own stories may be much the same as listening to other people's. Story-telling seems to be part of our mental equipment.

As well as being memorable, stories are economical. Since stories engage the listeners' and readers' minds, not everything has to be spelled out. The hearer works on the story, imagining details of his own as the narrative develops, just as the story-teller adds details of her own during her particular telling of the tale. To use the language of information theory, there is redundancy in stories which helps the receiver fill in a gap in the message. A gap may be due to a lapse in the listener's attention, or it might be that the story-teller inadvertently omits a piece of the story that she had planned to include, or that she had included when she told the story on previous occasions. In any case, there is usually no such thing as a 'complete' story. The sender can therefore change the message slightly, without harming its intelligibility or losing the receiver's attention. In an organisation with plenty of shared language and shared mental models, abbreviation can be extensive. There may be no time for more than a rapid-fire anecdote, but if the organisation has a tradition of story-telling plus lots of shared concepts, this may be a highly effective communication.

A story, with its more-or-less continuous narrative, actively engages the sensemaking faculties of listeners, making the story memorable and, when necessary, making it more economical than other ways of transmitting information. With a story, sensemaking by the listener is much stronger than when a list of items is simply read out. This active engagement of listeners has further advantages beyond being memorable and economical. By activating listeners' imaginations, their creative faculties become aroused.

Art and Emotions

Most northern European and North American organisations have cultures that severely limit any reference to the emotions of the people involved. The cultural norm is that there is a job to be done and personal feelings only get in the way. Of course, many people do feel strongly about their work, or about some aspects of it, at least. They love or hate various tasks they have to do. They love or hate their bosses, their immediate colleagues, or people in other parts of the organisation. Turf wars, resentment towards people in power, commitment to the goals of a sub-unit at the expense of the goals of the organisation as a whole – all of these are familiar and all have a strong emotional component.

In organisations whose official line is that feelings just hamper objective decision-making, people do have feelings all the same. But they are concealed feelings. So tensions build up, communications are a sham and poor decisions get made. For instance, competent people get fired, damaging the organisation's capabilities, because that seems the only way to deal with endemic, concealed conflict. The victim is the group's scapegoat and, since no real change has occurred, it won't be long before another scapegoat needs to be sacrificed, and so on. So most organisations would benefit from new ways to handle emotion. Greater skill in interpersonal processes helps a lot. And so does a well-established habit of story-telling, a particular interpersonal process in its own right.

The more skilled the teller, the more likely the listener is to absorb the emotional content of a story in a constructive way. That is one reason why a story should be entertaining, why there should be art in its telling. And finally, listening to stories develops our capacity to listen and learn from stories, making us a more receptive audience, which increases the overall impact of story-telling.

Sensemaking

Story-telling encourages people to think widely. The details that add interest and verisimilitude to a narrative are stimulants for the imagination. An analytical approach directs attention to quantifiable or data-related aspects of a problem. A narrative approach directs attention to simpler matters, to less precise ones, to those that may have been forgotten or repressed. Patterns start to be recognised amidst the surrounding tumult. And generally story-telling is more fun than analysis. Later in this chapter we make the point that stories ought always to be entertaining.

If a group gets stuck when trying to understand a difficult situation, it can try telling stories about various aspects of it. Gradually the situation as a whole becomes clearer. The members of the group start to make sense of what is happening, and become more confident about what they should be doing.

Complexity

Many organisations see that at the start of the twenty-first century they are immersed in complexity, uncertainty and rapid change. There is often little or no time for elaborate studies and, in any case, an analysis of a really complex problem can never be complete because there is too much that will always remain unknown. Nevertheless, action has to be taken, often quickly, and usually with others, which puts a premium on organisational learning. This is learning that must be shared and known to be shared by other organisation members – otherwise it would merely be an aggregation of individual learnings. Such shared learning determines an organisation's culture and helps it to evolve over time. A static culture is a potential disaster, deadening the ability to change, to do new things and to innovate.

In this dynamic situation, a flow of insightful, witty, memorable tales, shared among many organisation members, becomes part of the evolving culture of the organisation. They promote speedy comprehension, effective dialogue, humane values and good judgement. Stories are not a nice-to-have embellishment; rather, they are a vital resource for getting the right things done. They evolve gracefully over time, as different speakers and audiences use stories, and as the organisation changes. Stories and an organisation's culture co-evolve.

Respect for People

Even in an organisation that has an established culture of story-telling, there will no doubt still be cynics – of two different kinds. The first kind says, 'Yes, stories work, but who do they benefit? Only those at the top of the organisation, who now have yet another way of controlling and manipulating everyone else? Or do they benefit only the skilled tellers of tales, putting the less skilled at a disadvantage?' These are genuine fears. However, the power of the tale is less easy to misuse than other ways of communicating or sharing information. The nature of story-telling pushes the teller to think of the listener or the reader as a fellow human being, since failing to do this makes the story less effective. And although an expert teller of tales should be honoured for this skill, the practice of story-telling is natural to us all, making the emergence of any kind of elite group of tellers unlikely.

The second kind of cynic says, 'Yes, stories work, but should they be used everywhere? Don't analytical techniques and quantitiative methods still have their place? Must everything be done through the 'soft' practice of story-telling?' The answer to this is: of course stories should not be the only tools for appraising situations and for disseminating knowledge. Organisations must go on using the old methods alongside the new ones, picking the ones that are best for the particular task in hand. But the world is getting more complex and more interconnected, which will mean story-telling will be useful in more and more situations.

Luigi Pirandello's *Six Characters in Search of an Author* (1954) is a play famous for its multiple perspectives on fact and fiction. One of the six characters says: 'But a fact is like a sack. When it's empty it won't stand up. And in order to make it stand up you must first of all pour into it all the reasons and all the feelings that have caused it to exist.' Talking about the reality of personality, the same character says: '. . . each one of us believes himself to be a single person. But it's not true. Each one of us is many persons . . . With some people we are one person. With others we are somebody quite different. And all the time we are under the illusion of always being one and the same person for everybody . . . But it's not true! It's not true!' And again: '. . . it would be as well if you mistrusted your own reality . . . Because like the reality of yesterday, it is fated to reveal itself as a mere illusion tomorrow' (pp. 24–25, 57).

Story-telling like Pirandello's recognises the complexity of human personality and relationships. It makes us attend to other people, to understand them more profoundly; and frequently to respect them more, since to understand all is to forgive all. Box 1.2 lists the reasons why stories work.

BOX 1.2   Why Stories Work

Stories are: memorable
                     economical
                     entertaining
                     centred on people

and they: encourage creativity
                     help in handling emotion
                     help to make sense of puzzling situations
                     co-evolve with an organisation's culture.

Types of Narrative

The most useful way to classify a group of things depends on how you use those things. No classification is absolutely right or wrong. Not everyone will like the classification of types of narrative we propose below, although we think it is a relevant typology for stories told in organisations. Different dictionaries tell slightly different stories about the word 'story'. The same applies to the word 'tale', which is almost synonymous with 'story', but not quite.

Reality

One way of classifying stories is on the basis of how real they seem to those who hear or read them. The course of a person's life can validly be called his 'story'. So can a description of a particular incident, for example in a witness statement taken for legal purposes. These two kinds of story are supposed to be factual and will indeed often be judged to be 'real' or 'true'. Then there is the story as 'a narrative of incidents in their sequence' (Chambers Dictionary definition), in which the incidents can be either fact or fiction. Next is the story as fiction, clearly understood as such. Although, by definition, fiction is not real, there can nevertheless be extremely realistic fiction, while some other fiction is the kind no one could take for real. Finally there is the meaning of 'story' as 'lie', as in: 'That's a likely story!'

So we can construct a descriptive scale for different kinds of story, like this:

Real   **Unreal**

Factual account ↔ Legend ↔ Myth ↔ Fiction ↔ Fantasy

Legends are generally accepted as being true, albeit sometimes exaggerated. Myths are stories whose truth is accepted by some people and not by others, and also stories which everyone used to believe, but whose veracity is now questioned. Perhaps 'tales' and 'yarns' tend towards the (unreal) end of this scale of stories, as shown by the phrase 'telling tales', meaning 'telling lies'. However, stories that fall right across the scale can be told in organisations, to good effect.

The real–unreal scale is not the same as true–untrue. First, to say that a story is untrue carries the implication that the teller hoped you would believe it was true, even though it wasn't. Second, a story can be far removed from reality but still have a truth of its own. Bettelheim investigated how children perceived fairy stories, and found that generally they knew perfectly well that magic wands and flying broomsticks did not exist. All the same, certain fairy stories were true for these children, because the stories illustrated psychological truths they recognised or were beginning to understand.

Yiannis Gabriel's valuable study *Storytelling in Organizations* (2000), makes the point that story-telling ought to be truthful either to the 'facts' or to the 'meaning' it has for the listener.

Completeness

We agree with Gabriel when he says that, in an organisational setting, not all narratives are stories. He draws a line between proper stories and short narratives about a situation or a person which cannot be dignified with the name 'story', although they can be useful in helping people make sense of a situation. He calls the latter kind 'opinions' or 'proto-stories'. Gabriel also considers that purely factual narratives might better be called 'accounts' or 'reports', even though in everyday speech they would often be called 'stories'. We could simply call them remarks.

In this book we will be telling a lot of stories, real and unreal. Most of them will be told as sets of stories centred around a common situation, usually around a single organisation, and around a situation that changes over time. We need a term to describe sets of stories like this, and we will use 'history' as the term, without any suggestion that the stories told must be factual ones. On this basis, *The Thousand and One Nights* is a history, since it is a narrative that includes a lot of stories – 1001 of them, in fact.

This leads us to another scale for describing narratives, as follows:

Fragmentary   **Comprehensive**

Remarks ↔ Proto-stories ↔ Stories ↔ Histories

Entertainment

Gabriel claims that a distinguishing feature of stories is that they are entertaining. We would agree, provided that 'entertaining' means other things besides 'amusing' or 'diverting'. Stories can also be absorbing or engaging. They may also do things like provide moral education, advice or a warning, but for Gabriel a narrative is not a story unless it is gripping, funny, tragic or romantic. Thus a story must be capable of being judged as art, and its teller as an artist. Again we agree with this. Stories need not be 'great art' – they usually aren't – but they must be a bit artful.

This does not mean that stories have to be original. Linda Putnam and her co-authors (1996) say that good stories ('good' in the sense of being genuinely entertaining) are often familar ones, such as fairy stories or legends. They are entertaining because they give the satisfaction of fulfilled expectation; a sense of belonging over time and in different places. And there is art in the telling of a familar story. The tale can be adapted to different audiences, and may be abridged, extended or highlighted depending on the circumstances in which it is told. Audiences add to the tale with interruptions and laughter (p. 385). Box 1.3 explains the typology used in this book to categorise stories.

BOX 1.3   Dimensions for a Typology

The typology for narratives used in this book has three dimensions:

1. Real/unreal (which is not the same as true/untrue).
2. Fragmentary/comprehensive, which places stories along a scale from simple remarks to histories (which is what we call multiple stories based around a common situation).
3. Familar/novel (but in all cases a story should be entertaining).

Ways of Creating Stories

The council of a body giving grants for scientific research had a limited budget, most of which was committed to five projects. To find funds for new, innovative, work it was decided to reduce the grants to these projects. The five grant-holders were asked to submit plans for the future of their projects with reduced funding. Four out of the five responded that even a small cut would ruin their project. The fifth presented a plan that showed, although it would be very painful, they could still produce some good science if their grant was cut in half. At a meeting, most members of the council seemed ready to halve the grant to Project Five and leave the other grants unchanged.

Then one council member told a story. Imagine, he said, that you're the team leader at one of the first four projects. You argue to your team that accepting a cut of any size would admit the present level of support has some fat in it. You say we should tell the council that any cut will be devastating. Of course, there is a risk that if it's all or nothing, our whole grant may be withdrawn, but we can be sure that the council won't have the guts to close us down completely, as we're doing such good work. Now think about Project Five. That team was open about the possiblity of a radical cut to their budget. Why should we penalise them for their honesty? The council agreed, and found a fairer way to reduce the grants.

Why did a story alter the views of the council? Most members had themselves been leaders of similar projects so the story rang true. No doubt some of them had, in the past, made similar arguments about the impossibility of accepting a budget cut. The story made them accept that the Project Five team had been unusually honest. This was a story told on the spur of the moment to an audience the teller knew could empathise with it. It worked because it provoked a gut reaction from the listeners.

Following Etienne Wenger's term in his book *Communities of Practice* (1998), we can call this an 'emergent' story. It was a spontaneous tale, generated by the situation. Stories told in organisations are not all like this. Some are carefully thought through and refined. Again following Wenger, we can call these 'designed' stories. And not all tales are created by a single individual. For example, in scenario planning, dis-cussed in Chapter 8, scenario teams work together to construct stories about possible futures. This gives us a typology for story creation. On one axis (Box 1.4) is the distinction between emergent and designed stories, and on the other axis is the distinction between individual and collective story generation. Combining the two axes gives us four ways of creating stories. In thinking about stories, it is useful to be clear about which of these applies in your particular situation. But the four types are not mutually exclusive. Indeed, they combine very well.

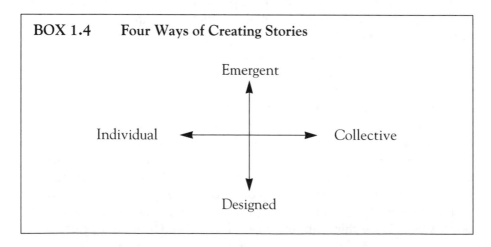

BOX 1.4   Four Ways of Creating Stories

Skills and habits learned through practice in one type of story creation are easily transferable to the others.

Story-Telling Skills

To be more than a simple narrative, a story should be entertaining – in the sense of being gripping, tragic, funny or romantic. The art that goes into inventing and recounting a tale gives it extra power. Of course, creators of tales need not aim to be Charles Dickens or Agatha Christie. But we can all improve our story-creation and story-telling skills. Rambling after-dinner speeches that bore or embarrass their audiences, and unfunny jokes or muffed punchlines are not necessary. They can be avoided with a little care and practice.

Today, many people in organisations receive training in the preparation of reports and in making presentations. For improving your presentation skills you don't need a three-year course at drama school, and you need not aim to become as persuasive as Henry Fonda was in *Twelve Angry Men* or Julia Roberts in *Erin Brokovich*. You can quickly learn how to organise a presentation so that its points are clearly made, its visual aids are simple and legible and your audience can hear you properly. We advocate a similar approach to improving your story-telling skills.

For individual, emergent stories, perhaps the best form of training is to watch how others do it. When you listen to someone whose stories hold your attention, watch how she does it. Watch for variations in pace and tone of voice. Watch for the pauses that both allow the teller to think of a good way of phrasing the next part of the tale and the listeners to absorb the last part. Listen carefully when someone you know is good at cracking jokes says, 'Have you heard this one?' Note how he makes an old chestnut worth listening to once again. Listen for the slight variations in each telling that make the joke particularly relevant to that day's audience. Watch his body language as well as listening to his words.

For individual, designed story-telling, you don't need a course in creative writing, but it is worthwhile paying attention to the various devices that help people remember the story. First, a repetitive structure. For instance, many fairy stories tell of similar feats performed in turn by three suitors (the first two fail, but the last succeeds). Second, alliteration and rhythmical form, particularly for spoken stories. Third, metaphors and symbols as story-telling elements. When reading the stories we tell throughout this book, it will be worth pausing to look at the structure and language of any story that seems to you to be particularly effective.

Here is a story still told today in the Czech Republic.

In 1940 the Germans were occupying a village in Bohemia. Their commander ordered his men to search all houses to make sure none of the villagers had any hidden arms. Three soldiers forced their way into one house. One searched the ground floor, turning out every cupboard in the kitchen. He found nothing. The second searched the bedroom floor, stripping the beds and turning out the drawers. He found nothing. The third soldier went up to the attic. At once he saw a gun in a corner. He waited a minute, went to the top of the stairs and shouted, 'There's nothing up here'. The soldiers then went away. In 1945, the Germans were retreating from the Russians. The soldier who had searched the attic in 1940 came to the same house, knocked at the door and asked for food and civilian clothes. He got these, dumped his uniform and went away, never to be seen again.

Like two of the suitors for the princess's hand, two of the soldiers behaved similarly, but the third does something different. This modern story has the form of a fairy-tale.

Generally, stories should be simple. When designing an individual story, you can do a triage of the things that you might include, classifying what you must tell, what you can tell when there is enough time and interest to embellish the story and what you should throw out because it is too detailed, too cumbersome or too obscure to be of interest to listeners and readers. Triage can also be used for collective stories (those that are designed by a group of people). Then you can think about what it is in a story that makes the reader keep wanting to turn the page. You can consider what, in an oral story, holds the listeners' interest. It's usually something that a reader or listener does not know. It might be a conflict between two people unresolved until near the end of the tale. It might be a mysterious situation, with a vague threat that could go away or might turn really nasty. A good story leaves something hidden until the very end.

Collective, emergent stories are frequently produced in workshops. Facilitators usually provide a device (like a collection of found objects or a common question) and ask everyone to use this device to create a story. They can also provide a framework that follows a simple plot line, such as the instructions for the Consequences game, which go like this: A female character meets a male character in such-and-such a place. She says to him . . . He says to her . . . The consequence is . . . These exercises stimulate the imagination, capture the collective creativity of the group and produce stories that pass the results on to others.

For all types of story you will find examples and exercises in every chapter. However, Chapter 10 is where practical exercises are gathered together. Whatever kind of story-telling you'd like to explore, there will be something for you in that chapter. Above all, learn on the job. The more stories you tell, the better you will tell them.

In this book we sometimes use 'story' as a verb. This is ancient usage in English, meaning 'to tell as a story' (Oxford English Dictionary).

Seven Histories

Following this introductory chapter are seven chapters (Chapters 2 to 8) each telling the history of a particular organisation. These chapters deal with story-telling as it relates to an important organisational practice. The seven histories and their practices are summarised in Box 1.5.

The first of the practices is communication, which to be really effective has to be multi-directional and interactive. This history is about a small but growing organisation, called M4 Technology, which uses story-telling for excellent communication.

BOX 1.5	Seven Histories	
Chapter	Organisation	Practice
2	M4 Technology	Communication
3	AutoCorp	Learning
4	Themis	Professional development
5	National Health Service	Resolving dilemmas
6	AutoCorp	Organisational evolution
7	LIFT	Innovation and collaboration
8	Kenya	Scenarios

The next history is about learning. Many organisations want to become learning organisations, but this is hard to do when an organisation operates with the old princples of command and control. The history in Chapter 3 is of a large organisation, called AutoCorp, that is trying to learn while retaining a strongly hierarchical structure. The history in Chapter 4 is about a group of professionals, called Themis, who use story-telling for the practice of personal and professional development. They develop their professional skills, share learning and pick up new tricks.The group itself is non-hierachical, but its members work almost entirely with hierarchical organisations.

All three of these organisations recognise established systems of control. M4 Technology has a hierarchy, centred round two charismatic founders, but it can learn because of its open style and skilled communication. AutoCorp struggles to learn and change in spite of its hierarchical constraints. Themis provides a space for its members to learn outside hierarchical situations, but they nearly always have to take hierarchies into account.

Chapter 5 describes the practice of dilemma resolution in the context of Britain's National Health Service (NHS). This chapter is a pivot between the earlier histories of learning in and around traditional organisations and the later histories that describe more complex, self-organising situations.

Chapter 6 takes another look at AutoCorp, this time in a history of a part of this large organisation, which is trying hard to evolve towards self-organised learning and change. The next history, Chapter 7, describes the London International Festival of Theatre (LIFT) and its practice of innovation. Innovation is the holy grail of many organisations today. We also show how stories can be vital in generating creativity and continuing innovation. The history of LIFT shows how stories help with collaboration across organisation boundaries, a practice now recognised as a source of innovation. In Chapter 8, the last of these histories, we show how stories can help in dealing with an uncertain future, through the practice of scenario planning on a national scale – in Kenya.

The Rest of the Book

Chapter 9 The Theory of Stories

In this chapter we describe some theoretical frameworks relevant to story-telling. People can use theory without knowing they are doing so; in fact, theories can be viewed as abstract stories about the world. Stories and theories are both items in the story-telling toolbox for people in organisations.

We describe the work of some of the thinkers who have particularly influenced our views on organisations and story-telling. Among other things we discuss metaphors and striking phrases, like 'the Golden Age' or 'the Red Queen', to show how the vivid language of metaphors creates precision, insight and memorable slogans. For readers who are short of time, this might be the chapter they choose to skip, unless they are keen to understand the intellectual background to the book.

Chapter 10 Tools and Techniques for Story Use

This chapter gathers together the various techniques for stimulating and improving story-telling, adding new ones to those described in previous chapters.

Chapter 11 The Future of Story-Telling in Organisations

This final chapter will summarise the lessons of the book, reviewing the ways in which story-telling can help organisational learning and discussing how to select the best approach for a particular situation. We will tell our own story – how our understanding of story-telling deepened during its writing. Finally, we will speculate about the future – where story-telling may go, and how its future may interact with the future shapes and roles of organisations.

What Readers Will Get from the Book

We hope that by reading this book you will develop your story-telling skills, and that you will learn from our examples of story-telling in a variety of settings and linked to varied practices. We hope you find useful the exercises and techniques we provide for generating good stories and for encouraging and developing the practice of story-telling in your organisation. We hope that you will gain a deeper understanding of the benefits that good story-telling can deliver, and that reading the book will change your views on organisation learning as a whole.

We hope, too, that you will be entertained by the stories we tell. Stories should be fun. Salman Rushdie's *Haroun and the Sea of Stories* is a modern story about stories. Haroun's father is a professional story-teller, with a seemingly never-ending stream of stories. Haroun asks his father where they all come from. 'From the great Story Sea,' he answers. But one day the source of these stories gets plugged. Haroun, with assistance from various characters, is able to remove the plug, leaving the source unblocked, so all the stories, even the oldest ones, now taste as good as new.

2

M4 Technology – Stories for Truth and Trust

It's the arrangement of events which makes the stories. It's throwing away, compressing, underlining. Hindsight can give structure to anything, but you have to be able to see it. Breathing, waking and sleeping: our lives are steamed and shaped into stories.

Carol Shields

This chapter is about real communication within an organisation, about practices that support it and about the role that stories play in making it trustworthy.

In several places in this chapter we tell stories about a business called M4 Technology plc. This is an imaginary firm, but its history is adapted from real-life situations. M4 Technology is a successful start-up company. Founded by a software designer called Peter Parsons and a businesswoman called Melissa Thorpe, in three years it has grown to an 80-person outfit. It has a good income from software development contracts with a handful of industry leaders around the world. Now M4 wants to raise capital, in an initial public offering (IPO) of its shares. The company wants the money in order to be able to produce its own software packages for general marketing. Following this fund-raising, it hopes to attract lots more talented technical staff, to go on working for its large customers and to release its own products as soon as they are ready for the market.

Melissa Thorpe, the CEO, has a reputation in the industry as a tough cookie, decisive and hard-driving. She holds monthly meetings of all staff at which she talks about the things – both good and bad – that have happened since the last meeting. Peter Parsons, the technical director, reports on M4's various projects. When a contract is secured there is a noisy cheer. When one is lost there is a sober discussion on what went wrong. Key decisions, like going public, are reviewed at some length. Policy developments are reported.

At one of the monthly meetings, Melissa announces her intention to pay bonuses to staff responsible for getting important contracts. 'These contracts are vital for our future cashflow,' she declares, 'and those who win them deserve recognition for this.'

'Wait a minute,' says a young software writer. 'It's our work that enables these deals to take place. It's the job of salespeople to sell, so why should they get special rewards just for doing their job? We don't.'

Melissa responds that in this industry salespeople expect bonuses. But that argument is not accepted.

'M4 isn't a typical company. This is a place where everyone works together. Don't destroy that by giving special treatment to one group of people.'

Melissa realises she's made a mistake. Her first reaction is to tough it out, because she doesn't want to demoralise the sales staff. Nor does she want to admit that she hadn't properly thought through her policy. But after a moment she says: 'OK. I'm probably wrong. Maybe any bonuses should be for everyone.'

This became a famous moment in M4's history, and a story that was told to people who joined the company after the event, as an example of the company's culture. From that small incident, and the stories that grew from it, M4's folklore now teaches that the CEO will listen to a sound argument and that company communication goes both ways, even when it means the boss gets egg on her face. The moment was never forgotten by those who were in the room.

So the organisation learned from the bonuses story, but what about Melissa? Before she and Peter Parsons started M4, she had worked in one of the Big Five consultancy firms. To make her mark in this competitive environment, she felt she had to adopt a no-nonsense style. She took decisions quickly. On key issues she always made her position very clear. She tried hard to avoid the weasel words that some of her colleagues used, in order that they might escape blame if things went wrong. She was polite, but very firm, about the things she expected from other people, and she let them know when she thought they had done a poor job. Melissa was respected by some people, and feared by others. In some ways, this style worked well at M4. In a start-up business there are endless things to be done, so speed and clarity are valuable. Melissa was a highly productive worker and people copied her no-nonsense approach. On the other hand, one of the reasons she had gone into the risky world of high-tech start-ups was her belief that most large, hierarchical organisations made bad use of the talents of the people who worked in them. She'd seen the harm dictatorial bosses could do.

The bonuses incident was therefore important for Melissa. It made her realise that the company had grown up. She no longer had to take all the decisions herself. Now there was time for consultation and careful thought. She knew that the story of the incident was being told in M4. It was a reminder to her that her own role was evolving as the business grew. In theory, she had always put a high value on listening to people. Now it was time to put this theory into practice.

Communication

Everyone talks about the importance of excellent communication within an organisation. For some, communication is a smart Website, regular newsletters or a jazzy slide show. For others, it is a manager's open door and plenty of management visibility. For others still, it is making available information, whether financial, environmental or people-related, often in voluminous annual reports, sometimes accompanied by solemn mission statements. All these can be valuable, especially when they are designed with specific audiences in mind. However, they do not necessarily promote open, multi-directional communication between all members of an organisation. For instance, professionalism in communication, usually such a good thing, can make non-professionals fearful of speaking because they feel they lack the skill to impart their messages effectively.

Most organisations now operate in highly interconnected situations. This makes it vital that every participant knows what the organisation is trying to achieve and what difficulties it is facing. Every participant may know important things his colleagues do not know, and may have bright ideas that haven't occured to the others. Therefore ineffective communication can cripple an organisation – any organisation. And communication that is inconsistent, manipulative or insincere will be ineffective. If listeners are cynical, bored or confused, they will not listen properly or respond to messages. Even if no lies are told, half-truths can be just as misleading and feed mistrust just as much. They stop people trying to understand what is actually going on or force them to rely on different channels of communication. However hard to achieve, the truth, the whole truth and nothing but the truth is the ideal for effective communication.

Gerard Fairtlough's book *Creative Compartments* (1994) shows how a consistent practice of openness creates trust.

Openness demonstrates that the person being open is willing to trust others. On encountering a trusting attitude, most people reciprocate with the same attitude. Likewise, when people encounter openness, they become more open themselves. Thus a virtuous circle develops, with openness building trust and trust reinforcing openness. The benefits for communication are enormous. When people know they can trust what they are told, they put their energies into understanding the message rather than wondering whether it is truthful or not. When openness is the norm, messages become more complete. Hidden agendas disappear.

The trust that truthfulness helps to create is also made more powerful through truthfulness of deed. In their book *The Soul at Work*, Roger Lewin and Birute Regine (1999) tell the story of Hatim's ride on a Honda. Hatim Tybaji was CEO of a rapidly growing high-technology company called VeriFone. His philosophy of care for others pervaded all that the company did. He cared for people working in the company, for business associates, for customers. And by his example, others in the company came to share his philosophy.

> On one occasion in Paris, during a downpour, Hatim couldn't get a taxi to drive 18 miles out of the city for a meeting. He couldn't leave the customer waiting and, instead of cancelling or disappointing the customer, he ended up going on a sales manager's 600cc Honda motorcycle. He arrived at his destination soaked but on time, which needless to say, impressed the customer. (p. 129)

An embedded practice of authenticity, truthfulness and openness, coupled with care and respect for others, works amazingly well. Lewin and Regine show why this is so. It works because in complex situations, effective relationships between individuals, teams and organisations are the only way to cope. What these authors call 'relational practice', the practice of authenticity and care, is demanding because it requires constant attention, even from those who wholly embrace its principles. But it is a great aid to success. Lewin and Regine recognise story-telling's big role in relational practice:

> The affiliative self is engaged by the narrative rather than the analytical mind. That means that to develop caring and connected relationships is to become genuinely interested in others and to invite conversations and engage people's stories . . . Engaging people's stories deepens the conversation and is a way of instigating the delicate work of building trust in an organisation . . . People's stories illuminate the diversity of their experience, challenge the plausibility of perspectives, and capture the flow of changing realities. (pp. 328–330)

This Chapter

The overall theme of this book is that stories are the best way to handle complexity, ambiguity, uncertainty and rapid change. In this chapter we show how story-telling relates to an underlying competence in communication. In exploring this, we take the view that truthfulness, openness and authenticity build trust, respect and care for others, and that virtuous circles can arise in which trust and truthfulness reinforce each other. Story-telling skill co-evolves with effective, multi-directional communication in and around an organisation. In short, the chapter describes how the power of the tale gets at the truth and nourishes trust.

In the following section we dig a bit deeper into the nature of authentic communication by looking at an influential theory of truth and trust. The subsequent sections describe six storying practices that enhance communication in organisations. The six practices overlap and interweave. A story that supports one practice could in many cases be equally useful for one of the others. A short concluding section then sums up the whole chapter.

A Theory of Truth and Trust

Barefaced lies may deceive people for a while, but are usually detected in the end. More common and more difficult to sort out are the concealing clouds of half-truths and distortions which are found in some organisations – and not only in organisations. Respect for politicians and for journalists is apparently at an all-time low in Western democracies. This may partly be due to particular scandals and cover-ups, but mostly it stems from a reaction to continuous news management and 'spinning' and from the selective use of statistics and sound bites. The public knows it is not being told the whole truth, but can't spot exactly what is wrong. The official line in an organisation may likewise be disbelieved without it being clear where it is faulty.

We should not be surprised at this. Even with maximum goodwill, it is hard to communicate truthfully. In complex situations nobody will know the complete truth, and even if someone gets close to knowing it, she may not be able to pass on that knowledge to others. Everyone makes simple mistakes, or fails to notice significant events, or misinterprets what is happening. Absolute truth is impossible and even approximate truth is elusive.

 So good communication is always difficult and always needs dedication and hard work. The German social theorist Jürgen Habermas, in his massive book *The Theory of Communicative Action* (1984), argues that speech would be impossible without an assumption that speakers are trying to be truthful. This is not being starry-eyed about the way human beings behave. Nor does it ignore the difficulty of getting at the truth. The argument is simply that the whole of our language is orientated towards finding and telling the truth. The way language is structured gives us a promise that, with enough effort, groups of people can achieve a reasonable degree of honest communication. Furthermore, as the practice of open communication develops, communication gets easier, as those involved become more competent in undistorted communication. Communicative competence must cover not only factual matters, but must also enable discussion about ethical and subjective matters. For full competence, we must learn how to communicate in all three areas – about facts, values and feelings.

How does story-telling contribute towards communicative competence? Because skilful, open communication in an organisation needs continued hard work, anything that makes the task easier is very valuable. Stories are much more memorable than more formal methods of communication and are often speedier to tell and easier to listen to. It is more fun to tell stories than to go through long lists of dos and don'ts. An equally important reason for using stories is that they so readily allow the teller to combine the three areas of communicative competence, that is, to talk about facts, values and feelings at the same time. It seems completely natural to mention a character's feelings when telling a tale, and in a well-constructed tale the value systems of the characters become clear through the telling. The very word 'character' has two meanings: it is someone who appears in a story and it is the distinctive collection of values and attributes a person possesses.

Box 2.1 contains an example of good, open communication in a meeting.

BOX 2.1 The Quakers

Geoffrey Vickers (1985) writes about the practice of the Quakers (the Society of Friends). By 'integrative solution' he means a conclusion reached through open and truthful communication.

> The most highly developed example known to me of the integrative process is the time-consuming but effective method by which the Society of Friends deals with its common business. Their procedure depends for its success not only on the belief that, given time and properly conducted dialogue, an integrative solution will emerge; but also an acceptance of the fact that time is indispensable to the process of restructuring reality systems and value systems, on which integrative solutions depend. (p. 209)

Here is a story about a particular Quaker Meeting.

It never ceased to amaze Mary the way Quakers fell into silence like other people fell into a swimming pool on a hot summer's day. Only twenty minutes ago she had arrived, frustrated by a day of office politics, to a house she had never visited before and nervous about her role this evening. It was her first Meeting as an Elder, and she was rather worried that she was a fraud.

She took a seat in the circle. Animated talk followed, about an argument at work and what had precipitated it, the problems of getting home in sufficient time to have something to eat before coming out again for the Meeting, about coping with a child's homework. The everyday stuff of being human, thought Mary.

Unlike most meetings she attended. Funny how the same word was used to denote two completely different activities.

'Well perhaps we'll make a start,' Martin, the convenor, suggested.

Instantly the group fell silent.

So much in just twenty minutes. Mary settled down and allowed her mind to become still. The silence was profound and she found herself feeling calmed and centred as she allowed herself to sink into it. Five minutes later, with no particular prompting, there was a general stir as people began to settle themselves for the task ahead. In a Meeting, agenda items were agreed at the start of the time together.

'I've put down a couple of things,' said Martin. 'I think we need to discuss whether we are going to meet up with the Overseers, since they have asked us for a joint meeting. And we also need to discuss the paper which was sent to us by Joyce about the needs of young people in Meeting. Has anyone got anything else that needs to go on?'

'Well, I think we need to discuss whether Meeting needs any other groups to encourage people to get together more outside Meeting for Worship. There have been several requests for this by various Friends.'

'And we also need to think about the Minute from Monthly Meeting about how we intend to approach conflict in our Meeting.'

Mary sat and listened, enjoying the way the agenda was being agreed, with everyone having a chance to speak and be listened to. There was so much to discuss and she felt a passing wave of anxiety – would there be time for everything; what was expected of her? At work she noticed that people tended to keep quiet. There, meetings were considered lengthy, unproductive, not a place to show your weak side, and a waste of time. But this wasn't a meeting. It was Meeting.

'I would appreciate it if you could fill me in a bit with what is expected of Elders,' she said.

There seemed space for everyone to have their say and be heard. Their words were received in silence and it gave everyone else the opportunity to think of their reactions before responding. Silence and listening: key to making effective decisions, building trust and a sense of community, making the most of what each person could offer. Why did it work so well here?

Mary leaned back. She felt comfortable and knew that her voice would be heard, when it felt time to speak.

Practices and Stories

In the next six sections of this chapter we will describe six practices that help to generate good communication in organisations, giving examples of stories that support each practice. The first practice is the willingness to accept that we all make mistakes, and that we're all vulnerable human beings, even the strongest and most competent of us. The second practice we call seeking empathy, which is putting yourself in other people's shoes, and thereby appreciating their viewpoints and coming to care for them. Accepting personal vulnerability helps the practice of seeking empathy, since both practices aim to develop understanding between fellow human beings.

The third practice is transparency, which is understanding achieved by openness. This understanding is not only of individuals, but also of the group's dynamics and of the purposes, tasks and competences of the organisation. The next practice is support of effective dialogue between organisation members, which is followed by the practice of spotting the false consensus known as 'groupthink'.

The last of the six practices is support for truthful politics. The term 'organisation politics' has an unpleasant ring to it, suggesting the pursuit of personal ambition at the expense of organisation goals, and the manoeuvres of backstairs cabals. Politics like that is not something to be encouraged. Indeed, one benefit of openness is that it makes politics of that kind very difficult. But there will always be genuine disagreements and dilemmas in choosing the best course of action for an organisation. What we mean by 'politics' is the process of resolving these. Truthful politics draws out good ideas from all, chooses wisely and convinces everyone of the wisdom of this choice.

All these practices are summarised in Box 2.2.

Accept Vulnerability

At the start of this chapter we told a story about Melissa Thorpe, a leader who changed her mind, who admitted in public that she was wrong. It was an instance of someone accepting vulnerability. There are many areas of life in which mistakes are sneered at or punished, so it is not surprising that we fear the loss of face that comes from admitting mistakes. Leaders want to get things right and to appear decisive,

BOX 2.2	Six Practices for Truthful Communication
The practice	**Stories you can tell from this book**
1. Accept vulnerability	The leader changes her mind
	Alfred and the cakes
2. Seek empathy	Hatim and the Honda
	Gossip, grooming and language
3. Seek transparency	Project selection
	Stories about the future
4. Promote dialogue	M4's away-days
	Daisy
5. Avoid 'groupthink'	Abilene
	Fred and the police camera
6. Support truthful politics	The Ethel rumour

which once again makes it hard for a leader to confess that he has fouled up something. It will often seem easier to brazen things out. But when we really want open and honest communication, it is inevitable that we will have to admit to mistakes, because everybody makes them. None of us can be right all the time.

Fear of talking about mistakes can breed lies. If an organisation's leaders cannot admit to error, then how much more difficult will it be for more junior and less powerful people to own up to things that have gone wrong? For proper organisational openness, essential for organisational learning, both leaders and followers have to be able to talk about mistakes: not to pin the blame on someone, nor to wallow in guilt, but to bring out into the open bad judgement and sloppy performance, in order to avoid making the same mistakes time after time. As Donald Michael put it in his book *On Learning to Plan – and Planning to Learn* (1973), we must be able to embrace error in a constructive way.

Leaders can be revered while showing their weaknesses. Take the well-known story of the Saxon King Alfred, hiding from his Danish enemies in a Somerset cottage. He is asked to watch out for the cakes cooking at the fire, but fails to do this and the cakes get burnt. A small error, perhaps, but serious if you are short of food. A worrying story for a leader who must convince his followers they can win their fight against a powerful enemy? Alfred may have realised that by telling the story against himself, he showed himself as a leader who shared some of the vulnerabilities and failings of his followers, who therefore would identify with him more closely and become more loyal than before.

Vulnerability may be more easily accepted if it is funny. Occasional self-deprecating humour, telling jokes against yourself, is a good way to admit you're not perfect. Of course, that should not lead to constantly putting yourself down, which is an unhelpful way of engaging with your own capabilities. Organisations with a tradition of Christmas parties with satirical sketches and the like, know how to bring faults into the open. Those little bits of pretention that a certain colleague shows, the mistake that luckily wasn't so serious and that has since been conveniently forgotten, these can be laughed at at the party – but remembered afterwards. Vulnerability reveals character, and knowing others' characters aids learning and working together.

Stories ought to be entertaining, and that means telling them at the right time and in the right place. Jokes that are funny in one context may not be when told in another context. The same applies to admissions of vulnerability – there are times when they shouldn't be made. The question of appropriate times and places is important – we'll return to it several times later in this book.

Seek Empathy

New recruits were often astonished to find that at M4 it was regarded as perfectly normal to discuss openly the capabilities and personalities of colleagues. Soon after she joined M4 as a junior accountant, Sue attended a meeting on project costing, which was chaired by Peter, M4's technical director. At one point in the meeting there was a debate about the accuracy of costings. Peter was holding out for the most accurate figures possible. 'That way you see the inconsistencies, and they give you a clue that something is wrong.' One of the project leaders, who was a lot younger than Peter, commented, 'Peter, you're being anal-retentive, as usual. That's fine for programming, but these costings are just a guide. We can have them a bit sloppy, the inconsistencies will still show up.' Sue gasped. In her previous job, no one would have dreamed of telling the co-founder of the company he was anal-retentive.

But why not? If the description is accurate, most people will know that. Peter probably knows it himself. We hold to the myth that leaders have no faults, and at the same time criticise them behind their backs. Obviously no one can do a perfect job all the time, so it is better that everyone's skills, strengths, inexperiences and weaknesses are widely understood. If we can think of ourselves in another's shoes, we might develop a feel for the point at which that person's boldness tips over into rashness, or when caution tips over into timidity. By being honest about our own and others' personalities and capabilities, we reduce mistakes and expand our achievements.

Honesty does not mean you have to insult other people. Genuine empathy produces a blend of frankness and kindness that guides a colleague rather than making her angry. Nor does it mean you always have to be hard on yourself, putting on a hair shirt whenever you fall below some impossibly high standard you've set yourself. Empathy is helped by the fact that we love talking about other people and finding out what others feel about us. We are deeply interested in how people think and act, what motivates them, whether they are stable or fickle in their behaviour. Acknowledged or not, these are endlessly fascinating topics in all organisations. Often discussion is driven underground, surfacing only in the pub after work, or in corridor gossip. These are the topics on everyone's mind. The effective organisation brings them into the open.

If you think this is an exaggeration, consider what we choose to entertain ourselves. Soap operas, novels, films, fly-on-the-wall TV, cartoons, news stories and scandals all feed our desire to witness the drama of human interaction. We also entertain ourselves constantly with stories of what we, our friends and our families are up to. This is the field where gossip blooms. To some, gossip is necessarily malicious, but that is not so. The term can cover all kinds of stories about people. Gossip explores and expresses our knowledge of people, and with those we know well it helps to build a deep and intimate knowledge.

 In his book *Grooming, Gossip and the Evolution of Language* (1996) Robin Dunbar writes:

If being human is all about talking, it's the tittle-tattle of life that makes the world go round, not the pearls of wisdom that fall from the lips of the Aristotles and the Einsteins. We are social beings, and our world – no less than that of the monkeys and the apes – is cocooned in the interests and minutiae of everyday life. They fascinate us beyond measure. (p. 4)

Dunbar claims that language evolved in order that we might gossip. In animals, particularly monkeys and apes, social bonding is achieved by mutual grooming. This is not merely hygienic – the removal of burrs and dead skin from another's back. Grooming changes the behaviour towards each other of creatures who groom together. But grooming takes time, especially if the aim is to bond with a large group. Gossip, Dunbar says, is much more efficient. Talking with others and about others provides bonding more quickly than grooming, and on a larger scale. Animals without language are thus at a disadvantage in wide-range bonding. Only humans have the advantage of being able to bond by gossip.

So if Dunbar is right, both grooming and gossip create bonding through the empathy that comes from repeated intimacy. The difference is that gossip allows a wider intimacy, which permits the maintenance of a larger group of well-bonded individuals. On this argument, gossip becomes the basis of human society, and since gossip is one form of story-telling, the centrality of stories is clear. Interpersonal relationships are the key to coping in a complex world. Relationships depend on empathy, and empathy can emerge from the stories we call gossip. Perhaps this is why humans are natural story-tellers.

We must again acknowledge that today 'gossip' has many negative associations. It's often felt to be no more than telling unpleasant tales behind someone's back, or speading nasty falsehoods. That said, there is a more positive current usage, as in the phrase 'a good gossip', meaning a relaxed and wide-ranging chat about people you know. In this book the word has the second, more positive, of these contrasting usages.

All this suggests that communicative competence is allied to the ability to gossip well. It needs both skill in story-telling and support from the group for story-tellers. To get the best out of gossip, it has to be a legitimate practice for the group. Sustained empathy requires a continuing alertness to others' feelings, but developing empathy also depends on the authenticity of the expression of feelings, for it is through such authenticity that true empathy, the accurate understanding of another's viewpoint, becomes possible. Gossip is the major means by which authenticity is constantly tested within a group.

Seek Transparency

When M4 Technology started to develop its own software products as well as doing custom development for larger organisations, Peter Parsons, M4's technical director, canvassed his staff for ideas about possible new products. He expected that one or two new ideas would be added to the four or five he had already thought up himself. To his surprise, he received twenty-three proposals, giving him nearly ten times as many ideas than M4 had the resources to work on. In some ways this was a nice problem to have, since it meant that he could select the most promising proposals, but how would the selection be made? In several cases the proposals were original and in many cases had been worked out in a lot of detail. People might feel angry if their ideas were ignored, especially if Peter chose mainly his own ideas. He decided that a transparent selection process was the only way to deal with the problem he had created for himself.

Peter devised a standard format for proposals, with several sections – resources needed for development of the idea, timescale for development, likely market size, competition, intellectual property, and so on. Proposals should be no longer than 1000 words. He asked that all proposals be re-submitted in this standard format by a certain date, and he re-worked his own ideas in this format as well. Faced with this more rigorous test, several of the proposers withdrew their ideas, and Peter found that one of his own ideas wasn't good enough either. By the deadline date, there were fifteen proposals left, all in the standard format. These were sent to every member of M4's software development staff, initiating an electronic conference on the proposals.

Staff were asked to discuss any proposal they wished, talking to the proposer and with other colleagues, and then to share their critique with everybody in the e-conference. Peter himself provided the conference with an initial critique on those proposals which he felt were lacking in some way. Several people modified their proposals as a result. After a couple of weeks, Peter asked everyone to rank the proposals in order of desirability. These rankings were submitted anonymously.

Peter then sat down with two experienced colleagues and devised a development programme, one that gave a good fit between the selected proposals and M4's resources and commercial priorities. Their choice took into account the rankings given to the proposals by their colleagues. The final programme selected four projects, two of them from Peter's own list, two based on other people's ideas. There was also a back-up list of three proposals which would be kept in reserve. The programme selectors wrote a short paragraph on each of the fifteen proposals, explaining why it had been chosen as a project, or put on the back-up list, or rejected. All this was shared with the conference.

After it was finished, Peter felt that the process had provided a stringent test for the proposals, had resulted in some of them being greatly improved, and had not been too cumbersome or time-consuming. It had also been great for the morale of M4's software staff. Everyone had been involved, had made their views known and knew the reasons behind the decisions that had been taken.

The lesson from this story from M4 is this: openness takes time and attention, but it's worthwhile and sometimes not as hard as you might expect. And when justice has been done and has been seen to be done, it gets easier next time, because trust has been built up by the previous openness.

Away-Days

Story-telling is particularly useful on away-days and similar events, when a group of people have to get their imaginations going, when they have to share the ideas they dream up, and when they have to understand sympathetically the ideas others put forward. As the company grew, M4 Technology found that events such as away-days were important, not least because they allowed busy people to spend time together. The purpose of one such meeting was to review business strategy. The current strategy was, on the whole, working well, but CEO Melissa's single-minded drive in a single strategic direction, amidst formidable competition, scared Jake, who was one of the more thoughtful of her colleagues. He raised his fears with Melissa and persuaded her to hold an away-day. The meeting was held in a nineteenth-century mansion which had been recently restored as a hotel and conference centre. The entrance hall was decorated with lots of figures carved in wood, depicting mythological heroes from ancient times. Melissa opened the meeting by saying that M4's away-days were usually held when there was an important problem to be tackled. 'This one is different,' she said. 'Our strategy is working, but Jake thinks it's all too good to be true.' Everyone laughed at this.

'I'm not proposing that we spend the day thinking about all the things that could go wrong,' said Melissa. 'So I've asked Jake to produce a set of three stories about the future of the company. Let's listen to them.' One story started off cosily with continuing success, but after a couple of years several unresolved problems came together to pro-duce an intolerable situation and the company was forced to find a larger firm willing to take it over. This was not a happy picture for the people participating in the away-day, but it was perfectly credible.

The next story painted a rosier long-term picture, but some imme-diate changes would be required to achieve it, involving investment in a risky new area of technology. Again the picture was a credible one, and at the away-day it stimulated a vigorous conversation about whether it would be possible to get the desirable end-result without the sizeable investment imagined in the story.

The third story in the set described an external event – the merger of two rival firms – generating stronger competition for the company. This story provoked a debate about the outside world. What other such events might happen in the future? How could M4's strategy take account of this kind of event?

None of the three stories was taken to be a prediction of the future, but all were seen as real possibilities, and together they led to a fruitful discussion. Jake reminded participants of the history of the mansion they were in. It had been built by a successful banker, but it became derelict after his death because the family failed to match his success and lost their wealth. It was the mark of a brilliant career, but soon started to fall into decay. 'That could happen to M4,' he said, 'if ever we allow ourselves to get complacent.'

Most people found the away-day a good experience, partly because it wasn't focused on a specific problem, and partly because using stories had proved an engaging and fruitful approach. A year later a second session of this kind was held, and a couple of the stories told the previous year were still vividly remembered by the participants, indi-cating that story-telling was now well embedded as an M4 practice.

Promote Dialogue

In the two years after M4 went public the company grew steadily. Melissa, Peter and Michael Saunders, the new finance director, were the executive directors, and Michael had become a trusted member of this team. They decided they needed a professional head of human resources and hired Lorna Buckley, who as a freelance consultant had worked for M4 from time to time. A month or so after she joined M4, Lorna said to her senior colleagues: 'Communication at M4 is great. But it relies too much on you people at the top and on a few old-timers. I'd like to develop skills in dialogue throughout the company.' She was given the go-ahead.

Dialogue was a term that hadn't been much used at M4, although a lot of it was actually happening. Lorna kept explaining the concept: it's about understanding other people's perspectives. That way you bring out the richness that the 250 people now working at M4 have through their combined understandings about the world and their work. It's for sharing tacit knowledge by making it explicit, and it's for revealing people's assumptions about the world. Dialogue creates new joint meanings through open discussion and the rigorous testing of ideas.

One practice Lorna introduced was to make clear when a group was in dialogue mode. This was best done by sitting in an open circle, with no tables or other clutter inside the circle, so everyone could see directly everyone else in the group. Arranging the group in this way was important, even for a half-hour session at lunchtime within a particular department. Lorna said: 'You don't need an away-day for dialogue. Just get yourselves in a circle. If you need a facilitator, I'll find the time to come and do the job, until you can provide your own or do without one.'

Lorna emphasised a few guidelines, including:

- Speak from your personal experience. Give your own views, not someone else's.
- When someone is talking, listen to him or her. Don't just sit thinking about what your response will be.
- Keep an open mind. Don't jump to conclusions or propose actions. That can come later. The point of dialogue is to learn how others view the situation.

As time went on, communication changed in the company. The practices that worked for a small, new outfit obviously depended a lot on Melissa and Peter – and on Jake, the wonderful teller of tales. But now there had to be dialogue without them. Lorna's intervention spread the practice to small groups, in departments, in project teams and elsewhere: 'The word dialogue doesn't only mean talk between two people. It means talk in any group that can sit together, in clear view, speaking directly to one another; perhaps up to twenty people.'

Lorna encouraged people to read Nancy M. Dixon's *Dialogue at Work* (1998) which is an easy read, giving clear guidelines for the practice of dialogue. Also, Lorna came to appreciate the story-telling tradition in M4, and how it supported dialogue. Stories were memorable, they were often enjoyable and they helped people to bring up matters that otherwise might have been too charged with emotion. She started to work on the practice of story-telling as well as the practice of dialogue.

When she was invited to be a facilitator for a dialogue session in the Marketing department, she told the group that she thought they already knew most of what she could tell them about dialogue. So she was going to start off with an exercise on story-telling, which should help them acquire some further skills, complementary to skills in dialogue. She asked the group to think quietly for five minutes about one or more of four questions that she'd written on a flip-chart. Then she said: 'Make your answers as playful as possible, and write them on a sheet of A4. After five minutes or so, swap answers with a colleague. Then make up a story about one of your answers, and after another five minutes swap stories with someone else.' This is what was on Lorna's flip-chart:

- If M4 Technology were a person, what stories would she tell?
- Which actors and actresses would star in the film about M4, and why?
- What colour is M4?
- If M4 were a building – from any period, past, present or future – what would it look like? How many floors would it have? How many rooms? Who lives there and who visits it?

Some amusing and insightful stories emerged from this exercise. They led Lorna to ask the group why they were having the session at this time. Sammy replied: 'I don't know exactly why the session was fixed. But the stories we've just been telling make me feel that Marketing is drifting away from the rest of M4. We're not in the same movie. That could be serious.' Sammy's remark sparked off a debate. Others said how they felt about this 'different movies' point. By the end of the session the department realised they had a potential problem – a problem that until today no one thought they had. How this exercise turned out, plus some further ideas and activities, can be found in Chapter 10.

Avoid Groupthink

Michael (1997) describes how individuals make an emotional commitment to a group and receive emotional support from it. It can then be called a sentient group. Sometimes the sentient group is the same as a work group, or at least overlaps with it; at other times the sentient group will be made up of family, friends or perhaps a professional association of some kind. The emotional support these groups provide for their members is valuable in coping with disorientating change, but there is a downside. Once a sentient group reaches a conclusion, no one wants to question it and the group tends to deny any difficulties which may arise.

Failure to question assumptions in a sentient group leads to one kind of 'groupthink' – when group cohesion becomes the main aim, and fear of disagreement overrides commitment to the group's task. The perils of groupthink mean that a group's aims and purposes have to be openly and rigorously tested by debate in a sentient group, to make sure they are clear to everyone and that there are no hidden reservations. Groupthink can also arise in situations of enforced consensus, and through lack of imagination or sheer laziness. The following stories illustrate these situations.

Fairtlough (1994) tells this story:

> [Groupthink] can happen anywhere. I have seen it happen at the top of a large pharmaceutical company when the CEO set out to check the in-fighting which had been endemic between R&D and Marketing. He called for less opposition and more cooperation between the two functions. The next time R&D staff made a proposal, the Marketing staff supported it, even though they didn't really believe in it. Later R&D developed doubts themselves, but because of Marketing's support they were now reluctant to abandon the idea. The project continued unconvincingly for months, until it finally collapsed, leaving Marketing and R&D as much at odds with each other as they ever were. (p. 82)

This is an example of enforced consensus, rather than the groupthink that arises in a sentient group.

There are lots of stories about Abilene. This one, set in a dusty rural township in Oklahoma, illustrates that you can find groupthink outside organisations.

Four men are lounging about outside a saloon. Pete asks 'What shall we do?' Chuck responds, 'Suppose we could go to Abilene.' Joe says

'I've got my truck, if you want to go.' Pete says, 'If you fellas are going to Abilene, I'll come with you.' Jake says, 'I'll ride along with you folks.' After a few minutes they clamber into the truck and start off down the road. It takes an hour to get to Abilene, which is another dusty hick town just like the one they came from. As they drive into town, Jake asks Pete, 'What did you have in mind to do in this dump?' Pete replies, 'Weren't my idea to come here.' 'Whose darn idea was it then?' says Jake. 'Weren't mine,' reply both Chuck and Joe. Since no one had ever wanted to come to Abilene, there was nothing to do but to turn right around and drive back home.

In his book *The Abilene Paradox and Other Meditations on Management*, Jerry B. Harvey (1996) uses a variety of stories, anecdotes and metaphors to highlight some of the absurdities of life in organisations. Starting with an Abilene story, Harvey points out the prevalence of groupthink in organisations, the paradox being that the excursion taken is in direct contradiction to anything the people concerned actually want to do. Furthermore their actions defeated what they were trying to achieve (a good day out, a successful business). The problem is not disagreement but agreement.

Melissa was fond of the Abilene story. It was her way of exposing groupthink. All she needed to do was to ask, 'Are we going to Abilene, then?' and when the group's consensus was phoney it quickly collapsed. Even when an agreement was more firmly grounded, saying the magic word 'Abilene?' allowed people at M4 to question an apparent consensus without seeming disloyal. The lesson is that when a group reaches an agreement it should properly understand what the basis is for that agreement. It should be normal to say: 'OK, but how did we get to this conclusion?' Then, if the agreement looks even a little phoney, we need the courage to say so, to stand out from the crowd, without diminishing our colleagues. And once again, stories help in dispersing groupthink.

M4 Technology devised a very clever solution to a problem posed to it by a customer, and its staff were full of hope when they went to present the solution to the customer. But the reception they got was cool, and a few days later the customer told them the project had been cancelled. This seemed incredible. The solution was neat and cost-effective, so the customer should have been delighted. Nobody could understand why they did not get the job. Frustrated fury gripped the company. Then Jake told a story.

Fred was driving his car past a newly-installed police camera on a road near his home. He kept his speed well within the limit, but all the same he saw a flash as the camera recorded his registration plate. Fred drove around the block and passed the camera again, at an even lower speed. Again there was a flash. Fred tried a third time, now travelling very slowly – again there was a flash. The local police station wasn't far away, so Fred went there to report the defect on the new camera. Information from the camera was automatically sent to the police station, so it was easy for the policeman on the desk to check what had happened. He got out his pad and booked Fred for driving past the camera three times not wearing a seat belt.

When Jake told this silly tale, it completely changed the atmosphere in the company. Of course they had been clever, cost-effective and all that. But had they forgotten something simple? Something necessary to persuade the customer that they would do a good job on the project? Going back over the project documentation, the project manager realised that some elementary features had been left out. It would have been easy to put this right, but presenting the proposal to the customer without these features made M4's work look careless. Jake's story had got behind the groupthink, changing the group's view that the customer was wrong to a realisation that the customer's rejection was rational. M4 deserved to be turned down.

Not all was lost. People at M4 learned lessons about humility and diligence from this mistake, and in future they could readily be reminded of these lessons by the pointed question: have you fastened your seatbelt?

Support Truthful Politics

When M4 had its initial public offering (IPO), getting its shares quoted on the London Stock Exchange, it had to recruit a finance director. Melissa was reluctant to do this. She felt that she and Peter, the founders of M4, should be the only executive directors of the business. The two of them often disagreed, but they had learned how to live with their differences and how to resolve them before they harmed the company. Their colleagues had also learned not to panic at the fights between the founders, and how to help in resolving the disputes. Melissa feared that the arrival of a third executive director might upset all this.

Schneiders, the investment bank which advised M4, insisted on a finance director. They told Melissa that she would be totally over-stretched if she tried to handle the extra finance and investor relations work that a public quotation would bring. In any case, investors who were putting money into M4 wanted strong financial management. A full-time, professional head of finance on M4's board was a precondition for an IPO. As she badly wanted the inflow of capital that the IPO would bring, Melissa had to agree. A couple of months before the IPO, Michael Saunders joined M4 as finance director, with a seat on the board.

During the run-up to the IPO Melissa appreciated Michael's fund-raising experience and it was great to have him around to take up some of the workload. The IPO turned out to be very successful: the timing was right, and M4 raised a lot of cash. Afterwards, M4's share price remained strong. Michael suggested to the board that they should take advantage of this good position to buy another company. Newbury Systems, a firm about half M4's size, was a suitable candidate.

Although she thought it wasn't a bad idea, Melissa was angry with Michael. He shouldn't have raised it at the board without telling her first. She and Peter had always talked over that kind of thing between themselves. After the board meeting she told Michael in no uncertain terms how she felt. His response was, 'I thought you were keen on openness.' Later, Melissa blamed herself for losing her cool. She still wished Michael had talked to her first, but she was indeed keen on openness. So, why had Michael's open suggestion upset her so much? Perhaps her anger was really about all the changes that had taken place in recent months. It used to be *her* business. Now there were non-executive directors to worry about, Schneiders, the lawyers, the PR people, the new shareholders. She hadn't wanted a finance director, and now this one was scheming behind her back, while *pretending* to be open. Well, she couldn't go back to the old days, when she and Peter ran things, but she'd stop the scheming.

The next morning the sun was shining. Melissa asked Michael to walk round the business park, to look for extra office space M4 might need in the future. She quickly came to the point.

'You spoke to the board about buying Newbury. Who else have you talked to?'

'No one but Schneiders,' replied Michael.

'Good God!' said Melissa. 'Of course they'd support your idea. Another lot of fat fees for them.'

Michael replied, 'When you hired me, you said that above all you wanted people at M4 to be open and creative. Now it seems that openness and creativity have to be under your control.'

'No. They have to be reasonable,' responded Melissa.

'Then please tell me what is reasonable and what is not,' was Michael's reply.

Melissa thought about the old days, when everyone knew what was reasonable. There were no secrets within the circle of M4's permanent staff, but outside that they all kept quiet. There were unwritten rules about who was 'family' and who was not. Perhaps Michael didn't know those rules – well, why should he? He probably wasn't the only one. M4 had been taking on lots of new people since the IPO. Yes, the rules should be clear. They'd have an away-day – hammer out guidelines about openness – tackle the question of buying Newbury at the same time – start with the senior people, then talk with the rest.

At the away-day, Melissa confessed that she'd been wrong in assuming life would continue as usual even though M4 was now much bigger. She said they should take nothing for granted. 'Is the old policy of 'no secrets' still possible? Do we need some kind of strategic planning? What about new ways of communicating?' In the discussion that followed, no real conclusions were reached. Neither Melissa nor Peter seemed ready to take charge as they would have done in the past. In the end, Jake asked if he could tell a story. Wanting a break from a debate that was getting nowhere, everyone said yes.

On the Eight and Ninth Floors

Jake's story went like this.

It was the headquarters of a big organisation, which was rather bureaucratic and very secretive. The eighth and ninth floors, just below the exective suite, were refreshed by Daisy, who brought them coffee in the morning and tea in the afternoon. She also brought them news. 'That Mr Simpkins has resigned. Couldn't stand the way he was being treated.' 'Sandra in accounts is having a baby. She was sick in the Ladies this morning.' People fed her ridiculous rumours. 'Next month we start work at six in the morning.' That one spread so fast that an official denial was issued. Some stories were planted in someone's self-interest, like 'Joe Smith is going to be promoted.' Soon after Joe started the rumour, he actually was.

Everyone on the eighth and ninth floors understood that Daisy's stories could be true, or could be false, but were always interesting. The day came when Daisy retired. They clubbed together to give her a great send-off. On Monday another tea-lady was there with Daisy's trolley. Over the next few weeks the eight and ninth floors felt increasingly disconnected from their work. They didn't know what was going on in their secretive organisation. Daisy's rumours were the best communication they'd had.

'That's my story,' said Jake. 'I'd just add that it feels as if Daisy's retired from M4, too. I'm not saying we're a secretive place – far from it – but we've got used to a particular style of communication. Melissa and Peter work out what they want to do and then ask us what we think. Mostly we agree, occasionally we ask them to change their minds. That style of politics has done pretty well up to now. But we'll have to change. Daisy's gone.'

Peter thanked Jake for his story. 'I've got a keen sense of loss – and I expect Melissa feels the same – we loved the informality of the old M4. But you're right, Jake, we must move on.' Michael, the finance director, then spoke. 'I feel like the new tea-lady. You're being polite to me, but really you're all missing Daisy.' Jake replied, 'We haven't had a farewell party for Daisy.' Melissa said, 'OK chaps. We'll have a party right now. I'll ring for some champagne.'

Gossip and Politics

The story of Daisy was told at M4's away-day, and was useful there in highlighting the importance of context for organisation politics – as the context changes, so do the politics. But it's also a story about gossip, because Daisy's rumours were often about people. In fact, communication in an organisation has to be about all these things – people, task performance, decision-making, false consensus, genuine consensus, and the resolution of dilemmas. So, as we said at the start of this chapter, the same story can be useful in more than one practice.

Gossip is about people, while politics is about the aims and actions of a group, large or small. Gossip can be malicious, and politics can be devious and self-interested. But neither gossip not politics need take those forms. There can be truthful gossip and truthful politics. Just as gossip validates empathy, so transparency validates politics. Both gossip and politics are needed by organisations if they are to survive in today's world. Politics may be less basic to human society than gossip, but it still comes naturally to many people. When people realise they really can influence their organisation's future their energy level leaps and a wave of constructive problem-solving appears.

M4 indeed had a tradition of truthful politics. All staff could be involved in deciding about the future of the organisation, and most actually were involved. There was strong leadership, but everyone could influence what was done. The openness that Melissa was proud of was genuine. In the early days, M4's politics had developed, unplanned, into a special pattern – based not on rumours but on a certain type of openness – a pattern that was now outmoded. No organisational communication completely follows a blueprint. Nobody had planned for Daisy either.

Just as some stories emerge from a situation, rather than being designed, so sometimes communication emerges very successfully. Of course, carefully designed communication can also be successful. The interplay between emergent and designed communication is illustrated by the story in Box 2.3. In this story the designed communication is rather manipulative, which is counter to the practice of openness and transparency. But Ethel isn't very serious manipulation – its aim is mainly lighthearted fun.

BOX 2.3   Ethel

The Daisy story isn't the only 'tea-lady' story on offer. Here is another story, featuring Ethel, this time highlighting the value of gossip in encouraging fun in an organisation. Ethel's function in this high-tech company is actually to be a low-tech human being, telling entertaining stories. As its Website will tell you, a company called AIT was founded in a room above Maurice the barber's by three people in 1986. It refers to itself as a community, and that community is now a successful listed company of some 350 people providing electronic customer relationship management (e-

CRM) solutions to the financial services industry. At the Association of Management, Education and Development's 'Frontiers' conference at Cranfield in the UK in August 1999, Richard Hicks, the chairman of AIT at that time, explained some of the practices that helped keep the community as a community in a time of rapid change. One of the stories concerned another tea-lady, called Ethel.

Periodically, says Hicks, we hire in actors to help brighten people's day. So people may turn up for work one morning and find there is a butler there to take their coats. Sometimes it's Ethel who comes round at tea-time with her trolley. She's dressed as a real caricature of a tea-lady, with a flowery apron and slippers, and as she goes round she not only dispenses tea and cakes but also provides gossip. This of course includes outrageous allegations about the chairman, among others – nobody is off limits.

'Aren't you worried that people might believe some of these things?' came a question from the audience.

'Well, it might not work in every company,' came the reply, 'but on the other hand I imagine you could say that no matter how outrageous Ethel gets, the truth could prove even more unbelievable; like all those stories they say they can never put in the plot of a soap opera because nobody would believe them.'

Conclusion

M4 Technology has more openness than you'll find in most businesses, and the company's tradition of story-telling is something special. Nevertheless, in most ways it is typical of a successful start-up company. The founders originally set the pattern for the company's culture and they retain a strong influence. People at M4 know who's boss. It has a hierarchy – a flat one, but a strong one. Alongside the hierarchy runs a certain amount of self-organisation. The company's storying tradition both supports and is supported by this self-organising strand. In fact, in a small organisation hierarchy and self-organisation can run quite smoothly together. And if there is a clash, M4's people have enough self-awareness and interpersonal skills to sort things out.

The six practices for truthful communication which we have pro-

posed in this chapter overlap each other, thus admitting your vulnerability can engender empathy in others; the practice of dialogue can
aid in spotting and avoiding groupthink; transparency helps politics to
be truthful. Story-telling easily skips over these distinctions, helping
to blend one practice with another, all to aid good communication.

The six practices will never be easy. Being vulnerable, being transparent and exposing groupthink all take courage. Genuine empathy,
truthful politics and good dialogue are not straightforward and require
great commitment and attentiveness.

After six years study, a novice asks his Zen master to tell him the secret
of life. The master replies: 'Attention.'
  'Thank you, honourable master, but what do you mean by attention?'
  'Attention. Attention,' says the master.
  'Attention, attention?' queries the novice.
  The master speaks again: 'Attention, attention, attention. That is all.'

Gregory Bateson (*Steps to an Ecology of Mind*, 2000) says: the banks
contain the river, but the river shapes those banks. Organisation practices determine what kind of stories can be told and the best times and
places for telling them. But the stories told shape an organisation's
practices, help the practices to change and allow them to withstand
the pressures of external events. Practices and stories together shape
an organisation's culture. It is possible for an organisation to plan for
change in its practices, and to take steps to encourage story-telling;
but most often both practices and stories co-evolve without any sort of
plan.

We need help in our practices – and we can get this help from story-
telling, which is for humans a natural way of doing things. A funny or
poignant story can change the mood of a gathering and can ease the
way for the acceptance of an unpalatable new truth. An insightful story
can often sum up a complex situation much better than a formal
analysis. A story with striking phrases is memorable and can constantly
be repeated without becoming boring. Almost everyone has the potential to tell stories. We should do all we can to help them tell their tales.

M4, being a start-up, had to learn lots of things very quickly. More
established organisations also need to learn, and in the next chapter
we tell the history of AutoCorp, which is struggling to become more of
a learning organisation.

3

AutoCorp – Learning

[The] recall of new facts is enhanced by the presence of certain degrees of emotion during learning. James McGough and his colleagues have led these studies whose results are now well confirmed. For instance, if you are told two stories of comparable length that have a comparable number of facts, differing only because in one of them the facts have a high emotional content, you will remember far more detail from the emotional story than from the other.

Antonio Damasio

In this chapter we tell a story about people in another imaginary organisation, this time a large multinational corporation. We show how story-telling helps individuals learn and survive in challenging and changing times.

AutoCorp is one of the six largest automobile producers in the world. Its head office is in the USA, but it has large operations in Europe and East Asia and sales offices throughout the world. Like all car makers, AutoCorp is facing fierce competition. It is a large and powerful organisation, but it has to improve productivity, raise the speed of introduction of new models, make design more innovative, restructure its procurement of parts, materials and services and deal with the advent of e-commerce. Indeed, continuous change is a feature of nearly all its operations.

AutoCorp is, of course, an imaginary firm, but we hope our description is close to the reality of all large automotive companies. The scene of our stories is a unit based near Birmingham in the UK. The unit has worldwide responsibilities, being AutoCorp's Design and Development Centre (DDC) for light vans and other commercial vehicles. Its task is to introduce a stream of new designs, implementing a product strategy laid down by corporate headquarters.

At the end of 1999, everything seemed to be changing at the DDC. AutoCorp's new Universal Costing System was about to replace the old UK system. For the moment the two systems were being run in parallel. The local system had been used since 1986 and people in the DDC were very familiar with it. The new system was much more sophisticated, but its spreadsheets were unfamiliar and sometimes it produced dubious results. Tommy Sprigett, the head of chassis design was heard to say: 'The official term for the system's output is 'counter-intuitive', but I call it completely bloody wrong.'

The costing system was only one of the changes facing the DDC. ACEP (AutoCorp's Electronic Procurement) was replacing the old method of purchase requisitions placed with the purchasing department. This new system allowed design engineers to place orders directly with approved suppliers. And the most radical change of all was Benchmarked Design Scheduling, aimed at cutting the time from product concept to commercial sale of a new vehicle to less than that achieved by the company's fastest Japanese competitor. It involved simultaneous work by many sections within the DDC, and lots of feedback loops between them.

Most of the staff of the DDC were engineers. The older ones were typically mechanical engineers who had worked both in manufacturing plants and in design departments. For them, the assembly line was the ultimate test, the one that separated the men from the boys. This group of people were used to hierarchical and sequential methods where engineering skills were applied in well defined situations. In the old days, you produced a drawing or a solution to a problem and gave it to the head of your section. You completed your task and handed on the job to someone else. But nowadays you have to work in teams, trust people and get them to trust you, switch rapidly from one task to another and then back again.

The younger people usually had plenty of computer training. They could write their own software, or at least work comfortably with software designers. Their thought processes were more systemic. What came naturally to them was thinking in terms of feedback, using concepts like system boundary, and applying systems ideas to social systems as well as technical ones. Older people, even if they held senior positions, could be envious or afraid of the younger ones, who seemed to be able to take change in their stride. And younger staff could not easily be ignored or patronised. It was hard to recruit good designers. You had to hold on to the ones you had, in conditions where headhunters were a constant threat. Increasing numbers of female engineers, and changing attitudes generally, meant that family-friendly actions such as crèche provision became necessary if the company was to be an attractive employer. Or, as some male workers would put it, you had to cater for women workers these days.

In spite of all this, the DDC was quite an exciting place to work. The Sigma project, for a revolutionary new van, was just getting underway, with an Italian design genius in charge. The Centre had a sparkling new building, built with computer-aided design in mind, which was a pleasure to work in. The new rules for design and development required staff from the DDC to spend time in the plants where the vehicles they were designing would be made. That meant occasional lengthy visits to Spain and California, and most people preferred these assignments to the type of flying visit between offices that had happened before. So, in short, some people felt better off with the direction things were going, although there were not insubstantial doubts in other quarters. How would the future turn out for AutoCorp? How could the company ensure its continuing success? What would the company and the individuals within it have to learn?

Individual Learning

In Chapter 6, AutoCorp Evolving, attention will be turned to work-group and company-level interactions, and the lessons of complexity theory. In this chapter the emphasis will be on individuals and the use of stories to support them in their organisational context.

An extensive literature from a range of disciplines including psychology, management and education covers the acquisition of skilled task performance, and how this may be supported. Readers are referred to the bibliography and references, where they will find a number of useful texts on this topic, which is too substantial to be reviewed easily here. A learning cycle is common to most approaches to learning, even if expressed as simply as plan–do–review. The cycle in Box 3.1 is widely used.

BOX 3.1   A Learning Curve

Four stages are shown in Figure 3.1:

1. Unconscious incompetence: Confidence exceeds ability, as in, 'Well, if Fred knows how to use the new software, it can't be that hard for me to pick up, can it?'
2. Conscious incompetence: Confidence drops as, after a first attempt, the phrase, 'I wouldn't have thought it was quite this complicated' springs to mind.
3. Conscious competence: As a result of successful learning, training etc., skill is consciously gained and confidence increases: 'Yes, I can do it.'
4. Unconscious competence: Here, the skill has become so automatic that expert performance can tip into unwitting bad habits. Confidence and ability have both peaked, and competence may start to decline. This brings us back to unconscious incompetence once more.

The curve has been drawn related to confidence levels. However, in terms of a learning sequence, the process is thought of as a continuing cycle.

Within such a framework, and in the light of what is known about skills development, the requirements for supporting learning include the following:

- share (and create) knowledge
- allow practice
- support learners through their conscious incompetence
- provide a means by which the unconsciously competent can continue to develop, instead of becoming out of date or developing bad habits

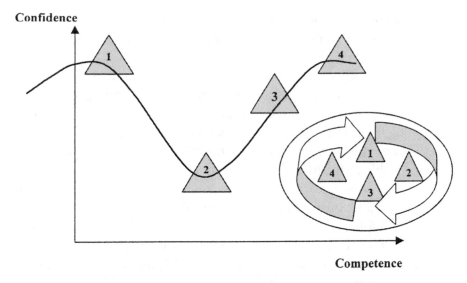

Figure 3.1 Stages of competence.

- finally, gather evidence for resulting behavioural changes and feed that back into the learning process.

To help our discussion of the uses of story-telling we will adopt some simplified categories. First, the Knowledge, Skills and Abilities (or Attitudes or Affect) terminology of occupational psychology (e.g. Tannenbaum and Yukl 1992).

Knowledge can be thought of as facts and figures, mental models and theories. It allows you to answer the question: what? In AutoCorp, it may be useful to know metal stress tolerances, employment law, or some theories about organisational culture, for example. Skills enable knowledge to be used. They may be specific to a task (manual dexterity) or more general (effective communication). They allow you to answer the question: how? At AutoCorp a skill-based component might be how to run a wind-tunnel test sequence, how to run workshops in managing change, or how to give staff useful performance feedback.

Abilities are an individual's general capabilities, which link in with attitudes, motivation and individual goals. Examples might be enthusiasm, curiosity and persistence. Abilities are connected to the question: why? AutoCorp may seek to make health and safety a central value in some areas, or develop self-efficacy (Bandura 1977) because of the consistent evidence linking high levels of self-efficacy with increased performance.

Knowledge, skills and abilities can be developed through training, coaching and mentoring, for which many overlapping definitions exist. This brings us to our second set of categories.

Training has traditionally been an activity designed to pass on knowledge. Often, this remains its main function. A good trainer will be knowledgeable in the field, and have the skills to assess trainees' current level of knowledge, to motivate them and to follow their progress. Coaching bridges into skill development. A coach will help a coachee review the application of a skill and consider developmental changes. This may also start to address some abilities requirements around motivation levels, goal setting and so on. This leads on to mentoring. While a coach may not actually be a specialist in the field he is coaching, a mentor frequently is chosen because of her particular knowledge and experience. Mentors can have a primary function in inspiration and example, perhaps even more so than skill development. In some definitions they would also be career champions (while a coach would be a development champion).

For simplicity, and without wishing to insist on the mutual exclusivity of these categories, we will use the word *training* primarily for a knowledge-imparting event, *coaching* for skills development, and *mentoring* for the inspirational and example-providing support of a junior by a more senior colleague (not generally in a line management relationship). Examples of how knowledge/training, skills/coaching and abilities/mentoring relate to story-telling are outlined in Box 3.2. The dotted lines between the categories denote the fluidity of these boundaries.

Whichever method of development the learner chooses, the evidence suggests that:

- it is beneficial to the learner if they can relate the new situation to a familiar one;
- it is beneficial to the learner to create rich cognitive connections (with already known facts, figures, sensations etc.);
- it is beneficial to the learner to be actively engaged rather than a passive recipient in the learning process, albeit with appropriate attention to different learning styles and preferences.

BOX 3.2   Story Use in Learning

Training, principally the transmission of knowledge	Enrich with a story about how somebody used the knowledge in practice. Encourage the learner to create a story about how he will use his learning. Both of these increase associative connections and encourage active engagement.
Coaching, principally the development of skills, often through reflecting on action	Creating and telling stories involves the practice of a range of skills related to creative thinking and communication, to name two generally valued competence areas. Coachees can be helped to practise these skills, and another use of story creation is to help illuminate values. Through using stories, a coachee can examine her value systems as well as the culture and values of her organisation.
Mentoring, principally the support of people's abilities, often through inspiration and role modelling	Mentors may use stories of what they or others have done in order to start conversations around options and vision. They may use stories about their mentee in order to promote them to others. They may use stories to encourage, help goal formation, promote trust and so on – the abilities or attitudes/affect portion of KSAs

Story-telling addresses these points and is valuable to a variety of practices important in assisting change in large organisations. And, partly because it is intrinsically interpersonal in nature – a story requires an audience, and requires a relationship with that audience in order to be a satisfying story – story-telling can promote interpersonal capabilities.

So, how might AutoCorp invest in developing people through a learning cycle and how might story-telling increase the possibility of useful outcomes? First, a story to reflect the context in which this must be done.

AutoCorp: the Past

Pete Binns is a training manager with AutoCorp. Learning and development, linked to business success, is his interest and his passion. He has a tale to tell about a learning curve of his own, when as a new graduate he joined the company, to discover he'd arrived just as relations between the unions and management had become particularly volatile.

Pete's Story

'I really wondered what I'd let myself in for. Shouting matches on the shop floor were common. All sorts was going wrong, and the guys at the top decided something had to be done.

'So, one Friday, I find myself comfortably accommodated at great expense, along with the best part of 200 AutoCorp staff, in a very nice hotel indeed for the weekend. It was all sorted out with agreement between the unions and management. Being new, I was just another participant. It was early evening and there was an organised gathering to hear from the management what was planned for the company.

'Now, I didn't know about training budgets at that time, but I can see expensive when I'm looking at it, and I knew that this counted as a training event. So I sit there in this great big hotel conference room with its stage and its plush seating and listen to the speakers – all top management who I hadn't even seen before.

'Ten minutes in, there's an interruption from the audience.

"This is complete ********, I'm off to the bar." Jim Barnes, leading trade union figure, left.

'Did I mention the free bar on the first evening?

'Well, I sat and listened to the rest of the presentation. And one by one, the shop stewards noisily headed off to join Jim. Over the course of the speeches, it wasn't just the shop stewards who headed off to the bar. And the remainder of the weekend passed off in a similar shambles as far as I could see. In fact, to this day, I sometimes hear people recounting the story as an example of how badly things can go wrong even if planned to the hilt.

'But I've got another story about it. Back in the office on Monday, thinking to myself that if huge budgets were spent, there should be some way to assess the benefit, I asked my manager how we justified the weekend. He told me what the total costs were – and they were BIG. I just looked at him, because I hadn't even realised.

' "You think that was expensive?" he said. "That's the total cost if the line goes down for just half an hour because there's a dispute. All the chats in the bar, the swimming in the pool, the free food and drink – and people feeling they're taking the mick out of the company. It's worth it if it means the line doesn't go down in the next month."

'The line didn't go down in the next month.

'So I tell this now to newcomers, not as a tale of failure, but as a pause for thought. I tell it as a kind of training story as well as a story about culture and history.

'I didn't realise when I was starting out that what you think you're involved in might not be actually what you're involved in. We had a budget to spend on staff development. It was poured into a hotel. The line stayed up. The stories are still told. Now, when I'm asked to look at away-days and so forth, I've learned to ask whether they are anything to do with development. Maybe they will be and maybe not, and both may be OK when you think of the business case and benefit to individuals. But we all need to be aware of the choices we're making.

'That shop steward saying it was all a load of * * * * * * * *. It wasn't at all. And it had all been agreed up front with the unions. He just wanted to be seen, it's all about flexing muscle. In the bar there wasn't a "them" and "us". Everyone was there together.'

Auto Corp: Stories for the Future

For AutoCorp to move towards its future, many tensions must be managed in a climate of fierce competition. The industry and company history of battles and winners and losers, of fearing to back down, of power struggles, is not so far back that people in the company don't know about it. It's not just AutoCorp that's changed but the job market, UK industry, European and global business priorities, political and social climates. People have felt the costs of change, and benefits take a while to be seen.

Now, failures need to be learned from and they need to be allowed – a blame culture is excellent for preventing the managed risk-taking required for success. In addition to the technical capability to perform their roles, AutoCorp employees at all levels need a range of capabilities concerned with working effectively in changing and uncertain times, and managing the inherent tensions of doing this. This requires some different ways of doing things.

The rest of this chapter explores how story creation and story-telling has been used to enhance learning (the development of knowledge, skills and abilities), in a number of ways:

- by a trainer, coach or mentor to aid the learning of others;
- by a trainer, coach or mentor to help themselves, personally, be more effective;
- by a participant, coachee or mentee to aid their understanding of a situation;
- by a participant, coachee or mentee to assist others.

Using stories in training and in coaching has a number of intrinsic advantages (which also apply to helping people become good trainers and coaches). These advantages include:

- engagement across a range of learning styles;
- a reminder of our common humanity. This is particularly important if people's past experience of learning has been unsatisfactory and they have come to feel defensive and unskilled in a classroom;
- entertainment. Teaching and coaching can be fun for all.
- being memorable. Inevitably, as the research shows, much of what trainees hear is soon forgotten, but they often remember a good story;
- practical experience, if story creation is used as a workshop activity, in such portable skills as managing personal risk-taking and effective communication;
- the opportunity for a new perspective. Where topics are complex rather than linear and there is not a 'right' way to be taught, stories encourage the juxtaposition of new and multiple perspectives;
- enacted creativity. Trainers and coaches can model effective story use and they can also provide an environment in which individuals can create their own stories. Where creativity and innovation are organisational requirements, this reinforces a creative approach.

We start with the use of story-telling in a training situation, then move on to coaching and mentoring.

A Training Tale

Here we learn about the experience of a consultant running a workshop within AutoCorp, appropriately enough on the topic of change. It's a training tale because the setting is a formal learning event that includes delivery of specific knowledge content. Fortunately for participants, they were not expected to sit through two days of lectures and presentations, but most people would recognise the event as primarily training for knowledge rather than coaching or mentoring for skills and abilities.

In this tale, not only is a form of story-telling used in workshop activities, but the consultant also uses stories as a personal resource for her own actions. And she re-tells a story she heard elsewhere in order to support learning. As it turns out, the story she remembers as a personal resource is only a version of what she actually read, and the story she re-tells to support learning isn't an accurate copy of the original she heard, but both still serve their purpose. This is a reminder of one of the useful qualities of story-telling, particularly in the oral tradition. A story is a fluid entity, told to suit the need or interest of the moment, and it may well change with each telling and re-telling.

Changes in the Telling: Leonora's Story

Leonora had been trained by Jeanenne LaMarsh to help others use LaMarsh's change management approach. Now she was in the middle of a managing change workshop at AutoCorp. The group was there under sufferance – after all, what is a change management initiative other than another thing to fill up the day instead of getting some real work done? There was a lot of anger at what was going on in AutoCorp, but the group, while hugely frustrated, were sufficiently good-hearted to have no interest in shooting the messenger. So they politely listened to Leonora, they did the exercises she set them, and all seemed well.

Leonora was relieved not to meet open hostility, but soon began to find the politeness level disconcerting. Two things came to her mind. First, her study of complex adaptive systems (not to mention life) led her to think that where there is nothing going on, then that's exactly what is happening – nothing. Then another piece of well-known life wisdom occurred to her: 'All is calm before the storm'. Perhaps if something did start to happen she might not like it; just as the participants didn't like what was going on at AutoCorp.

She remembered the folk tale of the Crescent Moon Bear in which a young woman, who is finding it difficult to deal with her husband following his return from war, goes to seek the advice of a wise older woman. The wise woman tells her that she can indeed help by making her a potion, but that it requires three hairs from the terrifying Crescent Moon Bear who lives on a mountaintop some days' journey away. The young woman sets out, receives various forms of assistance, camps out on the mountainside and overcomes her fear, returning with the three hairs. The wise woman burns them in the fire, advising her to recall all the energy, compassion and courage she demonstrated on the journey and saying that if she behaves likewise at home, her husband will soon show improvement (see Estes 1992).

Leonora decided not to let the false calm prevail but instead to set an exercise that would help bring some of the tensions to the surface.

LaMarsh's framework has descriptors of key roles in a change process. Individuals may take on different roles at different times, and it is useful to know where you are at any time. Two of the roles are 'Sponsor' and 'Target'. If Sponsors don't really do what they need to do, then Targets end up feeling as if getting shot at is their primary function. And since Targets, almost by definition, feel this way at least some of the time, it's easy to see that there was a lot of anger in the room towards 'the system' and those who could be described as Sponsors. And the Targets seemed to know what they had to do – smile, play the game, and then leave the room as unaffected as possible. And so far they were doing it very well.

Leonora split the participants into two groups: Targets and Sponsors. The next part of the exercise was for one group to explain, from the perspective of their role, what they expected of the other role, played by the other group.

Here is what happened. The members of each group rolled up their sleeves, became quite indignant about the actions of the other group and made lists of what those people should and should not be doing. Then the groups faced each other across the room. They took it in turns to make their requests of the other roles. Encouraged by Leonora, they didn't mince their words.

Then Leonora asked, 'OK, so do you think the requirements you have of each role are reasonable?' There were some more frank exchanges. In the end, with a few negotiations, the answer was 'Yes'. In other words, each role could see the merit of what they needed to do, and they understood what they should expect in return from the other group.

Often the underlying requirements around issues such as clarity, support and thanks were similar for each role. One central request was an end to 'malicious compliance', which means doing exactly what you're told even when you know that it is either ineffective or, worse, damaging. Towards the end of the exercise, the mutual interdependence of Targets and Sponsors was pretty clear to everyone. Then a participant asked, 'That's all very well here today, but what about outside this room, with Sponsors who haven't been told these things? I can't go to my senior manager and tell him he's not doing his job properly.'

'I have a story for you,' Leonora said. 'It's one of Jeanenne's. This is what happened to her one time, and here's what she says about it.

'I was called in to see a board of directors at a company I was working with. We talked for a while but basically what they were saying was, "We need to get this change to happen and people, the Targets, aren't doing what they should be doing. They whinge and they moan and they complain, and that's all. We want to get everybody together and we want you to tell them what they should be doing."

'So, I said to them, OK, I'll do it. But only under these circumstances. I will tell them what they need to be doing for this change to work, but I will also be reminding them what you, the Sponsors, should be doing. Is that OK with you?

'Well, they thought about it and decided it would be OK, so this is what we did. A huge hall was hired, there were presentations of all sorts, hundreds of people were there. And I had my turn and I said, "You have achieved a lot of good things, but it has to be said that this change programme is failing. Your board of directors called me in and asked me to tell you that you weren't doing what you should be doing. And they are right. You aren't doing what is needed. For this to work, you need to do – and I listed what that was – and you need to stop doing – and I listed what that was." By this time, as you can imagine, people weren't looking too happy. Anyway, I continued.

'Your Sponsors tell me that all you do is whinge and moan and complain, and nothing is getting done. If this continues, you will fail. *However*, your Sponsors also should be doing certain things. Here's what they are – and I listed them. And they should not be doing some other things – and I listed them too. So my message is quite simple. If your Sponsors don't do what they should, then I think you should carry on whingeing and moaning and complaining until they do. But if they *do*, and they have told me that they will commit to do the following – and I told the audience what the Sponsors had promised me – then you should shut up and get on with it."

'It wasn't the most fun speech Jeanenne had ever made, but it reminded everybody that they had responsibilities as well as rights. Six months after that, the change was pretty much through. Each of the roles had made the correct commitment to act.'

The AutoCorp group was quiet for a while. Then one person asked, 'Have you or Jeanenne explained to the Sponsors here what their role is about?'

'Yes.'

'Do you think they are doing what they should be doing?'

'No, not always.'

'Could I use that story?'

'Certainly. It's about what it takes to get the job done. And maybe at times when you're in a Sponsor role, somebody might need to remind you of it. Would it be OK if I did that?'

'Well, I don't think I'd like it, but it's better than what we've been doing so far.'

Jeanenne, Leonora, whoever else, won't necessarily be around. But their story can always be told. It has the power to help the person who heard it the first time, and also the people who hear the story when it is told afterwards in many different places.

This illustrates some of the main qualities of story-telling, namely:

• stories are memorable
• stories travel quickly
• stories can be, and are, amended to suit the circumstances.

Although Leonora is a fictional character, she is a representative of real-life consultants, some of whom were trained by Jeanenne LaMarsh. And Jeanenne LaMarsh is a real person whose work has influenced the writing of this chapter. You can find out about her, and read the original version of Leonora's 'board of directors' story in Box 3.3.

Box 3.3   Jeanenne LaMarsh

Jeanenne LaMarsh is the founder and CEO of LaMarsh Associates, Inc. of Chicago. Her organisation works to support effective change in a range of large global organisations, using a framework devised to be straightforward, especially within an engineering or manufacturing context (LaMarsh 1995). At first sight the change-weary can dismiss the framework as 'just common sense'. Jeanenne's view is, broadly, 'Yes, that's what it is. In fact it's profound common sense.' Jeanenne has built a successful consultancy in a hard area of business and, like the wise woman of a folk tale, she listens attentively, empathises with what's going on, and tells stories that she thinks might help people see things in a new light.

In Chapter 10, you'll find some of Jeanenne's story-telling tips, as well as some frameworks and additional tips from her colleague Joan Levey. For now, here is the story that Leonora borrowed after hearing it told just once by a third party.

Get Them To Stop Whining, by Jeanenne LaMarsh

A project manager called me, I think it was about six months ago. I remember it was still warm out because I was looking out of the office window at people bicycling down the street in their shirt-sleeves as I listened to his problem.

He was with a large retail operation based in the USA: specifically the warehouse and distribution centre for this company. He explained that they were making several fundamental operational changes in every centre in the USA in the next year.

'The problem,' he explained, 'is that people are not very happy about some of the changes. I can understand why.' We're going to dramatically reduce our workforce and the new operations will require a great deal more computer literacy than people currently have. But we have to make these changes.

'While I have sympathy for their concerns, I cannot tolerate how they are dealing with the changes. They are slowing us down, making things even worse by standing around every day at the coffee machine or at the lunch table or at the forklift parking stations. They spend a tremendous amount of time just complaining and whining about all the changes. Why don't they just get over it?

'We've decided to put a stop to this behaviour. Here's our plan. We're going to go warehouse by warehouse across the country. Starting with Los Angeles, we're going to pick a day and shut the whole operation down about two in the afternoon. I know this is going to cost a lot of money, but we've got to do something. We're going to bus the whole group to a hotel; rent a big ballroom and get them all assembled there.

'What we're looking for is someone who could get up in front of them and knows how to get them to stop all that complaining and whining and crying. Could you do that?'

I smiled a little, then replied, 'Of course I can. But let me tell you how I would go about this and see if you are still interested in talking further. I'd start by explaining to them that they are Targets of change. As Targets, they have a very well defined role to play. In fact, there's even a job description for them as Targets. And I would pass round that job description. But, I would explain, they are not the only ones with a defined job. I'd explain about Sponsors and Change agents and give them the job descriptions for those roles as well. I'd ask them to read all three.

'If the Sponsors and Change agents at their operation are doing their jobs according to the descriptions they have just read, I would tell the Targets to stand up, file out of the ballroom, get back on the bus and go back to work and follow the Target job description. I would remind them it does *not* include whining and crying and complaining.

'But, if the sponsors aren't doing their job, and if the Change agents aren't behaving like the ones on the sheet of paper they have in front of them, I will ask them all to stand up, to tear their Target job descriptions into little pieces and let those pieces fall on the floor. Then I will tell them to get back on the bus and go back to work and continue to whine and cry and complain all they want.'

There was a long silence on the phone when I finished. Finally, the project manager said, 'Well . . . that's a very interesting approach. We hadn't thought about anything quite like that. We'll consider it and get back to you.'

It's been six months. I haven't heard from him. I don't expect to.

A Coaching Tale

This story starts out partly as a training tale, arising from events that happened as an internal consultant tried to deliver a workshop day. But it is told from the perspective of a coaching session in which the consultant reviews her experiences and, prompted by a coach using story-based methods, considers what she has learned. Within the story itself is reference to some earlier coaching support that was crucial to the outcome.

This story is about dragons, which all organisations seem to have – or people think they have (see also Chapter 6). The characters in the story are as follows:

> Faye, an internal consultant for AutoCorp
> Leonora, the external consultant from the previous story, in her coach role
> F. Breather, a very senior person indeed
> Faye's line manager
> Faye's guardian angel
> Assorted citizens (workshop participants, colleagues, etc.)

Lost in the Woods: Faye's Story

As part of a particular AutoCorp staff development project, Faye was invited to run a workshop day with the finance function, to explain something about the project and see if they wanted to take it on. She was asked to do it in such a way that everybody could decide if they wanted to take part, without any senior staff breathing down their necks, and in a genuinely voluntary way.

So Faye devised a day in which some finance line managers and people from a different area already trying out the scheme could do a short presentation. They would then leave so that the delegates could have open discussions about the costs and benefits, and work out what they might want to take on. Over a buffet lunch the delegates would be joined again by one or two senior development staff responsible for the finance area, and by people from other departments who had already tried the scheme. The afternoon was then confidential time to work in groups on any planning they wanted to do. At the end of the day, they would make a presentation to their managers.

Below are Faye's words from a coaching session, with some thoughts (in **bold**) from her coach Leonora.

Faye begins her tale (**Leonora listens quietly**)

'I was nervous, really, because I hadn't done anything like this before. But I knew I was well prepared, and once we'd started I felt a lot better. It was a really good group, and all went well until lunch.'

But not after lunch?

'At lunch I noticed a platter of sandwiches. I mean a platter, not a little plate. It was covered over and had a label saying 'F. Breather ONLY — vegetarian'. [F. Breather's name has been changed!] Well, quite a few of us were vegetarian, and this person clearly hadn't turned up, but we decided to make do with what we could find on the other plates. Although I'd never met him, I knew he was a very senior manager, but I wouldn't have recognised him unless he'd been eating his sandwiches.'

That's dragons for you. Some don't even have wings and scales these days.

'With twenty minutes to go before the afternoon session, I went around the groups of people chatting and eating their sandwiches, and let them know that there were twenty minutes left. Then I went out to get some materials. When I came back, the group had reconvened and there were just two people left talking — a line manager and somebody I didn't recognise. I went over, and just jokingly, because everything had been pre-agreed, I said, "Very sorry, but I'm going to have to kick you out now".'

I can see the curls of smoke starting to form . . .

' "What did you say?" said the person I didn't know. Well, I repeated myself, with an extra apology, explaining we had to restart the session. I felt confused and worried but I was in charge of running the event so didn't think I should let myself be intimidated.

"Do you know who I am?" he shouted. "Who the hell do you think you are? Nobody tells me what room I can or can't be in."

Bully!

'The line manager I did know said nothing. I said I needed to start and turned to go back to the group. As I walked away, I heard this man saying again, "Who does she think she is. . ." So, maybe I shouldn't have but I really thought I couldn't let that go. I turned back to him: "I'm sorry I didn't know you. . . there is an agreement for only the group to remain after lunch. . . it's important, that's why I have to ask you to leave. . ."

'He turned bright red, practically exploding, volcanic, he stepped to within a few inches of my face, he shouted at me to just get on with my job. . . I couldn't believe it, I was shaking . . . the line manager just said, "I think you had better get back to the group, Faye." Well, I went back, started them on an activity and then left the room. I got myself a drink of water and tried to get composed again, and then I telephoned my own line manager to say how unacceptable I had found this. Then I went back. Thank goodness, they had both gone.'

So what then?

Now, when Faye told that story to Leonora, she didn't mention dragons – that was Leonora's imagination, responding to what she heard as the fierce heat and level of amazement reflected in Faye's voice. And the order of everything wasn't quite so clear – occasionally Faye would leap back in time as she remembered some important detail from earlier in the proceedings.

Like all stories of organisations, the factors affecting any individual's actions at any one time are legion and interconnected. When the action really happened, Faye was making the best sense she could out of what was going on. So was everybody else. When Faye told the story later to colleagues, over several days and on several occasions, she was continuing her sensemaking and hearing the sensemaking of others. When she told the tale to Leonora, many more events had happened and her story was different once again.

We'll come to whether everyone lived happily after in just a moment. But, after listening to this, and after some general conversation about the whole situation until Faye had returned to the here-and-now from her very vivid memories, here's what Leonora asked Faye.

'Would you be interested to explore this experience in a slightly playful way, using stories as an approach to enquiry?'

Faye said she would. Leonora said, 'OK, then I have a story question for you to try out. If you find it interesting then we'll keep going, and if not then we'll try something else.

 'If you were to think about the situation we've been talking about as if it were some sort of folk tale or fairy story, who would you say were the main characters?'

'Little Red Riding Hood is me,' came the reply. 'The group were trees. That line manager was a waterfall, not a character, all wet and not very solid. He wasn't a character but he should have been. And F. Breather was the wolf, although as the whole story developed [see below], it turned out he was Grandpa dressed as the wolf, not the usual way. And I had a guardian angel who asked me a very good question at a difficult time. Everybody else involved was, for the most part, those little grey plasticine characters that just melt away and change – Morph.'

For location, Faye felt she was in a cardboard box with figures inside, like a puppet show. At the time she was at one side of the box, looking in, because the whole situation had felt 'so surreal. A mixture of textures – plasticine Morphs, material puppets, photograph trees. It was as if they were all mixed together, like you do with paints, and swirled.'

'Thinking about it all now, and using these characters, I can look down into the box from the top. It seems like a play because there was a very clear sequence, different acts, beginning, middle and end. And there is a happy ever after.'

In recreating the story with Leonora, Faye highlighted other themes, such as the feelings of Red Riding Hood, and how the threat had been hidden in the guise of 'maybe a wolf puppy, but the animal became suddenly very angry and had fangs'. Faye also explained how her guardian angel (her coaching scheme 'buddy') helped her make her way out of the woods by asking her what was really important to her and sending her on a new journey. 'Everyone was busy telling me that this was to be expected, that everyone knew what this dragon was like, and that you weren't really an AutoCorp person until you'd been flamed by the dragon. I didn't want to hear that – to hear that this is all OK. It wasn't OK. I had done nothing wrong. I had been shouted at, during an event I was running, by a man who put his hands on his hips and came within two inches of my face in order to make his point, and what is more, by the time I got back to my desk at the end of the day there was a note from my manager saying this man had made a complaint about me. Well, I thought this was too important to ignore. In fact, I'd be prepared to lose my job. But I wouldn't go without a fight.'

All's well that ends well

Faye sought a meeting with the dragon/wolf. As already indicated, the wolf turned out to be a grandfather in disguise. Instead of a loud, tough guy, she found somebody who explained his context more fully and apologised for over-reacting. He said he'd behaved inappropriately. The fire-breathing, girl-eating monster were gone; instead she saw an older person reflecting on his career and giving advice. Faye still was not prepared to condone or accept his earlier behaviour: 'he dealt with me in a monstrous way, but behind the monster there was a person.' They parted on friendly terms, each having explained their position.

Two months later, there was an announcement of grandpa wolf's retirement. 'When we had our meeting,' explained Faye, 'we had talked about the pictures on the walls, and it turned out that he had painted them or taken the photographs. I saw an artistic side to him that I would never have guessed at. He was quite self-deprecating, said he'd probably get rid of them one day, and I said jokingly that he should call me before he did that because I'd have them. He must have known when we met that he was leaving. His secretary called me when the announcement was made, to ask if I wanted a picture or photograph from his office.

'So I went and I chose a picture. It was a lovely black and white photograph, just of a garden spade leaning against a wall. And I asked him to sign it for me. This is what he wrote: "A nice light makes ordinary things nice".

Narrative benefits

 The use of this story by Faye, as well as by others involved, by Leonora, and in its telling here, highlights a variety of themes, including the following:

- An individual can think about a narrative in fictional terms, for example by drawing on fictional characters, to clarify the central emotions and themes of an event.
- A story is created through a sensemaking process and, conversely, stories promote sensemaking, in a co-evolutionary way.
- Core values can rise to the surface through reflecting on a story, because the creation of a story, whether done formally or inform-ally, requires consideration of the motivations of characters involved.
- A coach can help a coachee decide on the best actions to take through making enquiries about (not imposing analysis of) a story a coachee is telling. See Chapter 10.
- Through stories, events can be reframed both as journeys and as opportunities for learning.

Faye reflected on this story and others she had experienced or been told, to explore her own values and the values of AutoCorp. In management terms, she compared evidence of theories-in-use with espoused theories (Argyris 1992). She also reflected on AutoCorp's past traditions and the emergence of a new story for its future, as grandparents, wolves and dragons either went away or were integrated in new ways. She discovered benefit in going to visit the wolf, and found that her courage in going (well prepared) to the wolf's lair had a transformational effect on the wolf. She learned what was needed for going walking in the woods, and she realised how to find and use a guardian angel. This was not a tale in which a fairy godmother waved a wand to make everything better again, and Faye didn't tell it that way. Instead she found a helper for the journey whose main contribution was, as in all good fairy tales, to put her in touch with her own values and resources.

Says Faye, 'I probably will still go into the woods naively, but I'll be able to deal with things differently. Also, I am learning how, as a character, I can choose my actions, including perhaps having more understanding of the actions of other characters. I can have higher regard for people if I start with the notion that they are doing what makes sense to their character. Like Rogers' unconditional positive regard.' [a reference to psychologist Carl Rogers (1951)].

In some ways, F. Breather, as a senior figure who was not Faye's line manager, missed a mentoring opportunity. Perhaps he could have updated his behaviour to suit the changing times rather than what had supported his success in AutoCorp's history. Then he might have continued to provide both inspiration and a role model in real life, even though he clearly had a significant effect on Faye's learning before he left. The next two stories are of people who, in different ways, highlight the contributions of a mentor.

A Mentoring Tale

Here you will find one inspirational tale of companionship and one work tale about being a positive role model. In our simplified use of the term mentoring, we refer to a relationship that may include both inspiration and example. Coaches and trainers are, of course, not exempt from practising what they preach and providing effective modelling, nor from inspiring people. However, a mentor figure, particularly, may provide these.

Betty and Adele

Two terminally ill cancer patients lay in adjacent beds in a very caring hospice. Betty was unable to sit up, and she told Adele that she regretted not being able to look out of the window. Adele began to tell Betty what was going on outside the hospice. Her stories were so vivid that Betty sometimes wondered whether it all could really be happening, but as she enjoyed Adele's stories that didn't bother her. After a week or so, Adele died, but Betty recovered a little and at last was able to look out of the window. She was amazed to see a blank wall in front of the window, and told a nurse that Adele must have had a wonderful imagination. 'She told me all those wonderful stories when all she could see was a blank wall!' 'You're right about the imagination,' said the nurse. 'Adele became blind a few months ago.'

Adele's imagination was an inspiration to Betty, and the fact that it was not based on the mundane happenings in the street outside the hospice didn't make the slightest difference.

In teaching, the Socratic method aims to make explicit to the pupil the knowledge the pupil does not know he has. In coaching, much benefit is drawn from the confidence it gives to the coachee as he comes to see how he is able to develop the skills he wishes to have from his existing skills. In mentoring, inspiration can play a key role, and can do so – as the story of the cancer patients suggests – in difficult times.

Tommy and Mike

At AutoCorp's DDC, there was a policy of encouraging engineers to study for extra qualifications. AutoCorp paid the fees for selected courses, provided that the student actually gained the qualification. Quite a few people took part-time MBA courses, and old-timers like Tommy Sprigett didn't much like this. It meant that the best people spent time on study leave when they could have been working, and once they got their qualification they usually went off to work somewhere else, either another department in AutoCorp or in some other firm. Tommy asked the HR department why they had this policy. He was given the answer that without it AutoCorp wouldn't be able to attract the best engineers.

An informal mentoring practice had grown up within AutoCorp's

DDC. Experienced members of staff looked after those studying for qualifications such as the MBA, on a one-to-one basis. The more experienced people often did not have the qualification themselves, but they were nevertheless able to help their younger colleagues through the arduous process of combining study with work. Mentors helped by discussing how to juggle the requirements of work and study, and how topics of study might relate to tasks at work.

Groups within the DDC were encouraged to mark the successful completion of someone's course of study by a small ceremony. In the chassis design group, this took the form of the presentation of a metal object, made in the DDC's workshops, symbolising the qualification. A newly qualified MBA might get a shiny plaque in the shape of a pound sign. When Tommy was involved at such gatherings, he made a very short speech and then told a story. His favourite story was the old, slightly off-colour, one about the three dogs.

One evening in a bar, an engineer, a doctor and a lawyer were boasting about the skills of the dogs they each owned. After a few drinks, they decided to hold a contest to decide who had the cleverest dog. A big pile of bones was provided for the contest. The engineer went first, calling to his dog: 'Come here, Sliderule!' [Tommy always remarked here: 'I told you it was an old story.'] Out ran Sliderule and used the bones to build a model of a suspension bridge, with all its ropes and girders in place. The audience gasped – this dog would surely win. But the doctor smiled and called to his dog: 'Come here, Stethosope!' Out ran Stethoscope and built a complete human skeleton, with every metatarsal and carpal in place. Again, there was a gasp of admiration from the audience. Then the lawyer called to his dog: 'Come here, Loophole!' Out ran Loophole, who ate up all the bones, screwed the other two dogs and was declared the winner.

One of the people who had mentored a successful MBA student this year was Mike. After Tommy had told his story of the three dogs, Mike spoke up. 'You know what, Tommy, it's a good story, and I'm glad us engineers can take a joke, but I don't reckon Loophole would get a look-in these days. These lads here, who've just got their MBAs, show that we can be capable in two fields – technical and administrative. And we don't need to cheat either.' This raised applause, and Tommy retired the story from his repertoire.

Such small changes told quite a big story about how AutoCorp was starting to change, and the unexpected impact of learning. Mike spoke up and provided an example to others. Tommy lost some ground, but in choosing to retire the joke he could soon be setting a better example once more. At AutoCorp, 'Tommys' were beginning to realise that their talents were still valued but their humour would be better appreciated without the cynicism. 'Mikes' were starting to realise that they could speak up in support of the future.

A Cautionary Tale about Not Learning

Sometimes we haven't learned what we think we have. This is why review is important and why outside perspectives are valuable. Sometimes being incorrect in our assessment of what we have learned matters and sometimes it doesn't – after all, opportunistic learning of all types can and should be of benefit. However, it's good to stay aware of the possibility.

You could talk about unconscious incompetence, or of not knowing what you don't know, or even of rearranging the deckchairs on the Titanic. Or you could think about the two travelling frogs from Japan.

The Two Frogs

This tale concerns two frogs, each of which, quite independently and coincidentally, set out on a journey to see the home town of the other. [Original spelling has been retained.]

Once upon a time in the country of Japan there lived two frogs, one of whom made his home in a ditch near the town of Osaka, on the sea coast, while the other dwelt in a clear little stream which ran through the city of Kioto. At such a great distance apart, they had never even heard of each other; but, funnily enough, the idea came into both their heads at once that they should like to see a little of the world, and the frog who lived at Kioto wanted to visit Osaka, and the frog who lived at Osaka wished to go to Kioto, where the great Mikado had his palace.

So one fine morning in spring, they both set out along the road that led from Kioto to Osaka, one from one end and the other from the other.

The journey was more tiring than they expected, for they did not know much about travelling, and half-way between the two towns there rose a mountain which had to be climbed. It took them a long time and a great many hops to reach the top, but there they were at last, and what was the surprise of each to see another frog before him! They looked at each other for a moment without speaking and then fell into conversation, and explained the cause of their meeting so far from their homes. It was delightful to find that they both felt the same wish – to learn a little more of their native country – and as there was no sort of hurry they stretched themselves out in a cool, damp place, and agreed that they would have a good rest before they parted to go their ways.

'What a pity we are not bigger,' said the Osaka frog, 'and then we could see both towns from here and tell if it is worth our while going on.'

'Oh, that is easily managed,' returned the Kioto frog. 'We have only got to stand up on our hind legs, and hold on to each other, and then we can each look at the town he is travelling to.'

This idea pleased the Osaka frog so much that he at once jumped up and put his front paws on the shoulder of his friend, who had risen also. There they both stood, stretching themselves as high as they could, and holding on to each other tightly, so that they might not fall down. The Kioto frog turned his nose towards Osaka, and the Osaka frog turned his nose towards Kioto; but the foolish things forgot that when they stood up their great eyes lay in the backs of their heads, and that though their noses might point to the places to which they wanted to go, their eyes beheld the places from which they had come.

'Dear me!' cried the Osaka frog, 'Kioto is exactly like Osaka. It is certainly not worth such a long journey. I shall go home.'

'If I had had any idea that Osaka was only a copy of Kioto I should never have travelled all this way,' exclaimed the frog from Kioto, and as he spoke, he took his hands from his friend's shoulders and they both fell down on the grass. Then they took a polite farewell of each other, and set off for home again, and to the end of their lives they believed that Osaka and Kioto, which are as different to look at as two towns can be, were as like as two peas.

Reprinted from *The Violet Fairy Book* by Andrew Lang, with permission, in *The Art of the Story-Teller* by Marie L. Shedlock (1854–1935).

Conclusion

This chapter has explored the ways in which story-telling can be helpful in supporting individuals in organisations. Some stories are warnings, like the two frogs, others help us to see things in different ways, like Pete Binns' and Faye's tales, and others concern the support for formal learning and putting learning into practice, as with Leonora and Jeanenne, or even Tommy Sprigett's retirement of his off-colour joke.

Stories help through making learning events more memorable and engaging, through helping individuals gain perspective and become more effective, and through their ability to cross boundaries from formal/designated learning situations to the wider everyday world in which we learn, and vice versa. They remain useful even when not precisely recalled and retold, because they are suited to the circumstance of here and now.

Story-telling can be used to address knowledge, skills and abilities. It accepts and deals well with the often sidelined emotional life of organisations and organisational change, and supports best practice in training, coaching and mentoring.

4

Themis – Using Stories in a Professional Development Community

Be with those who help your being
Don't sit with indifferent people, whose breath
Comes cold out of their mouths.
Not these visible forms, your work is deeper

Rumi, Ode 2865

This chapter explores the use of stories and story-telling in a professional development setting. Key story uses include sharing knowledge and experience, creating a community of (learning) practice, and using a story-like structure as a framework for development days. This last practice was found to be very useful in addressing the need for both fluidity and structure.

Collaborative learning requires individual and collective commitment, supported by appropriate skills and processes in order that maximum value can be derived from the experience. Here we describe how a group of professionals, which we'll call Themis, came together to support and learn from each other by sharing their stories and experience. Not only did they create and use stories during their day-long meetings but, over time, as *they* shaped stories from their experience, *stories* shaped the group. In this way, the format and process of the entire day co-evolved to be a story structure in itself.

Later in the chapter we look at how the structure of the day matches a typical story structure, but first we tell the story of a Themis day, from the point of view of Lyn, one of the participants.

Lyn's Story

 It is 7 am on a winter Saturday. A persistent noise builds somewhere off to the left. 'Something is happening this morning,' Lyn thinks.

She starts to recall taking three hours last night to get home through traffic jams on a journey that should have taken an hour . . . going straight out again to the late-opening supermarket for . . . a contribution to today's lunch. Today's lunch. It's still dark and Lyn can hear rain outside. Feeling as if she's only just got to bed, Lyn is now thinking about getting up for the hour-and-a-half drive to join Themis, her peer learning group. To meet for a full day each month with a group of fellow professionals is, Lyn knows, a wonderful opportunity. But it doesn't always feel that way. Ten more minutes . . .

It's 9.30 am. The weather is looking up, Lyn has managed somehow not to fall back to sleep and has arrived at her colleague Sarah's home in good time for a 10 am start. Gossip, stories about her journey, the snowdrops in the garden, the new colour scheme, are swapped as a cup of tea is made. Lyn is pleased to see her colleague looking well after a recent illness, and to hear she has started painting once more.

Taking her drink and bags through to the living room, Lyn chooses a comfy chair with a view to the garden. Through the window she sees Helen drive up, with Mike and Howard as passengers. Mike often stays at Helen's on the evening before these events because of his four-hour journey to reach most of the venues. Once a year, for the last session, the whole group makes the journey to his seaside house for a sociable weekend of reviewing and planning.

Lyn goes with Sarah to greet the new arrivals, who have just been joined by Luc, making his first visit of the year. There's plenty of to-ing and fro-ing with car parking since most people live around forty miles from Sarah's house and public transport doesn't serve her particularly well. By the time they are ready to start, eight of the twelve possibles have arrived, the kitchen is full of food and the living room is full of people plus an assortment of books, papers and other items of interest brought by participants.

It's 10.15 am – not too bad for timekeeping thanks to Elemeik's nudging. Elemeik is this month's designated 'facilitator' who, among other things, takes responsibility for reminding the group of passing time. The group begins the work of the day. Materials of interest are briefly introduced by those who have brought them, and notice given of forthcoming events. This time these include a book launch for one of the group members, a singing workshop, a recommended film and a range of books including ones on landscape photography, gardens, African society, complexity, organisational change, clinical governance in the NHS, working with addiction and qualitative research methods.

Sarah conveys messages from those not present. Roy is not expected today since his agreed contribution to the group is to host once a year, when he also makes some presentation of his work. Other no-shows are Kaye, Esther and Tessa. Tessa again. Lyn frowns. According to Sarah, Tessa was going to call Lyn for a lift. Great, thinks Lyn, so I'm implicated now. 'Well, she didn't call,' states Lyn, not adding 'and in any case I'd only have had to listen to a long list of woes on the way here.' Tessa has been a sporadic attendee and there are mixed feelings in the group about whether she's really a member or not. Lyn wonders if she should be more concerned to include her – after all, she didn't call her and offer a lift. If only Tessa's cup wasn't so loudly half empty.

Torn between irritation and concern, Lyn takes out a pad of paper. She is today's note-taker, collating facts, stories and her impressions of the day for circulation before the next meeting. She gets ready to listen to the news of those present. Since the notes will go to people not there (should she really still send them to Tessa?) Lyn tries to be careful about personal information and in the write-up will provide only broad details of this section. The group's guidance is that the note-taker should show consideration and the speaker should indicate when they particularly wish to be off the record.

Lyn always feels moved by what people have to say in this part of the day. She is very aware of the general excellence of her colleagues' professional practice and she listens once more to recent achievements including the setting up of a research agency, the completion of a chapter for a forthcoming book, and ensuring the safety of a threat-ened child. She listens also to experiences of attempting to make a change or complete a project and failing, or of others taking credit for work they have done. And she hears how all these issues and more have been addressed through times of family or personal illness, bereavement, house moves, job moves, and individual challenges such as overcoming a fear of public speaking. She is reassured to find out that some enterprises do indeed run smoothly from start to finish, that people she regards as being quite brilliant nonetheless experience and overcome prejudice, failure, overt aggression, exhaustion and humiliation. Even that sometimes they don't. She celebrates people's successes with them, knowing how much they mean, and benefits from the same attention in return.

Coffee time. Conversation in the kitchen is of business and book writing; in the living room it's of overseas travel and cultural contrasts. Lyn peruses a book filled with beautiful photographs of the natural world and scans the contents page of another one about organisational complexity. Like the issues that were coming up before the break, and the conversations going on around her, the books also have a perspective on how patterns emerge as a product of interrelationships.

There will be a presentation after lunch, on a topic not yet known to anybody except today's presenter, Lisa. The time before lunch is given to exploring the main themes to emerge from the day's activities so far. Lyn is intrigued by how often the themes from that discussion link in with the as-yet-unannounced afternoon slot. Will that happen today? Back in her seat she looks forward to the process of collective exploration and sensemaking: individual stories of actual experiences, references to theoretical frameworks or literature, and reflection on how the themes apply to the group as a whole.

The themes of the discussion before lunch are of inclusion and exclusion, who belongs and who does not.

She is the first to notice a green Mini stopping outside the house. . .

At lunch, around the large kitchen table, conversation turns to enquiries after people's families and holiday plans, or to world events and news of mutual friends. An hour and a quarter also allows a little time for book browsing or quiet discussion. Then there is a brief focus/preparation activity that in the past has included music, different types of meditation, a short walk or a venture into the garden, depending on weather, mood and inspirations. Today Elemiek has brought along some Aboriginal music with its distinctive rhythms and story-telling purpose.

Now comes the presentation. Yes, thinks Lyn, the theme was there all right, as Lisa outlines a session she will lead on in-groups, out-groups, diversity and cohesion. A subject matter expert in these areas, she has chosen to help the group explore the Stephen Lawrence inquiry and the McPherson report. She has brought a range of publications and also materials from the local government Internet sites. Her question is, 'What do you know of the enquiry and the report, and how does this relate to your work in organisations or with people who are part of organisations?' There is silence for a while. Then one voice says, 'You know, a lot of my information has come from television news reporting . . .'

Lyn is struck by one of Sarah's thoughts: 'What does it mean in the McPherson report when it refers to prejudice that is "unwitting"? If I am asked to run a session on leadership, for example, how unwitting am I if the definitions of leadership I use are all based on a Western culture? Or a Japanese culture? Whose responsibility is it to become "witting", or whatever the word should be, and act accordingly?'

And so the session continues, thought-provoking and challenging, as each person considers their knowledge and capability in addressing discrimination. By the end it has broadened into issues of power and responsibility, the role each person takes within the group – including Tessa, whose green Mini it was – and the role they want to play outside it.

The day is drawing to a close. Lyn collects book references and spare copies of Lisa's presentation notes and newspaper article to be circulated to group members who were absent when her own meeting notes are posted out to everybody. She knows she will find writing the notes challenging because she wants to feel that she has done some measure of justice to the day and to everyone's contribution. She also knows that there is another value to the notes, which is to highlight significant differences in perceptions of the same event and in the learning experienced, even among close colleagues.

'See you next time – at Helen's.' 'Hope you get that new job you're going for, it sounds really good.' 'Thanks for the story you told, it's made me feel quite different about things.'

On the way home, a poem that was read out in the meeting comes back to her:

Ring out the want, the care, the sin,
The faithless coldness of the times;
Ring out, ring out my mournful rhymes,
But ring the fuller minstrel in.

Tennyson, *In Memoriam*, CVI, 17–20.

She realises how easy and comfortable it is to believe that because she did her bit today, being there and sharing stories, that this is doing enough. But what might it mean to ring in the 'fuller minstrel', the many stories and the deep stories?

That is Lyn's story of one day in the life of Themis, the peer learning group she cherishes as a source of learning.

Perspectives and Practices

Lyn's story is about a day that is both demanding and rewarding for her, not just because of the knowledge she gets from her colleagues, but because of the opportunity she has to reflect on her values, beliefs and practice, and in the way that group dynamics can be used for learning. What she takes from the day is different from what others take; the experiences of other participants are inevitably somewhat different from hers. For instance, for Lyn the issues of inclusion and exclusion are important in her work at the moment, while her thoughts about Tessa posed her an additional challenge.

There is no single view on the facts of the day and while Lyn's story, as told here, would be recognised by others in the group, it is a personal account. We see the day through her eyes. It leaves out things that another story-teller would have included; and this is a vital aspect of story-telling. A transcription of a tape recording, although 'accurate', is usually much less compelling than a story told from someone's point of view. Personal authenticity is much more powerful than trying to put everything into a story – which is impossible, anyway. Understanding this is a useful lesson in story-telling. As Bettelheim pointed out about fairy-tales (1991), a child hearing a fairy-tale (or an adult reading the above story) can know that while it is not 'real' in precisely duplicating factual detail, the story is nonetheless able to contain some truth.

So far in this chapter, we have given one perspective on how an individual might make sense of, and gain value through, the interweaving of stories, past and present, fact and fiction, professional and personal; how stories can be used to pass on knowledge and experience, and promote reflection for learning. Box 4.1 lists a range of the narrative techniques used by Themis to support this. In addition, what Lyn doesn't talk about because it isn't her focus, is the way in which story-telling intrinsically requires practising of key skills that are often preached: personal trust, responsibility, valuing experience and acknowledging multiple narratives, for example.

BOX 4.1   Narrative Techniques Summary

- Making a place (time) for 'everyday' stories and the use of active listening
- Making a place for appreciation of a storying format (day format and structures)
- Attending to boundaries, including physical comfort and psychological climate
- Supporting and valuing reflexivity/an enquiring orientation
- Developing ritual
- Boundary spanning through sharing tales of first-hand experience in a variety of environments outside the group
- Multiple narratives and the use of action research
- Archetypal reference
- Traditional story reference (fairy-tale, folk tale and other)
- Imaginative exercises and experiential learning opportunities

---

As already indicated, and as Lyn's story starts to explain, a story-telling structure emerged as an effective and appropriate format for Themis learning days, and this is what we will explore next. A story-telling framework was found to attend to declarative knowledge (the acquisition of 'what') and support skill development, or 'how', alongside 'when' and 'why' (see Kolb 1984, Andersen 1985, Kraiger, Ford and Salas 1993 and Chapter 3 of this book).

The Story Structure of the Themis Day

The structure of the day is the structure of a story (see Box 4.2; the bold in the box is the story). As stories have a beginning, middle and

end, with some signposts on the way, so the day's structure provides
this sense of journey.

	BOX 4.2	The Structure of the Day	

Time	Section title	Activities
10 am	Administration time (*Once upon a time in a land where . . .*)	Sharing of books, articles and the dates and titles of forthcoming events and opportunities
10.15 am	Check-in: (*There lived . . .*)	'Headline news' from each participant and messages from those absent
11.30 am	Break	Refreshments, conversation, book browsing
11.50 am	Processing 1: (*The inhabitants lived happily except that, from time to time, they were all beset by the visitations of . . .*)	Dialogue and discussion building on what has been said since the start of the day. Discovery and reflection of key themes and key challenges, including the dynamics and effectiveness of the group
12.50 pm	Lunch:	Food preparation and eating, chatting, book browsing. A community activity that has developed its own ritual quality over time
2 pm	Post-lunch: (*They made preparations . . .*)	Use of poetry, music, quietness, physical movement, voice . . .
2.15 pm	Presentation: (*. . . and sent across the kingdom to find what could be done . . .*)	Individual presentation of some theoretical material or viewpoint, with exercises and reflection. This part of the day has one speaker or story-teller, who shares a learning story in whatever way it seems appropriate to them to do so. A whole story-telling format is generally used here. The teller explains the title of the particular tale, the reason for its existence, the characters involved, what was involved in the journey and how things have turned out (so far). The particular nature of a learning group is that most stories are To Be Continued. Often, after some brief story-telling, participants are invited to join in with an exercise of some

Time	Section title	Activities
		sort. This may be so that they can experience some aspect of the story, or the purpose may be to create a new story
3.45 pm	Break	Refreshments, conversation, book browsing
4 pm	Processing 2: (*Having heard the wise woman's tales they decided to . . .*)	A facilitated discussion covering the whole day's events. The format is generally discursive or dialogic although any appropriate format can be chosen
5 pm (close)		

The early parts of the day provide opportunity for the context and characters to be introduced, as in a story we would find out where we were and who was there. Then follows some negotiation and collective sensemaking between the characters (group members) about what is going on and what is important. These narratives develop a sense of plot through the perceived connections providing 'turning points', and the engagement with live issues engenders the type of mental processing and interactions that increases connections and creates memorable learning.

This all leads to a shared event (lunch), a valuable 'space between' according with the view that the majority of learning takes place outside the formally designated learning times or zones, and a focus period of preparation for the afternoon. Then comes the acquisition or creation of knowledge (presentation), after which all the preceding events are taken into consideration and some new meaning arrived at (processing/close). The presentation in particular enables learning through attention to moving back and forth between explicit and tacit knowledge (Polanyi 1967, Boisot 1999), and through the realisation that a theory can be regarded as a type of story (Clarkson 1996, p. 203), particularly in the wider context of who was involved in creating it and why. Furthermore, individuals can gain some practice and feedback on their way of story-telling, should they wish it.

Of course, within this framework there is room for many unexpected turns of events and connections, as Lyn's story demonstrates.

The account of a day can be seen as an event in an overall history. The story of the day ends but the characters do not. They go back to their lands to undertake whatever aspect of the task they choose to take on. The results of their activities will be brought back to the next story-telling, and the first sentence of the story – 'Once upon a time there was a land in which . . .' – will have a changed ending because the nature of their lands will have changed. The histories of the individuals, of their working and personal lives, and of Themis, co-evolve over time.

The framework above developed as Themis tried to negotiate the different preferences of its members for flexibility, structure, spontaneity and so on. The framework can be altered as needed on the day; however, it gives a sufficient starting point and often runs exactly as Box 4.2 indicates. Using the story format, and using stories within it – 'storying' the group – was found to develop capability in dealing with uncertainty. It also attends to the role of individual responsibility and choice in acting with others to evolve and continue a self-managing group. These intra- and interpersonal skills are exactly what many organisations seek to develop to help them deal better with the current business environment.

Lyn's story has valid themes and representative happenings in it, to which her colleagues could attest. But it is not a factual narrative. True or untrue, it would remain incomplete and any illusion of object-ivity would be just that – an illusion. Its validity lies elsewhere.

Themis doesn't limit itself to one story and neither will we here. In Themis, individuals keep, and share with each other from time to time, their own notes and stories of their professional development days. The circulation of 'official' notes from the days forms a part of this multiple narrative.

Here is another view on the same day. It doesn't represent a true 'multiple narrative' contribution since it isn't told fully in the per-spective of a different person. However, it is a contribution towards understanding the multiplicity of 'windows' available on any learning experience and shows how using stories within peer learning can help maximise the benefits to be gained.

A Different Perspective: The Story of Tessa

Over time, stories came to be used to address difficult issues within the group, and to be used quite spontaneously. Here is an elaboration on Lyn's story, about what happened when the green Mini arrived. A conversation about in-groups and out-groups was in full swing.

'Why on earth does the government have a social exclusion unit instead of a social inclusion unit?'

'I'm fed up with Tessa not being clear about whether she wants to be in or out, and I'm angry that she's not here to discuss it again.'

'We don't mind Roy only being here once a year.'

'Yes, but we all know that's what he's doing.'

'And it's a question of what people are prepared to contribute when they are here.'

A green Mini stops outside the house.

'An African tradition says "I am because we are" '. . .

The doorbell rings.

Sarah opens the door. Tessa is standing there. Tessa doesn't have a green Mini, thinks Lyn. So she's not ill after all and wanted to come and I didn't bring her. Great. She smiles; they all do. 'Hello! What happened? Come in. Do you want a drink?'

There's a gap as everyone settles. 'We were discussing inclusion and exclusion, in-groups and out-groups and so forth,' offers Elemeik. The room is quiet. 'Oh,' says Tessa, smiling. 'Well, I'm in now.'

'I'm not sure whether I want to take time up on this,' says Luc, 'but it seems to be the topic of the day. I don't like the way you behave towards this group. I don't know really why you come or whether you want to be in it.'

'I'm sorry I'm late today. A misunderstanding about getting here. Lyn, I left a message last night which I'm assuming you didn't get, then I slept in this morning so missed you. My car's in for repair but fortunately Chris lent me this one for today.' Lyn confirmed she hadn't got the message. Now, what else should she say? Sorry? She wasn't really. She was feeling ungenerous. Sarah faced Tessa. 'If it's not one thing, it's another, Tessa. There's always something and I wonder what that says about your wish to be here or contribute. Perhaps you don't realise the time we've spent on discussing your relationship with the group, or the influence you have.'

'Well, I think we've spent enough time on it,' said Howard.

'And I don't want to discuss it now,' said Tessa. 'I won't be labelled the scapegoat or the outsider. I'm here, I'd like to stay, and I've only just arrived so I'd rather settle before saying any more.'

Lyn summarised this for the notes, realising the issue remained unresolved yet again. It was lunchtime, prompted Elemiek. . .

After lunch, during the discussion after the presentation, Tessa had a story to tell. 'I went to Helen's house last weekend to help with setting up her new computer. We went to this fantastic greengrocer with just about everything you can think of all stacked in trays so you could choose what you wanted. There were quite a lot of vegetables I didn't know – there is a real ethnic mix there. Anyway, we left with all sorts of things to try – the chap who owned the shop knew how to prepare each one – and he gave me something to try for free because I'd never seen it and it was his favourite thing. Anyway, that's not the real point of what I want to say, although we had a really great time and he was so generous and I can't believe he makes a living if he gives everything away the whole time.

'This is about when we were back at Helen's. I was complaining about my sister-in-law who had been staying with me, saying how exhausted I was by the time she left because she was so obsessed with nothing going right and how little she has and how things won't get any better. I couldn't believe how she never came up with a single positive thought and always looked on the dark side.

'Helen just looked at me. Then she said, "Now you know how we feel."'

Lyn glanced over at Helen, who was now looking at Tessa with admiration. 'I'm so glad you could tell that story,' said Helen. 'I know how badly you were feeling and I was sad when I thought you weren't going to turn up again.'

Tessa's voice was trembling. 'I've really been thinking about what I contribute to the group and I know you haven't been happy with me. I haven't been happy with myself, and I just thought how well you are all doing and that I didn't have anything to offer at the moment. . . But this group really is important. And I do have things to offer. I don't have to be that sad person feeling sorry for myself and wondering what I'll say if I turn up.'

Lyn felt a tear in her eye. 'Thank you for your story,' she said to Tessa. 'I can see how difficult it has been for you. And Helen, I have to say I also admire your turn of phrase. I've been thinking the same things but not knowing what to say because I was feeling too annoyed.'

'Well, I do keep coming back to this,' said Helen. '"I was angry with my friend, I told my wrath, my wrath did end." That's it really.'

In this chapter we have now attended to the format and content of a Themis day, and heard two different stories about the same event to offer a brief insight into how stories have been used in the service of professional development. Now we will look at some particular aspects of stories and how these relate to the ways in which Themis works.

The History of Themis

In this book we use the word history to denote not just 'times past' but the past, present and continuing evolution of entities such as organisations through their collected and growing set of stories.

A Beginning

One attractive feature of stories, particularly in learning contexts, is that their format works in many scales and in an iterative fashion. The very same tale can be considered in relation to an individual, a group or a society. While a Themis day has the history of previous days and starts with the equivalent of 'Once upon a time', there is also a wider history to be told, another origin point with echoes into the present. As with all stories, beginnings are important. In life, a beginning is often something that is realised only after the event; in stories, beginnings are designed in.

Some of the Themis members recall that a respected colleague familiar with a number of 'start-ups' warned them that such groups did not usually last. There were a number of individual reactions to this including increased determination to 'succeed', irritation, and curiosity about what would make the difference between continuing and not continuing as a group. But it has continued for more than four years as a voluntary, self-managing, emergent property of participation, and it continues to be experienced by individuals as valuable in supporting their continuing professional development. As with a story, it perpetuates because it is valued.

Although the story of Themis is fictional, a variety of real 'Themis' groups exists. The one which developed the story framework for their days outlined above has a particular origin, explained in Box 4.3.

Box 4.3   Physis

Physis is a Greek word that concerns growth, beginnings, generation. It is the name given by Professor Petruska Clarkson to her centre for learning and research in London. Professor Clarkson is a widely published author on subjects including psychology, psychotherapy, organisational change and ethics, and she has done much to aid the development of fellow professionals in these fields.

One group, used as an inspiration for the Themis story, emerged from Physis. The group came together in order to maintain contact with colleagues who were moving on from a programme called Dierotao (learning by enquiry) run by Professor Clarkson at Physis. Initial membership was open to anybody who had attended at least one of the Dierotao years. There was therefore some shared knowledge base and some shared history that arguably reflected the presence of some underlying interests or values.

Such was the import of the origins that, as with many stories in the oral tradition, the group evolved in the telling while retaining kernels/shades of its original form. For example, a group member coined the pet name 'physlings', and emphasis on responsibility and ethical behaviours continued to be an important concern.

During research for the Themis story, here is one story that a participant told:

'After the session I did some reading about responsibility and ethics. The book was *The Bystander* by Petruska Clarkson (1996). It includes the well-known case of Kitty Genovese, which I learned during my original degree. This woman was murdered in broad daylight, in open ground, with lots of people around her, but nobody helped her.

'I am reminded that these issues and their stories re-emerge because of their significance and importance. And this is also why the oral tradition works. Quite simply, stories are told and re-told because they continue to be relevant and useful. Their written form, however, is an additional touchstone reminding me that I have passed this way before and asking me to consider what else I now know.

'Clarkson's poem "The Killing of Kindness" is a powerful reminder of the value of telling stories, in poetry or otherwise.

There was a child, bruised like a plum, terrified like a wounded thrush, sick
from fear and lack
of concentration, stretched like a deerskin in the sun between a father's secret attentions and a
mother's whimpering cry for help and nobody knew or they said they didn't
know and the
teachers couldn't have known, but she never undressed for swimming and nobody ever asked her the reason.

There is an old man near you or a young woman, a child or a baby, a dog, a friend or a place,
absorbing the violence, the viciousness, the vileness and the vice and someone is standing by
passively looking, merely observing, inwardly cringing, finding good reasons for not engaging,
estrangingly ever from feeling the kind-ness, our human kindness, the sameness of being and pain.

Excerpt from 'The Killing of Kindness' by Petruska Clarkson (in the preface to Clarkson (1996)).

Some Characters

If the 'Once upon a time' of a story is held to be important, then so generally are the characters involved. The inaugural Themis had a dozen members, three of them male and nine female. The age range was 27 to 63. Diversity considerations would further include five nationalities and seven ethnicities, with two of those who counted as UK nationals having spent significant periods of their life in other continents. Educational attainment was typically a first or higher degree(s) plus at least one professional qualification or accreditation. Occupations represented (not necessarily mutually exclusive) included student, social worker, psychotherapist, organisational psychologist, local government advisor, lecturer, educational psychologist, SME (small to medium-sized enterprise) owner and priest. All had training and qualifications in a psychological or psychotherapeutic discipline.

From a story point of view it is easy to imagine that one could cast most archetypal roles from such a group. Furthermore, from a practice point of view, all of the individuals were familiar with using narratives to a greater or lesser extent in working with people. There was therefore some core overlap of interest as well as a diverse range of cultural influences and application areas.

Worth noting was the growing realisation as the group was in its second year that additional members would be valuable in many ways, not only for their knowledge and practice areas but also for their impacts upon the group as a system of relationships. In order to thrive rather than simply survive, the group would need to choose diversity, challenge and fresh viewpoints. New plot points would be needed or the story would be frozen in time. A decision was taken to open the group to others, including those who had not spent time on the courses from which the group originally evolved. This is an experiment that continues at the time of writing, which is highlighting the importance of beginnings and histories, and which will be storied in due course.

Story Space and Community

Themis functions through its story spaces and the capacity of its members to work within them and create them. In this example, the group members (story characters) are involved in using stories and narratives in some way as part of their professional lives. It is therefore appropriate to use them in the peer group, and this provides the experiential opportunity to use themselves reflexively as the subjects of their own practice in this regard. However, this does not exclude the use of this framework by other types of group who through virtue of joint activity or enterprise may be regarded as a Community of Practice (Wenger 1998). The important factor is that the group is a product of participation and its members share an enterprise or practice in common. In Themis we see a number of joint enterprises, in particular those of professional support and learning: 'learning . . . depends on opportunities to contribute actively to the practices of communities that we value and that value us, to integrate their enterprises into our understanding of the world, and to make creative use of their respective repertoires' (Wenger, p. 227).

In order to achieve this, the group uses stories in a number of ways. The meeting days involve the unfolding of a variety of stories in such a way that each individual may engage in meaning-making for themselves and collaboratively. In participation throughout the day, the group story as an ongoing enterprise is evolved, with the participants forming the cast. And the structure of the day gives a format within which individual stories may be told and a collective history evolved. Each person and each section of the day makes a specific contribution. The use of these different story types has the effect of extending individual repertoires in their negotiation with other communities and systems (for example the use of story-telling in organisational development or large-scale change programmes).

Development of an Appropriate Climate for the Day

The phrase 'are we all sitting comfortably?' is well known in the UK as a precursor to storytime at school (originally from the radio programme 'Listen with Mother'). One reaction to such a phrase is rejection of its hackneyed qualities and nursery-school connotations. However, it's not an insignificant requirement. Themis attends to physical and psychological comfort levels through some simple but effective tactics. Some specific roles are rotated among group members in order to support group functioning, and some informally held behavioural requirements. One role, the 'facilitator', attends to timetables, break times and is a resource in the whole-group 'processing' sessions; the 'host' ensures there will be sufficient liquid refreshments throughout the day, kitchen facilities, appropriate seating etc.; the 'presenter' offers to make a specific contribution on a topic of her choice, with sufficient accompanying notes for everyone; the 'scribe' takes notes, writes them up and distributes them along with any additional materials before the next meeting. Key attitudes that are appreciated by the group are constructive challenge, generosity, curiosity, honesty and integrity. And there are stories about this too. Here is one:

The going has not always been comfortable or easy. A mini-story in the form of a saying was brought by a participant who was challenged by the degree of fury she felt on several occasions while in the group. It was of benefit to everyone on more than one occasion, both within the group and at work or with loved ones: 'I was angry with my friend, I told my wrath, my wrath did end. I was angry with my foe, I told it not, my wrath did grow.' ['The Poison Tree' by William Blake]. Told with evident feeling, the story challenged everyone to attend to the effects of 'letting things slide' and, in organisational contexts, with going along with the prevailing 'undiscussables'.Undiscussables are those things that an organisational culture deems as things not to be discussed. The fact that they are undiscussable is usually also not to be discussed, so the situation is difficult to change.

Development of Community

The iteration of the process through the year(s) creates an informal group (hi)story and, through doing so, a community. Negotiating meaning and sensemaking do not necessarily mean agreement, but there is a striving towards the capacity to hold disagreement and tensions. Individuals and the group as a whole need to be reflexive, and the process also teaches and supports reflexivity.

Development of Ritual

Story and ritual are often intertwined, with story-telling having rituals of its own, and stories being told about rituals. When somebody says 'once upon a time', this is an invitation to attend in a particular way and is a ritualised beginning that children quickly learn, indicating a particular type of event to follow. Attention can be focused. Within the structure of the day, lunch takes this ritual function, mirroring the significance accorded to sharing food together that is found in many communities around the world, for example in Jewish spiritual celebrations. It is allocated a generous amount of time, everybody brings some food to share, and the meal is eaten together.

Sharing Knowledge and Skills for Application

Within the day, stories have been used as a method for supporting learning, and to support the use of stories in professional practice by group members working in three main areas, as below. Where individuals have learned from a day, they bring back a story of the subsequent application so that it too may be learned from.

1. Supporting individual creative work.
2. Organisational development, including managing change, addressing innovation, and working effectively in groups and teams.
3. Therapeutic work with children and adults.

In addition, the afternoon presentation slots often include story-telling practices. Presentation slots in Themis have been used by individuals for a variety of purposes including to receive feedback on papers, book chapters or course materials; to share interesting or intriguing aspects of their current work practice and/or philosophy; to practise skills in giving presentations and to experiment with new approaches or ideas in progress. Theoretical input has generally been combined with some experiential learning, with an invitation to share related stories and reflect on their implications. A rich juxtaposition of influences always emerges.

Each year of Themis gives the opportunity for ten particular learning stories to be told by those working in the appropriate areas. These have been wide-ranging and have included: complexity in social systems and organisations; Jung and Christianity; cognitive analytic therapy; a book for children about suicide; evaluating therapeutic communities in prison; psychosomatic disorders; ethics; neuro-linguistic programming; leadership and self-management.

Storying the Group as a Multiple Narrative

Themis is engaged with writing or producing a record of the learning group to date as an individual and collective story-telling. This involves each individual choosing the way in which she tells 'her' story of the group, with some initial starting-point questions she may use if she finds them useful. This form of action research is ongoing, and a description of one of the 'starting-point' activities included may be found as a practical exercise in Chapter 10. In addition, attention is given during each session to hearing individual perspectives, including the discipline of hearing perspectives very different from one's own.

Personal Narrative

These are the stories of everyday life that group members share at the start of the day. The learning from these is both tacit and explicit, and the stories are of triumphs, failures and work in progress. As the group goes on to explore emergent themes connecting the stories, this helps individuals to gain new perspectives for themselves and also engages them in community sensemaking.

Archetypal Reference

Themis can draw on a range of psychological and cultural traditions and learn through reference to symbolic or archetypal stories. For example, one group activity used during the morning 'processing' slot involved naming any specific archetypes, symbols or representations that group members associated with each other. Examples included: the still point of the turning world; the watcher at the gate; anansi; sprite or water spirit; artist; court jester; Mercury/Hermes; mad professor; autumn.

This is a collective way of storying, and one that moves away from personal narrative into more metaphoric realms. The exploration of individual roles can be made more explicit by relating the archetypes to real-life activities, or they can remain tacit with an exploration of the qualities associated with the archetype.

Box 4.4 includes an example of one of the tales discussed by Themis as the group considered a number of issues concerning what the impact might be of Jung's inferior function on individuals and the group. The examination included conversations around the role of the 'wise fool', the benefits of 'going underground', and implications for professional development and the quality of learning.

BOX 4.4   The Three Feathers

This is a version of a tale from the Brothers Grimm and represents a number of tales that include a 'Dumling' or 'stupid' brother. In these tales, a number of brothers (often three, including one who is the youngest or the least bright) must go on a journey and complete some tasks. It is the youngest who succeeds, generally by being diligent rather than lazy, kind rather than cruel, brave rather than cowardly, and able to find and receive help from magical or 'underground' sources.

An old king, aware of his advancing years and approaching infirmity, began to wonder which of his three sons should inherit his kingdom after his death. Two of his sons were strong. The third, and youngest, son was a weakling. He was called Dumling or Blockhead.

The king decided on a contest. Each son had to blow a feather in the air, follow in its direction, and return with a carpet. The one who brought the finest carpet to him would inherit the kingdom. The first son blew his feather to the right. The second son blew his to the left. But Dumling's feather fell straight to the ground. The other two set off, jeering at their brother.

Dumling stood where he was. Then he noticed a trap-door with steps going down into the earth. Descending, he met the Toad Queen and when he explained his plight she gave him a carpet finer than any other. When Dumling and his brothers returned, it was clear who was the winner. His brothers had brought the first things they had found. But Dumling's brothers objected so loudly at such a fool becoming King that their father set another task.

This time they each had to follow their feather and return with the most beautiful ring. The same thing happened again. Dumling returned with the most exquisite jewelled ring, while his brothers, not learning from their previous defeat, brought only plain metal. Again he was the winner, and again the brothers complained so loudly that the king set another contest.

Each brother was to follow their feather and come home with the most beautiful bride. The brothers set off and returned with the first women they met who would come with them. Dumling returned with a dazzling princess who, underground, had been one of the Toad Queen's attendants.

But still the brothers complained, and a final contest was arranged. This time it was the brides who had to take part. The brothers thought they would be bound to win a competition in which the brides must demonstrate not their beauty but their strength – the women they had first met were hard-working local peasant women. They persuaded the king to require a demonstration of strength. 'So be it,' said the king. 'Whichever can jump through a hoop highest and best will be the winner.' Of course, the toad bride won, so the youngest brother married his princess, and ruled well for many happy years.

A Note on Written Stories

Themis members have individually and jointly written stories of their experiences of the group, of professional practice and of their lives. However, much of their development, and the focus of this chapter, has been about a combination of oral and written forms rather than writing as the only discipline. Gillie Bolton, poet, researcher/lecturer in medical humanities and Quaker, among other characteristics, is a leader in the field of using the written form for professional development, particularly in medical contexts (Bolton 2001). Of her work, she says:

We live our lives as if they were story. We tell stories from our lives the whole time – to ourselves and to others – in bed, in the car (bus), over coffee, beer, in the bath. We reconstruct our lives unwittingly in this way – to create a coherence with which we can work, rather than the chaotic muddle which is how life-as-it-is-lived happens. These stories are constructed mostly with the classic structure of beginning, middle, end, with a dynamic bit in the middle, and the end probably a slightly changed state from the beginning. Some of these stories are told and retold many times. These ones particularly help us to feel secure – to know who we are.

Writing these stories down helps them to become other, separate from us. We can then relate to them as 'other', and REWRITE them! This is of value because they can get stuck, and then we are stuck. Perhaps we need to rewrite our understanding of who we are. Our stories are plastic, malleable. They are not chunks of fact lifted from our lives, but particular ways of viewing particular bits of our lives.

A story is not just a story, but a way of understanding myself and my relationship to my world. (personal communication)

 The following chapter, on the NHS, includes further examples of the use of written stories, while Chapter 10 includes one of Gillie's reflective practice writing exercises and tips for getting started.

Conclusion

This chapter has explored the evolution of a peer learning group for professionals. It started with a fictionalised story told from an individual perspective, then explored the ways in which the format of the Themis day was in itself a story format, touched on the multiple narratives that interweave to create a learning community and examined important elements in the ongoing history of such a group.

The role of story in creating and maintaining community and learning could be seen to be working in various ways, and in a variety of formats. In combination they created an effective learning environment. Such stories may be factual or fictional, personal, a news item or a theory, told in words, in pictures, or a combination of the two, or can deal with the past, present or future, be musical, poetic . . . What is important for a learning community is that the singular and the many voices are attended to. The skills for doing this are often the skills required to notice, re-tell, and gain insight from, the stories available to us.

A variety of narrative techniques was discussed in this chapter. In summary, these are:

- the power of the individual perspective
- engaging 'reality' as distinct from photographic 'truth'
- using the multiple narrative (spoken and written)
- using uncertainty to promote enquiry-based learning (rather than tying up all the ends)
- using archetypal and other tales to promote the use of metaphor and juxtaposition
- attending to the appropriateness of the space/place, whether through rituals around food sharing, values around listening, challenging and so on, or being in the appropriate frame of mind for learning (from stories or anything else)
- dialogue
- writing
- how the format of a story provides an effective framework for a learning or development event.

Wenger's 'communities of practice', with their active inter-relationships around some common activity (for example, families, work groups, sports teams) are the communities that readers of this book may well be most concerned with. The process of writing and/or telling a community's history is a powerful support for that community; perhaps it even *is* the community.

Discourse, creativity, imagination and community: all are built through stories and all are important for a world in which communication and learning are increasingly seen as key. The new model for life and work is moving increasingly in line with concepts of sharing, co-evolution and sustainability not simply through the imposition of rules and designs but through creating individual capability, organisational forms and a climate rendering success an emergent property, a verb rather than a noun. The 'storying' behaviours of the peer learning group are one demonstration of what it means to attempt this.

We close the chapter with some quotations. The first is from *Creativity* by Mihaly Csikszentmihalyi (1997), and the second from Wenger's *Communities of Practice*.

> Whether we like it or not, our species has become dependent on creativity . . . evolution has been transformed from being almost exclusively a matter of

mutations in the chemistry of genes to being more and more a matter of changes in memes – in the information that we learn and in turn transmit to others. If the right memes are selected we survive; otherwise we do not. And those who select the knowledge, the values, the behaviours that will either lead into a brighter future or to extinction are no longer factors outside ourselves, such as predators or climatic changes. The future is in our hands; the culture we create will determine our fate. (*Creativity*, p. 318)

Learning cannot be designed. Ultimately, it belongs to the realm of experience and practice. It follows the negotiation of meaning; it moves on its own terms. It slips through the cracks; it creates its own cracks. Learning happens, design or no design. And yet there are few more urgent tasks than to design social infrastructures that foster learning . . . Those who can understand the informal yet structured, experiential yet social, character of learning – and can translate their insight into designs in the service of learning – will be the architects of our tomorrow. (*Communities of Practice*, p. 225)

5

Matters of Life and Death – Using Stories in the National Health Service

And so, from hour to hour, we ripe and ripe,
And then, from hour to hour, we rot and rot;
And thereby hangs a tale.

Shakespeare, As You Like It

The practice of medicine generates dilemmas which can pose dire problems for those involved. This chapter shows how story-telling can reveal these dilemmas and help in resolving them. The chapter ends with a brief discussion of complexity thinking.

Britain's National Health Service (NHS) is huge – the largest organisation in Europe in terms of the number of people working in it. It delivers over 85% of all health care services in the UK, since the scope of private medicine (including complementary medicine) is relatively small. Most people in Britain have contact with the NHS at some time, as patients, as relatives and friends of patients, as employees or as providers of goods and services to the NHS. The NHS is a constant theme in UK political debate. Medicine is obviously a regular setting for drama, comedy and satire in media of every kind. So, not surprisingly, story-telling is ever-present in and around the NHS.

A mother was in hospital with her three-month-old baby, whom she was breast-feeding. The policy of the ward was that if babies were being breast-fed, then the mothers should be given food from the meal trolley. She had to get her food by subterfuge because the nursery nurse who gave out the food would say that she would serve the children first and come back to the mothers, but she never did. She had to find ways round this nursery nurse to get her food. The mother's interpretation was that it was as if this was the only thing the nursery nurse felt in control of, and she was going to exercise her power using this mother. She made life difficult for someone who already had to cope with her child's illness. (Story No. 11)

Two junior doctors were on duty at two o'clock in the morning. They were treating a baby, and were waiting for the results of a test to come back so they could start treatment. They decided to wait on the ward so that they could respond as soon as they had the results. Since they had not eaten they ordered a pizza from the local takeaway [the canteen was closed], to eat while they were waiting. The parents complained that the doctors were eating pizza. They felt it was unprofessional of the doctors to be eating whilst they were waiting for the test results. It was the fact that the doctors smelled of pizza that bothered them. (Story No. 20)

These are two stories drawn from a book by Becky Malby and Stephen Pattison (1999), titled *Living Values in the NHS: Stories from the NHS's 50th Year*. Food is central to both stories – breast milk for the baby, food from a trolley for its mother, pizza for the doctors. In both stories there are strongly held values which in practice appear incompatible. One value is the need to care for fellow humans who are in difficult situations, whether this is care for a sick baby, an anxious mother or two overworked doctors. The other value is the need for a system that delivers an effective, fair and professionally judged outcome. The nursery nurse in the first story may have acted wrongly but the story implicitly supports the value of a system that gives food first to patients, then to carers. In the second story, the system is expected to set professional standards, even if 'good doctors don't smell of pizza' is one of the less important of these.

The apparent incompatibility of values may be driven by lack of time, lack of resource or by poor communications. The clash is probably not fundamental, but to those involved it feels real. The contrast between simple care for humans and the demands of a huge, complex, scientific, technological and administrative system is what makes these stories poignant. In many organisational settings, stories are told to show up the system as clumsy and bureaucratic. But the NHS stories do more than this. The relatives who objected to the smell of pizza may have been acutely worried about their baby. They had a strong need to experience doctors as calm and clinical, even as superhuman beings whose expertise would ensure the survival of their child. In life or death situations, the system may be something people want to believe in rather than ridicule. So both humanity and professionalism are rightly held to be important.

Value Conflicts

Incompatibility of values creates a dilemma. Charles Hampden-Turner (1990) has studied the resolution of dilemmas. He writes:

> The history of contending values within an organisation can often be 'read' by uncovering corporate stories. A story repeatedly told within a corporation, especially to recruits, may be regarded as an important message about how protagonists have tried to mediate dilemmas and succeeded or failed in these attempts. Nearly all stories have recurring clashes between people and/or values in which one side wins, the issues are resolved or both defeat each other. Twists and turns of fortune or joke collisions between values improve the story. (pp. 197–198)

Hampden-Turner describes how story-telling reveals the strong feelings and powerful insights of individuals. These feelings and insights make clear the active dilemmas within the organisation, which are often far from trivial. Conflicting values may be held by the same person. When value-conflicts are brought to the surface, people wish passionately for their resolution, through new ways of seeing the situation and through better ways of doing things.

When the group or organisation refuses to admit these dilemmas and to respond to people's hopes, this leads to a vicious circle. Those in power enforce bureacratic rules, so as to keep the illusion of control. They intend to resolve dilemmas by edict. But allowing one of two values to trump the other is futile: conflict remains, and eventually re-emerges somewhere else, provoking more rule enforcement and continuing the vicious circle.

Hampden-Turner believes, and we agree, that the only constructive way out of the inevitable dilemmas generated in organisations is to open them up. Rule enforcement hides conflicts. Openness brings them out for everyone to see, to understand and to reframe. When the organisation recognises crucial dilemmas and accepts that, with good-will, differences can be negotiated, this may lead to a virtuous circle. It then becomes possible to find ways to reconcile dilemmas, formulating new rules that support both values. Organisations driven by values, like the NHS, should strive particularly hard to move towards virtuous circles. The first step in doing so, and an essential tool in keeping the virtuous circle going, is telling the organisation's tales.

The stories of the nursery nurse and the pizza-eating doctors revealed a conflict of values, both strongly held: care for people and a pro-fessional system. The stories recognise both values, which is the first step towards the resolution of the dilemma between them.

Embracing Error

Another story from Malby and Pattison is of a nurse who had given an injection at the wrong time. 'It was the right dose, the right patient but the wrong time of day. She had got the most appalling disciplinary action, for this very small drug error, and she said what happened was that the whole staff were left feeling, well we are not going to report any errors now.' (Story No. 65)

Embracing error is hard enough when a mistake costs money or makes someone look stupid. When the error could kill someone, it might seem to be almost impossible. Errors with life or death conse-quences are not confined to medicine. An army unit taking part in a peace-keeping operation, say in the Balkans, faces this situation. So do workers on construction sites – think of a mistake made in attach-ing a cable to a skip. And something as common and simple as driving a car carries the risk of killing someone, or being killed.

In air traffic control, as in medicine, in the military, on construction sites and on the roads, there are rules intended to prevent mistakes. When things do go wrong investigations take place, and today the public demands that those reponsible are held to account. Thorough investigation, allocation of blame and no cover-ups are a strongly held set of values. And without these values, carelessness or complacency might allow avoidable mistakes to be repeated.

But over-stringent application of rules means that 'near misses' may not be reported, and the opportunity of learning from these will be lost. In *Candide*, Voltaire tells of a country which, from time to time, finds it pays to shoot an admiral to encourage the others. (He meant England.) But finding someone to blame seldom helps to improve the system, and doesn't necessarily encourage the others.

Amy Edmondson (1999) writes of the need for psychological safety if learning is to take place in work teams. She defines psychological safety as a shared belief held by members of a team that the team is a safe place for interpersonal risk-taking. It does not mean that everyone in the team is always nice to the others, but it does mean people respect each other's competences and genuinely care about each other as well as wanting the team to succeed in its tasks. And safety within the work team is a good basis for risk-taking outside the team.

Although it is an instance of non-existent psychological safety, the story of the nurse who gave the injection at the wrong time also reveals a genuine dilemma. There are two strongly held, but apparently anti-thetical, values: public accountability and learning from mistakes. Later in this chapter we will consider how this and other dilemmas might be resolved, but now we would like to tell two more stories about the NHS.

The first is about a woman in her sixties, who saw her GP because of shortness of breath and tiredness. She also felt thirsty at times, and wondered if she might have diabetes. The GP referred the patient to a respiratory consultant at a nearby hospital. After a number of scans and blood tests, the consultant diagnosed emphysema. The patient was a moderate smoker – two or three cigarettes a day. The consultant was very fierce about this: 'If you go on smoking, you'll be a respiratory cripple.' Steroid inhalation was prescribed.

The next week the patient went back to her GP, who also spent some time warning her of the perils of smoking. The patient asked whether the tests had shown any signs of diabetes. The GP turned away to look at a computer screen and said, 'No. Nothing like that. And, oh yes, you've got a hypothyroid condition. You need thyroxine.' The patient was about to move house to a different area, and took advantage of this to change her GP. Her new GP prescribed thyroxine, and over the next few months the patient's health improved greatly, including her respiratory problems. She felt that her first GP had been so concerned to berate her over her smoking (possibly encouraged in this by the consultant) that her thyroid problem would have been overlooked unless she herself had raised the possibility of a problem unrelated to her lungs.

The second story is about a man, also in his sixties, who was referred to a local hospital with suspected diabetes. The consultant confirmed this diagnosis and showed the man and his wife how to inject insulin. They were told that it might be difficult to get the insulin doses right to begin with, but after a week or two everything should settle down. This didn't happen, and the patient again consulted his GP, who checked that the insulin injections were being made correctly and assured the patient that his problems would soon pass. Another week later, the patient's wife read an article about pancreatic cancer in a newspaper. The symptoms described seemed exactly like her husband's, so she contacted the hospital and asked whether the problem might be cancer. The consultant was absent, and a registrar told her there was nothing to worry about. But the patient was so ill that his wife took the newspaper article to the GP and insisted that she read it. Having done so, the GP immediately got the man admitted to hospital. Pancreatic cancer was diagnosed, and two weeks later he died of it.

The patient's wife felt bitter about the fact that she received no apology from the hospital for what was obviously a misdiagnosis. She realised that the mistake probably made no difference to the eventual outcome, but she and her husband had had several anxious weeks struggling with insulin injections and wondering what they were doing wrong. She also felt that her fears about cancer should have been taken seriously. Subsequently she heard through a contact in the hospital that there had been 'an almighty row' over her husband's case. So why couldn't they have said sorry to her?

These stories suggest there is a powerful taboo within the NHS about admitting to a patient or relative that a mistake has been made. No doubt, this is partly due to fear of formal complaints or claims for compensation. But it must also be connected to the medical profession's need to keep up a pretence of being infallible. This is not just a self-serving pretence, since a patient's recovery will often be helped by his faith in the doctor and his treatment. Call it 'faith healing', 'the placebo effect' or what you will, there is plenty of evidence that belief in its efficacy can form an important part of a cure.

Trusting your Judgement

A hospice agreed to admit a patient who was dying. The patient died in the ambulance *en route*. The patient should have gone straight to the city mortuary, but out of consideration for the family the hospice admitted the dead patient and rang the GP to come and certify the death. This way the family had a better experience of death and the staff could care for them in their grief. The hospital manager complained that the staff had not followed hospital policy. The medical director of the unit said that, given the circumstances, he would expect them to do exactly the same if it happened again. (Story No. 40)

A junior nurse was in charge of a ward. A lady had a CT [computerised tomography] scan that showed a tumour. The lady and her relatives suspected the truth about what was wrong with her and asked the junior nurse. It was the weekend and there were no senior medical staff available who knew the patient. The junior nurse decided to tell the patient, but felt out of her depth. While she was sure it was the right thing to do, she was still anxious on Monday when she told the medical staff what she had done. (Story No. 64)

These are two more stories from the Malby and Pattison book. On the theme of 'taking responsibility', they comment that situations of this kind are inevitable in the NHS, and yet the culture appears to be one of blame and fear – and low learning. Individuals are expected to take responsibility, but are not trusted or supported.

Adler and Borys (1996) make a distinction between enabling bureaucracies and coercive bureaucracies. In coercive bureaucracies, the rules are all-important. Rule-breakers are punished regardless of their motives and of the effects of their action. In enabling bureaucracies there are rules and staff are expected to know them. However, if in a particular situation a strict application of the rules goes against the values of the organisation, the rules can be broken. Staff are treated as intelligent human beings, capable of judgement. Adler and Borys comment: 'Enabling procedures help committed employees do their jobs more effectively and reinforce their commitment.'

A Positive Approach to Dilemmas

To resolve dilemmas you need to know what they are. But what they are is normally far from clear to those involved – their emotions are stirred and they hide problems from themselves. Surfacing dilemmas can sometimes be done by wise and insightful outsiders, but perhaps the most reliable method for doing this is story-telling. Therefore, an organisation that faces serious dilemmas, and most do at times, if not continuously, should seek to establish a tradition of story-telling as part of its culture. People may find this difficult to start with, but telling one story usually produces several others, and a habit gets going. Nonetheless, getting story practice established does need support and encouragement.

Eventually, stories should produce organisation change. But this should not happen too quickly. Malby and Pattison recommend: '. . . living in story-telling mode without recourse to analysis and discussions about causes for as long as possible, until key themes emerge . . . more subtle causes, we think, can be uncovered in story-telling.'

When the time comes to draw out the themes underlying an organisation's stories, this can be done quite simply (for example, in a small organisation) or in a more structured way (as Malby and Pattison did for their NHS stories). Either way, it is important to check that the themes identified really are the ones that participants (permanent and temporary) are concerned about.

Having selected key themes and validated them in feedback sessions of various kinds, the next step is to identify the dilemmas behind them. There will almost certainly be these dilemmas, since dilemmas generate emotions and emotions generate memorable stories. Rather than produce a full list of dilemmas, the aim should be to spot the most important one, where there are two apparently conflicting values, both fervently advocated by lots of people. Identification of the important dilemmas usually needs a workshop of some kind, and pictures as well as stories help to bring them out. Drawing a pair of horns and writing one value on each horn is an obvious device. The green line/blue line in the Kenya scenarios story in Chapter 8 is an example of a pictorial representation of a dilemma.

Now comes the step that needs the most imagination and creativity.

The task is to take a completely new look at the situation. What deeper value could there be that enfolds the present two conflicting values? Can the two values of the dilemma be subsumed into one, more fundamental value?

There is no single method for doing this. In most cases a combination of methods is needed. These might include a deep understanding of the organisation's present culture, mainly derived from its stories, slogans, symbols and ceremonies. Workshops may be held to study the concept of dilemma resolution and to review examples of the successful use of the concept in other organisations. Brainstorming may have a role to play, as may creative people from outside the organisation. (See the discussion of 'remarkable people' in Chapter 8.)

If a new value emerges that appears to resolve the dilemma, it must be tested in the organisation. If the new value isn't easily understood and widely accepted, then the dilemma will not be resolved. Further iteration may be necessary.

The final step is to imbed the new value in the organisation's rules and practices, so that a virtuous circle is created, reinforcing the value and making it part of the organisation's culture. Story-telling can help with this process of embedding, particularly telling the tale of how the new value emerged from the old values. In a large organisation, watching how current stories evolve is a good way of monitoring the change. The process changes the culture and self-image of the organisation. Box 5.1 contains a list of the steps to take in resolving dilemmas.

BOX 5.1   Resolving Dilemmas

1. Make story-telling a normal part of life.
2. Draw out themes from the stories which are often told or which have a big impact.
3. Define a dilemma that the stories pose.
4. Reframe the situation so the two values of the dilemma are subsumed into a single, more fundamental value.
5. Seek to generate a virtuous circle of support for the reframed value.

Stories about Stories

In this and the following section we describe three instances of the use of stories in changing behaviour and resolving dilemmas. The first of these is a report by Dr Trisha Greenhalgh published in the bulletin *Wellcome News* (2000). In the early 1990s, Dr Greenhalgh became interested in patient empowerment. In clinical trials in California it had been shown that patients' control of their diabetes improved if they were taught to argue with their doctor. She wondered how she could help a much less empowered group: the Bangladeshi community in East London, where diabetes is a major health care problem.

In a research project, Dr Greenhalgh collected stories from patients. Forty Bangladeshis with diabetes were asked to 'tell the story' of their illness. One surprising finding was that whenever the informants talked about a change in their behaviour, it was never linked to an instruction given by a health professional. Instead, it was always linked to a story told by another Bangladeshi – often friends and family members. By listening to patients' stories she was able to discover how patients learned to change their behaviour – and their learning was, in turn, achieved by listening to stories.

The second story is about a management consultant who was brought in to support change in an NHS specialist baby unit. There was a culture of blame in the unit, there were clashes of personalities, conflicting messages passing amongst staff and a high degree of anxiety in performing all types of task. Resignation letters were handed to the lead physician and unit manager on a daily basis and, overall, there was a sense of powerlessness in the unit.

The consultant used narrative-based approaches to raise awareness of the interpersonal dynamics in the unit. The story in Box 5.2 is one that he created for himself and told to staff. Having told his own story, he then started to listen to the stories told by the staff.

BOX 5.2   A Family Concern

Once there was a woman who was not well. She was unhappy. She was disruptive and very childish. For example, she would blame others for her own mistakes. She would be impatient with others and often get into fights over nothing at all. Grandfather was very worried about her. In particular, it worried him that her job in the village was to take care of infants, which needed patience, care and maturity. Also, he was concerned about her eligibility for marriage. In those days, a family that couldn't forge good links with other families was not in a happy position.

Grandfather made discreet arrangements to get help from outside the family. He chose an outsider who he heard had experience of such difficult situations, and brought him into the house. The outsider knew that in a family situation, one person was often blamed for things that were not of their making. But they learned that mostly he asked questions, and they decided to do their best to answer.

'How is life here for you?' asked the outsider. 'What would you like it to be like?' The questions were simple enough, but the answers didn't always seem so. Some family members had to admit that they did not like each other. They also realised the impact of some of their behaviours on others. They acknowledged that if they did not change, the family would have no friends, no money and no future. And they came to trust 'their' outsider. They had not been feeling very cared for – the young woman felt that she had to be perfect, day in and day out, with no help, and many of the others felt that if Grandfather spread his attention around the family a bit he would see that the young woman wasn't the only one who needed help.

The outsider listened carefully to every story he was told. And later, at a family gathering, he used his skills to tell a story in return. A story about trust, respect, unused talents and wasteful behaviour. A story about a hard and unforgiving environment, and about what infants needed in order to thrive.

Listening to the story, the family could hear that almost all the words he used were words that they had told him. Still they argued and cried, sometimes too upset to address what they were hearing. But little by little they were able to see that the harsh environment was one they had created, and that the one they needed was quite different. They decided that they must have a sanctuary, which they would use to take proper time to reflect on their actions and important family business; a place where they could be creative and build a healthy future. With help from the outsider they made some plans and they attended to putting their house in order. When he saw they were busy and doing well, the outsider went away.

Postscript: Now, if this were a fairy story, the end of the tale would involve them all living happily after. And this isn't really a fairy story. They couldn't have Cinderella to sweep up the dirt and get blamed for everything, or Snow White to look after them all, and they had to live in the village rather than fly off to an enchanted land. But they are living a good deal more happily than previously, and although they couldn't live a fairy-tale, they no longer had to survive in a horror story.

The stories included tales of fear and bullying, and the management consultant witnessed grief, tears, pain – and threats to himself. This was a difficult task but the stories gave the outsider profound insights, as well as helping trust develop since he was very clear about confidentiality. And there was another effect – at this early stage, the unit calmed down and people became positive about the change process.

Later, the initial listening done, it was the consultant's turn to re-present the stories, with quotes from the characters involved:

'There is lack of respect for others.'

'Senior staff overload junior staff.'

'There is no real training/development. Junior staff feel they can't get help from more experienced people because there is no time.'

The stories were not easy to hear. And telling and hearing the stories, then re-telling and re-hearing them, was only the start of the process. In almost all organisational situations where stories are used, the telling is not over after the first time around, and the sensemaking continues individually and collectively over iterations. Nonetheless, the tales are catalysts. Using fictional tales as part of the process helps people to acknowledge and come to terms with their emotions. The initial gathering and re-telling at a group level has its own emotional cycle on the road to community efficacy. A crucial moment was when staff admitted that they were not treating each other respectfully, that they did not help and communicate with each other well enough.

Barchester District

This is a longer story, with several episodes. In fact, it is what we call a history. It is about an imaginary unit in the NHS.

Gilbert Sammler arrived a year ago at the district hospital at Barchester. His appointment was as head of a newly-established unit, set up to study the efficacy of cancer treatments. This was part of a joint initiative by the NHS and a national cancer charity. This initative, called the Oncology Outcomes (OO) project, funded six such units around England and Wales, all in medium-sized general hospitals like Barchester District Hospital. The idea was for these units to be sited away from major specialist hospitals, in an average clinical environment.

Gilbert came to Barchester from a world-renowned cancer centre. His was an unusual move for an ambitious young research-orientated physician, who'd already built quite a reputation for himself. His friends asked him why he was going out into the sticks since, from the point of view of a medical career, Barchester was a rather ordinary place to work. His reply was that to be ordinary was the point of the project – the aim was to raise the standard of treatment across the whole country, not just to do spectacular things in a special centre.

There were two ways in which this would be done. First, the OO units would be centres for knowledge transfer to and from the hospitals and clinics in their regions. Second, the centres would gather information on cancer incidence, treatment and outcomes and the relationships between these. By discovering how variation in patient populations inter-reacted with variation in treatments to produce different courses of disease and different outcomes, it should be possible to make big improvements in cancer care.

Gilbert Sammler was 34 when he made the move to Barchester. He knew he was taking a risk, but liked the idea of being responsible for knowledge management, which he felt should have a greater part to play in medical practice. The OO unit at Barchester had a staff of nine, and was housed in a new building next to the hospital's oncology wing. Others at Barchester, who worked in inferior conditions, were envious and as the OO unit was monitoring the outcome of treatments, it was seen by some as a spy in the camp.

After a few months in the job, Gilbert noticed that his work was being subtly constrained. Everyone was polite, but all seven oncology departments in his region, including the one at Barchester District Hospital, responded slowly to his requests for information and visits, and gave him and colleagues in his unit the minimum of help. The usual excuse was overwork. The pattern was too regular for this to be chance. The heads of oncology departments had mostly been in post for many years and knew each other well. They could easily have agreed to freeze him out.

Irritating as this was, Gilbert made up his mind to cause no fuss. His own research into the genetic influences on lung cancer was not being hampered. The statistics his unit needed to work out the history of cancer incidence in the region were readily avilable. Also there were gaps in the iron curtain – a few doctors realised that Gilbert and the OO unit were a valuable resource. As the word got around that the unit was helpful and could be trusted, more people started to make contact.

The OO unit set about building up a set of case studies illustrating successful and unsuccessful practices in cancer diagnosis and treatment. Anne Proudfoot, in charge of knowledge management in the unit, wanted these studies to do more than the usual dry scientific reports. They should tell a story about the patients' lives, before and after cancer was diagnosed. Outcomes should be described in wider terms than survival times and other clinical facts. Anne organised a series of seminars, held in rotation in the oncology departments in the region. Gilbert's contacts ensured that well-known oncologists came to talk, which meant that the seminars were well attended.

Anne used these occasions to arrange small story-telling sessions before or after the seminar. Participants were set the task of telling stories of incidents about which they felt either glad or sad. She taped the sessions and subsequently she and Gilbert separately played the recordings thorough several times to extract what each considered to be the dominant themes in the stories.

(This was an abridged version of the methodology used by Malby and Pattison to produce their pioneering work on story-telling in the NHS.) Anne then grouped the stories by themes, turned them into anonymous versions and published them in a booklet, which was widely circulated in the NHS and elsewhere.

Story Themes

Some of the themes that emerged from the story-telling sessions were:

- the doctor as magician – or faith helps the cure.
- patients' understanding can often be part of the cure.

- learning needs honesty, which needs safety.
- stress can damage clinical judgement, care and learning.
- the cure isn't everything – especially if it lowers patients' quality of life.

Another theme was the technique of triage: the division of patients into three groups. In extreme situations like wartime, the first group is those who may get better without any treatment; the second is those who are so ill they will probably die regardless of treatment; the third is those for whom treatment could make the difference between life and death. Only the third group gets treated. A milder kind of triage is practised throughout medicine. People who come for treatment but who seem to have nothing wrong with them are given placebos. At the other end of the scale, when nothing more can be done for a patient, palliative care may be all that is given – a situation sadly familiar in oncology.

Anne and Gilbert suggested that the stories they heard made them think of a different kind of triage. Patients could be assessed for the extent to which they were able and willing to get involved in the detailed rationale for their treatment. One possible category was patients who didn't like medical details and who wanted to leave everything to the expert. Medical mystique and faith in the doctor was particularly helpful for this group. The opposite category was patients who wanted to understand everything they could about their illness and the treatment they were getting. They were the people who used the Internet to find out things that the doctor might not know. In the middle were those patients who just accepted they were sick and hoped to get through the treatment as best they could.

Avoiding a Fight

Three months later, Anne had collected another set of stories. She put her head round Gilbert's office door. 'Look at this,' she said. 'We've extracted the themes from this lot. One strong theme is bureaucratic interference with the judgement of senior clinicians. As you know, this has never figured much before now. It's gone up to be the top theme. The other is not so prominent but completely new. This one we've labelled "pride comes before a fall". Something is happening. A change of mood, perhaps. Or maybe someone's been planting stories in our collections.'

'Umm. That's what's called story viruses, isn't it?'

'Yes. Do you think these stories are aimed at us?'

Gilbert thought for a moment. He felt under threat.

'We could start planting stories ourselves,' he said. 'Although that would make nonsense of using stories as a research method. Still, I'd love to see a few reports of reactionary consultants resisting the spread of new knowledge.'

At the next meeting of the OO unit's staff, Anne told the others she thought stories were possibly being planted. Gilbert asked the group what he should do. Should he bring everything out into the open? Should he tell the world that the present sensitive approach of the unit, trying hard not to tread on people's toes, was at an end? Should he expose the lack of co-operation and the apparent planting of stories? Should he reveal the poor practices that he'd tactfully suggested might be changed, but which still seemed to be continuing? If he did all this, there would be a terrific row. The unit would probably get powerful support. And it might stimulate some kind of revolution by junior oncologists, forcing the old guard at the top to change their ways.

Gilbert reminded his colleagues that the unit was in a strong position. Together with Nichole Hardy, a senior researcher in the unit, he had just published a major research paper in genetic influences on lung cancer. It had appeared in the *International Journal of Pulmonary Oncology*, and had led to Gilbert being appointed an assistant editor of the journal.

'Have we been patient too long?' asked Gilbert. 'We spread knowledge about good practice. We suggest concepts – like that of assessing patients' willingness to get involved in the details of their treatment. But nothing seems to change. Perhaps we should come out fighting.'

Nichole spoke up. 'I know very little about knowledge management. What I've learnt is by chatting to you lot. And I know nothing at all about political in-fighting in the NHS. What I do know is that the secret of good scientific research is to ask the right questions. Gilbert, you're asking us whether you should fight the old guard. I can't possibly help with the answer. But I would say: are you sure you're asking us the right question?'

Anne stepped in before Gilbert could respond. 'That's it, Nichole.

It isn't the right question – at any rate until we've thought a lot more about the whole thing. We should consider whether the dreadful old guard do have a point. I'm as keen as anyone on learning new ways. But doing that takes time and energy. Perhaps there isn't much space for learning among the people we're trying to influence. Before we start a fight, we should be sure that the consultants' resistance isn't just a power play.'

'What might it be – other than self-interest?' asked Gilbert.

'Well', replied Anne, 'the throughput of cases in this region's oncology departments, and the waiting lists for operations, is OK by NHS standards; better than some famous teaching hospitals, in fact. The outcomes could be improved a lot, of course. But they do manage to get things done. That could be due to the style the consultants use. They make rapid diagnoses, stick to a fairly simple pattern of treatment, make the best of what they've got – by muddling through. And actually the overall result isn't too bad, considering resources are limited.'

'Are you saying we shouldn't rock their boat?' was Gilbert's comment.

'What I've saying is that these departments have a method that more or less works. They may feel they haven't got the time or the skill to find a better way. If they abandon their present way of working, things could go really wrong, and they'd get the blame, not us. There may be a genuine dilemma here. The best could be the 'enemy of the good.''

'Or the enemy of the mediocre and shortsighted,' said Gilbert. 'OK. I don't much like it, but I'm willing to give it a try. No fighting. Diplomacy instead. Try to resolve the dilemma.'

A Virtuous Circle

A few days later Gilbert hurries along the corridor and runs into Robert Brown, the senior consultant oncologist. Brown says: 'Congratulations on your pulmonary oncology paper. I suppose you'll soon be leaving us for a chair in some distinguished university.'

'Oh no,' Gilbert replies, 'you won't get rid of me that easily. I've lots more work to do here.'

'You don't mean your knowledge management rubbish? That's just NHS politics – not science or medicine.'

'Robert. Why would I need to spend my time on politics? Actually, knowledge management is more important for medicine than my genetics work. If we had the chance to talk I'd tell you why. Shall I buy you dinner sometime?'

'There's no such thing as a free lunch. What on earth do you want from me?'

'To tell you my point of view. And to hear yours. How about the Barchester Arms – next week?'

The wine is good, the atmosphere mellow. Robert tells his story.

'I came to Barchester 22 years ago. I was about the age you are now, and like you I was keen to put the world to rights. Things went well at first. More beds than now, fewer cases, lower expectations. But for the last ten years we've been struggling. Struggling to give a half-decent service. We're short of everything – especially short of time. My high ideals have been knocked out of me, just as yours will be if you stay in a place like Barchester. And on top of everything the administrators try to tell us how to do our jobs. They send all sorts of management consultants – who produce nothing. You're an excellent oncologist, Gilbert, but why should your lot be any better at telling me what to do?'

Gilbert asks Robert: 'May I tell you a story? It's about a man from the Basque country – the mountain region in northern Spain. The stereotype of a Basque is someone very tough and stubborn. A Basque forester went into a hardware shop to buy a chainsaw. The man in the store told him he'd be able to cut down 20 trees a day with it. A week later the forester returned to the store. "You promised me I could cut down 20 trees a day with this saw, but try as I will I can't do more than 10." So the next day the man from the store and the forester went into the forest together. The man pulled the cord, and the motor started immediately. "Good God!" said the forester, "What's all that noise?"'

'So you're trying to sell a chainsaw to a stubborn old consultant?'

'Look,' says Gilbert, 'I know you have to work damned hard to keep the show on the road. You have to make rapid diagnoses, decide quickly on treatments. All under pressure. But suppose I came along with a new tool. Say a computerised decision-support system. Something really user-friendly. It wouldn't tell you a whole lot of things you've known for years. But it would prompt you to think about alternatives, and make it easy for you to get information about these. It could be like the computer systems advanced chess players use. Suggests various moves, but leaves the player to use his judgement. Capable of learn-ing, too, and able to take into account the resources that you've got at the time. And help with record-keeping.'

'Sounds too good to be true.'

'If you and the other heads of oncology think of us as self-interested politicians, we won't be able to help you. But if you'd work with us, I think we'd be able to develop this sort of support.'

Robert grunts and says: 'I accept you're trying to help. Sorry I doubted your motives. I'll see what we can do. And thank you for an excellent dinner.'

Over the next few weeks, Anne notices a thaw in relations with the region's oncology departments. She's invited to some departmental meetings. She organises a workshop on Enabling Bureaucracy and Learning and to her surprise, several clinicians turn up. She makes the point that organisation procedures can be shaped in response to the real needs of an organisation and that listening to the stories told in the organisation is a great way to understand these needs. A lot of knowledge transfer can be informal. But formal systems can be highly effective too, providing they are user-friendly, robust, light and enabling rather than ponderous and coercive.

Gilbert realises that he and his colleagues have a lot to learn about the best way to improve medical practice. It isn't enough to be clever and helpful; a deep understanding of the existing culture is also necessary. It really was important to work in the environment of an 'ordinary' hospital like Barchester District, but you had to understand what daily life is like in this environment, and how people cope with the workload, the bureacracy and the politics of their jobs.

Openness to new ideas remains a key value for Gilbert. Now he adds a new one: learning within a particular background, a back-ground that is shaped by a huge range of past experiences. He realises that changes in practices are shifts within a complex system. Unless the system is reasonably well understood, attempts to change it can be dangerous. Another realisation is that the Barchester unit ought to be learning from the experiences of the other units in the Oncology Outcomes project. Apart from formal reports and scientific papers, there had so far been little interchange between the units in different regions, at least since Anne's early initiative of the book of stories. So Gilbert and Anne visit other units and agree to work together on the design of a decision-support system, to be called 'Grandmaster'. Gilbert asks Robert Brown and a couple of other oncologists at Barchester to help with the design. In the Grandmaster project, actual clinical practice would feed back into the system, so that it evolved to meet user's needs.

Various themes from the Barchester story collection would be taken into account when designing 'Grandmaster'; for instance, the cover-ups, organisational and mental, that restrict people from learning from their mistakes, also the value of considering in what way the patient wanted to be involved in his treatment, the pressure of scarce resources, and the importance of the patient's dignity and quality of life. It wouldn't be easy to fit things like these into an expert system alongside genetics and cell biology; but they were highly relevant to medical practice, so they could not be left out.

Complexity

During the 30 years since Robert Brown took his doctor's degree, things in medicine have become increasingly interconnected. Thirty years ago there was less knowledge about cancer, fewer kinds of treatment, and cancer patients didn't expect much beyond good nursing. Public accountability for the actions of doctors and other NHS professionals was hardly an issue. Decisions in one area of activity could be made separately from decisions in another. A hospital consultant wasn't much concerned with administration, with the efficient use of resources, or with public relations. Little was then known about the ways an individual's genes affected his chances of getting cancer. More was known about the ways an individual's environment (say at work) affected those chances, but much less was known than is known today. And practically nothing was understood about the interaction between genes and the environment. So things were simpler in the old days. Now, increasing interconnectedness is experienced as a perennial shortage of resources, as interference by others while you are trying to do your job, as a loss of control.

Highly interconnected situations have the property known as 'complexity'. In a complex situation, the old management method of command and control breaks down, because the situation has become incomprehensible to those at the top. The skills needed by organisation members used to be technical and task-orientated, and they had to be willing to carry out orders from superiors in a hierarchy. Now the key skills are different. Vital now are strengths like the ability to recognise patterns within a complex situation and the ability of small groups to organise themselves. Networking with others has started to replace obeying orders from the top. A new vocabulary and set of concepts is required.

To think constructively about highly inter-related situations, attention has to shift from objects to relationships. The properties of objects (mechanical, biological or social) used to be the key to understanding, and they do, of course, remain important. But in complexity thinking, the properties of objects are less important than the relations between objects. Complexity is thus the science of connections and relationships. In a social situation we think, not about the characteristics of individuals, but about the quality of the interactions and the network of relationships between them. Complexity thinking has many implications. Here we will consider only two: the need for skill in recognising patterns and the need for skill in self-organisation.

A highly interconnected social world is constantly changing. It becomes difficult to recognise new patterns, particularly when we cannot extrapolate them from past experience. Refining the ability to 'see' new patterns as they emerge is a valuable skill, enabling individuals and organisations to survive and thrive. The multiple interactions within a complex system sometimes lead to the emergence of a pattern of behaviour that human observers can recognise. This emergence cannot be predicted, and even when it has emerged, the pattern may vary in unexpected ways, but it nonetheless remains recognisable and valuable in deciding about future actions.

Perhaps the most important idea within the whole of complexity thinking is the concept of self-organisation. To many people, especially those who have been trained as managers, the idea of self-organisation may seem bizarre. We find it hard to believe that things can successfully organise themselves. Of course, in some situations – like a fire in a crowded theatre – someone still has to do the organising. But often an extraordinary degree of organisation can arise without anyone designing or controlling the situation. The most striking example of this is biological evolution. Since Darwin formulated his theory of the origin of species there has been argument about whether the unplanned interaction of a huge range of factors really can, over time, result in the emergence of such amazing structures as the human eye, or the peacock's tail, or the hummingbird's flight. But today the overwhelming evidence is that unplanned self-organisation does indeed produce marvels like these.

Self-organisation does not arise whenever we would like it to. That is why the system of market forces does not always produce an immediate solution to economic problems, as illustrated by the slow emergence of viable market economies in the countries of the former Soviet Union. The study of complexity is slowly revealing the conditions needed for self-organisation. We know that experiments in self-organisation should be encouraged, and when self-organisation emerges it needs protection. An enabling infrastructure can be put in place that supports self-organisation. Open communication and interpersonal process skills play a big part in this infrastructure. With so much to communicate about, story-telling skills are essential, because stories provide such economical and memorable communication.

In this chapter, we have given a glimpse of the effects of increasing interconnectedness in the large organisation that is the NHS. Telling stories about this organisation has produced some suggestions for useful behaviour in situations of complexity. The following three chapters will also consider complex situations – of varying kinds – and will also show how story-telling helps to cope within them.

Conclusion

1. To make useful changes in a large, complex system is not easy. The culture of the system may be opaque even to those who have worked in it for years. Complete understanding is impossible, but a sensitive try should be part of any change process.
2. Committed staff are a marvellous resource for any organisation, but committed people have strongly held values, for which they will struggle.
3. Organisations have to have rules and procedures – what is called 'the system'. The system can either be enabling or coercive. An enabling bureacracy is more difficult to construct, but well worth the effort.
4. There is sometimes a problem in following both of two values in a particular situation. This leads to a dilemma. As a way of coping with dilemmas, bashing people over the head is useless – the

dilemma goes underground and generates a vicious circle of conflict. However, organisations can learn how to resolve their dilemmas, and to shift into virtuous circles, in which new, more fundamental values subsume the old ones.

5. Listening to an organisation's stories is the first step in uncovering the real dilemmas. Futhermore, story-telling helps when finding ways to resolve dilemmas and in embedding the virtuous circles started by their resolution.

6. In passing, we can note that medicine is rich in stories. Kenneth Calman, a distinguished doctor as well as a cartoonist, wrote about laughter in *A Study of Story Telling Humour and Learning in Medicine:* 'It causes the nostrils to flare, the diaphragm and abdominal muscles to contract . . . A good laugh stimulates a number of muscle groups and improves the circulation . . . and the immune system may respond more appropriately to disease' (Calman 2000, p. 39). Gillie Bolton, who was quoted in Chapter 4, also writes extensively on the use of stories in medicine.

The following chapters give the histories of three more organisations. Each of these includes a struggle with complexity, and shows how story-telling helps with this.

6

AutoCorp – Evolving

We spend our years as a tale that is told.
Psalm 90:9

In this chapter we revisit AutoCorp, the imaginary corporation we described in Chapter 3. Now we look at how a segment of this organisation uses stories to evolve towards a culture of self-organisation, as a response to increasing complexity.

The seven or so major automobile manufacturers battling it out in the world market are all looking for ways to differentiate themselves from their rivals. They would like their strategies, products, operations and public images to be distinctive. If all the majors are the same, it is likely they will all have a hard time gaining a majority market share. AutoCorp's top management's keenest wish is to have more innovative design: they want a stream of new product concepts; they want the design process to be speeded up to match the best of the Japanese companies.

A wish and its fulfilment are often far apart. Like the Red Queen in *Alice in Wonderland*, AutoCorp has to run hard to stay in the same place, let alone move ahead of its competitors. Each of Autocorp's product divisions has its design department. Each of these departments is under pressure from its divisional CEO to become more innovative and speedier. One or two are spending a lot of money recruiting famous designers, usually along with their own design teams. Another has relocated its design centre to Italy. Several have set rather arbitrary targets for design improvement, justifying this by benchmarking exercises that compare AutoCorp with other firms. None of this is working very well. AutoCorp knows it is in a perplexingly different world than the one it knew ten years ago, and is finding it hard to respond successfully.

Alongside the divisional structure is a central unit called Global Design Systems, located in Detroit and headed by Chuck Mascone. This unit's job is to discover new approaches to design and to sell these to the design teams in the divisions. (There are some similarities between Mascone's task and that of Gilbert Sammler in the NHS, described in Chapter 5.) Global Design Systems is expected to shift AutoCorp design operations from the old hierarchical style of management to a complexity-related, self-organising style. But in an organisation that has a hundred-year old tradition of hierarchical management, and divisional CEOs who mostly adhere to that style, this is an unrealistic expectation.

The cynics in Detroit see Mascone as a sacrificial beast. Setting up his unit looks like to them like a futile gesture towards the gods of complexity. The cynics anticipate that after a few years Mascone will be fired. This would, of course, be another futile gesture, but one that top management might choose so as to give the impression of decisive action.

Facilitating Change

In a large, highly automated manufacturing plant the natural tendency is to want everything to run smoothly. Once the complex machine is working well, it seems safer to leave it alone. Of course, small improvements can be made, and once in a while a completely new plant may be built, but generally change has worrying connotations for the plant's managers. Major organisations are a bit like these large plants. Change can easily upset the way they function, especially if the change ignores the contribution tacit knowledge makes to effective operation. To use the language of complexity theory, most managers in large organisations want to keep close to equilibrium.

Some big organisations can survive for years without much change.

A culture of continuous improvement, for which Japanese industry is justly famous, can sometimes go on providing better and better performance, which can postpone the need for drastic change. But even in organisations that maintain their rate of small-scale change, radical change ultimately becomes essential, as the current state of much of Japanese industry illustrates. The tension between keeping things running smoothly and the need, sooner or later, for radical change is characteristic of most large organisations, in both the private and public sectors.

During the first half of the twentieth century the command-and-control approach to organisation, originally derived from military models, largely went unchallenged. Increased turbulence and complexity now mean that this approach is dying. But accountability for performance still remains, and for some people this is more difficult to live with than command and control. At least in the old days someone told you what to do and if the command led to disaster, you might escape blame. So, interwoven with the tension arising from the need to combine stability and change, is another tension, generated by the need to combine accountability and innovation.

In well-managed organisations initiative and innovation are encouraged and rewarded, and attributing blame to others is discouraged. But it is still possible to blame yourself when things go wrong. For people whose goals are closely aligned with those of their organisation, organisation failure becomes personal failure. This can be a stressful situation. Some failures are inevitable, so learning to live with them is important. Fear of failure can inhibit useful action, and this fear can stop an organisation from learning the lessons that failures can teach. As we have said, large organisations are permeated with tensions between the wish for stability and the need for change, and between accountability for performance and the need to take risks. There are a number of ways in which members of organisations can learn to cope with these tensions. Improving personal skills is one way, since this can shift individuals onto a virtuous circle – greater capability gives greater confidence, and greater confidence, gives greater capability.

Central to personal skill is story-telling. Stories need to be entertaining, to some degree at least. The story-teller can hold the attention of listeners or readers with tales that are gripping, tragic, romantic or funny. Tales can emerge or be designed and can be individual or collective. Whichever they are, some art is called for in the telling. This can be learnt by training but, above all, a story-teller learns the trade by practising.

Story-telling may not always work as expected. Sometimes stories may be ineffective or inappropriate. Anecdotes, for example, are not always representative of the whole situation. Rival stories can illustrate different viewpoints, highlighting dilemmas, which can be good if they are dealt with constructively, but bad if they continue to fester. Sometimes rival stories may exacerbate conflict rather than painting a richer picture of the organisation. However, even when story-telling does not work as hoped, the failure can be highly informative. Story-telling can help us in the process of 'embracing error'. Story-telling can turn a mistake into a learning experience.

Stories provide the opportunity for a new perspective. Where topics are complex rather than linear and there is no 'right way' to be taught, stories encourage the juxtaposition of new and multiple perspectives. And stories are enacted creativity. The right setting provides an environment in which individuals create their own stories. Where creativity and innovation are organisational requirements, the experience of story-telling reinforces a creative approach.

In today's organisations we have to develop interpersonal process skills, skills in open communication and skills in boundary spanning. We must learn to tolerate uncertainty, to benefit from ambiguity, and to engage in dialogue with our colleagues. The capacity to reach political agreement and thus to initiate collective action is critical. For this we need simple rules for resolving disputes and for giving feedback in constructive ways.

All this is easier in face-to-face situations, but with the right skills and with agreed rules for reaching agreement, for defining boundaries, for taking action and for reviewing results, a capability for political agreement can be developed in a large organisation or even in a whole society. For effective self-organisation, it is important that everyone's skills are developed, not just those of an elite. Studies done by Barbara Heinzen (1994) on the processes of national development show that when a large proportion of a population achieves a reasonable standard of health and education, the nation becomes capable of self-organisation, and therefore of economic development. Development of skills precedes economic development. Likewise, in organisations, skill development precedes self-organisation.

Coping with Complexity

Dense interconnections generate complexity. Looked at from the perspective of complexity thinking, no event has a simple cause. All events result from multiple influences, some of which are feedback from earlier events of that type. In such a multi-causal world, there are no levers to pull which produce a predictable result. No one has sure-fire answers to the problem of management action in complex situations. Chuck Mascone has been charged with finding answers, but in reality he will not be able to find anything simple to recommend to AutoCorp's design teams. We, the authors of this book, certainly don't have formulas that are guaranteed to work. We believe you should be alert to new patterns. You should talk continuously, openly and probingly to your colleagues, mainly by story-telling. You should keep trying new things. Although we believe these ideas will be very useful, they are not panaceas.

Modelling of complex systems shows that order often emerges from an apparently chaotic situation. Practical experience shows that this does indeed happen in the real world. So it is reasonable to hope that new types of order will emerge in your organisation, but unreasonable to expect that this will happen whenever you want it to. Complexity is marked by uncertainty and is often best described in ambiguous terms. Life in a complex world is largely uncontrollable and unpredictable. The sensible management response is to create an enabling infrastructure that gives a good chance for self-organisation. You don't design a solution, you design a capacity for solutions to emerge. There may be no firm rules for coping with complexity. However, some hints, new perspectives, possible experiments and encouragement are available, so if you try you may find your own solutions.

Lewin and Regine (1999) write:

> Complexity science implies that CEOs and managers must give up control – or, rather, the illusion of control – when they are trying to lead their organisation towards some goal. But they need to create an environment in which creativity can emerge; *some* structure is necessary if a company is to avoid slipping into anarchy and out of business . . . The complexity-guided style of management is hard – very hard – to do, especially for managers who seek safety in a command-and-control practice. It is hard even for those who embrace its principles, because the everyday urgency of business can make time spent interacting and nurturing relationships seem like a waste of time, a distraction from tough business realities. (p. 44 and p. 50)

These writers stress interpersonal relationships, which are indeed vital for coping with complexity. This is understandable because complexity arises from relationships rather than from objects. In this book, we stress story-telling, which both facilitates the building of sound relationships between co-workers and enables the understanding of complex situations. Stories are the means for appreciating the factual, ethical and affectual aspects of a situation. In Chapter 2 we discussed Dunbar's view of gossip as the verbal equivalent of grooming for creating bonds between people. This is an instance of story-telling as an enhancer of relationships. In Box 6.1 we draw on the work of Antonio Damasio to suggest why story-telling has such cognitive power – how it enables us to appreciate complex situations.

BOX 6.1   Is the Brain Hard-Wired for Story-Telling?

In his book *The Feeling for What Happens: Body, Emotion and the Making of Consciousness*, Antonio Damasio (1999) sets out a novel view of the human brain. Damasio links the rapidly expanding understanding of the brain provided by cognitive science to his years of experience in treating patients who have suffered brain damage through injury or illness. He tells how human consciousness arises out of emotion. The core of consciousness is the feeling of self and what happens around the self. Some of what he says is speculative, but the speculation is always careful, subtle and humane.

Damasio believes that the basic function of consciousness is to link the non-conscious biological machinery that keeps our bodies working to the constant activity of imagining what may happen in the future. He says that consciousness 'is valuable because it centres knowledge on the life of an individual organism'. He sees humans as having an 'autobiographical self', made up of a huge collection of autobiographical memories. For him, a key part of consciousness is the interaction between what is happening at a given moment and the autobiographical self in the background. This link between the self and the world is an essential, life-preserving asset, presumably developed during evolution.

From the point of view of story-telling, Damasio's thesis is interesting because of the central roles it gives to autobiography and imagination. Autobiography is the history of the self. The structure of the autobiographical self is a series of stories; so is the structure of the imaginative views of the future that the brain is constantly constructing.

To this, we can add the words of Michael Milburn and Shree Conrad (1996): 'if a person can experience no emotion, then all concepts lose their meaning' (p. 41).

Another Virtuous Circle

In Chapter 5 we described Charles Hampden-Turner's work on the resolution of dilemmas. The aim of dilemma resolution is to move from a vicious circle in which conflict is hidden by repression to a virtuous circle in which two apparently antithethical values are integrated into a new formulation that honours both.

Here we present another virtuous circle. The circle starts with an organisation facing a complex situation. Because story-telling is such a natural activity for human beings, complexity tends to produce lots of stories within the organisation. This stream of stories is an active response to the complex situation, an attempt at sensemaking. In this context, story-telling and sensemaking sometimes merge into a single activity. If the individuals concerned are reasonably skilled in the narrative arts, and if the organisation's culture is reasonably supportive, then story-telling strengthens its capability in two directions. First, sensemaking becomes collective. Tellers of tales are not fazed by uncertainty. Indeed, a central technique for holding readers' attention is the last-minute denouement – the identity of the murderer is not revealed until the last chapter. Listeners welcome variety, they enjoy mystery, metaphor, patterning and ambiguity. All these are features of a complex situation. Thus tale-telling develops a collective capacity for pattern recognition, for living with uncertainty, for making sense of what happens.

Second, story-telling strengthens the group. The inter-connections between people in an organisation are dense, which generates further complexity. Story-telling (in this case we may call it gossip) helps us to understand fellow members of our group. Gossip is informal investigation into what makes someone the way he is and why someone else behaves in the way she does. We come to see that all members of the group must be included. Gossip can, of course, be malicious, and in that case it fails to aid learning, because it does not present the truth about a fellow member of the group.

We come to relish the diversity within and between people and the value of diversity to the group. We come to realise that group effect-iveness depends on constant renewal of group bonds, and therefore on constant story-telling. Through stronger relationships, we find how to work together constructively, how to reach public judgements, and how to agree on collective action.

Capabilities for collective sense-making and collective action lead, in turn, to effective self-organisation. In the final stage of the virtuous circle, self-organisation allows the group to tackle other complex situations, and the circle begins once more. Box 6.2 has a diagram of the circle.

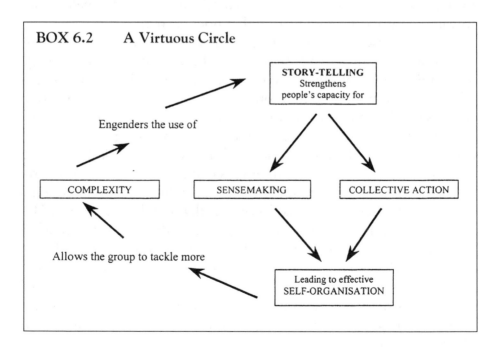

BOX 6.2   A Virtuous Circle

STORY-TELLING
Strengthens
people's capacity for

Engenders the use of

COMPLEXITY   SENSEMAKING   COLLECTIVE ACTION

Allows the group to tackle more

Leading to effective
SELF-ORGANISATION

This picture tells us that we don't have to throw up our hands in horror at the uncontrollable, unpredictable, uncertain world of com-plexity. We can use diversity and ambiguity to help us cope. We can expect some kind of order to emerge, even if it does so in unexpect-ed ways. We can expect to get into a virtuous circle that links increasing self-organisation and increasing ability to handle complex situations.

The social learning theory of Bandura (1977) emphasises the importance of observing the behaviours, attitudes and emotional reactions of others, and using them as models. The new behaviour is learned by first rehearsing it symbolically (in imagined stories) and then enacting it overtly. Clearly, people are more likely to adopt a new behaviour if it results in outcomes they value and if they admire the person whose behaviour is used as a model.

AutoCorp's Change Programme

AutoCorp decided to use a range of strategies to develop people's capacities. This included Functional Excellence – a performance management system that involved regular appraisals against agreed measures. This resulted in individual performance being rated as out-standing, on target or unsatisfactory and was supposed to lead to appropriate training, coaching and mentoring. The system was getting the mixed reception generally accorded to such schemes.

Story-telling was used during some of this development work. Participants were invited to create and tell short stories about organisational life, to give them an introduction to the liveliness and effectiveness of telling simple stories. This activity encouraged a creative approach, which AutoCorp wanted to develop, and prompted fruitful discussion about the positive and negative effects of the culture or climate in different areas of the organisation, and what to do about it. Some stories had to be constructed overtly as learning stories in order to share best practice ideas between representatives from different areas; others were left more open to allow people's immediate interests to emerge. Here is what happened at a development workshop attended by senior staff primarily responsible for strategy and policy across different functions such as process development, human resources, CADCAM (computer-aided design/computer-aided manufacture), finance and sales.

To create their story, participants were given a range of materials and props to choose from. They were encouraged first to share personal experiences of things they found helpful and unhelpful about the corporation. The following story was one that emerged. The story-telling group used a narrator to comment on the action.

Narrator: 'Once upon a time there was a new recruit, fresh and chirpy with lots of energy and enthusiasm for the tasks ahead. [The story-tellers used a fluffy yellow chick puppet to play this character and, deftly manipulated by a first-time puppeteer, the puppet quickly endeared himself to the audience.] Chirpy made friends and, after looking with his fresh eyes at how things were done, came up with some alternatives. He got to work on some of his ideas.

'For a while all went well. Chirpy enjoyed his work and people enjoyed having him around. But one day his efforts attracted the attention of the finance department [much booing at the finance department, represented by a little model of Bill the Pirate and his chest of gold]. Chirpy was summoned to see Bill. "You scurvy land-lubbing spend-thrift," shouted Bill, waving his cutlass. "Roast is how we usually have our chicken around here. You'd better hope I don't need to call for you again or you and your ideas will be taking a very long walk off a very short plank – if I'm in a *good* mood."

'Chirpy turned pale and fled so quickly he nearly got tangled up in his own legs. Back in his own corner, a tear trickled down his beak. He thought he'd been doing OK. His friends consoled him. "We should have warned you," they said. "But we can help you now. Pirate Bill does have some bad moods but if you submit a proper budget you might get what you want." After some consultation and hard work, Chirpy plucked up the courage to enter Bill's lair once more.

'Wobbly on his feet from nerves, he presented his case to Bill the Pirate. It was a good case and Bill handed over two gold coins. Now, Chirpy had needed three, but until he learned to fly he thought he'd take what he could get and, thanking Bill, he left.

'Chirpy got to work. And as word spread that he was good and enthusiastic, people came to him for help. One after another, projects arrived until Chirpy – who, being a dedicated sort of chick, had taught himself to juggle [quick demonstration using juggling balls provided] – was quite exhausted. And he hadn't managed to complete his original project that he'd worked so hard to get his gold coins for.

'Of course the day came when Chirpy dropped one of his balls.

'As it happened, this particular ball was a health and safety issue. There was a very big fuss. Chirpy was horrified at what he had done but he also realised that nobody had been looking after his own health and safety. Nor had they let him properly use all his new skills, like juggling and getting money from pirates while not getting roasted or having to take a long walk off a short plank. And there was something else. Not only had his balls dropped, but he'd learned to fly. And fly was just what he did – to a competitor who knew how to treat a growing chick properly.

'Bill the Pirate, his seafaring days over because of the threat from the new dragon at the edge of the world, tried never to give away so much as a brass farthing ever again because he never knew where his next doubloon was coming from. And in any case, he had formed the distinct impression that people who asked for your money were all cousins-of-parrots who never finished what they started.

'And Chirpy, in his new home, lived happily ever after doing things that really messed up life for his previous employers.'

This was an engaging exercise that provoked great debate between those who recalled their own days as Chirpy, and a couple of Bills who were in the room.

But not all story seeds get such fertile ground, and very deliberate support for them needs to be maintained. For example, on another occasion, a Chirpy-like story was told and received general agreement. However, another view prevailed, which was, 'But we can't tell that story in public'. The fear was partly of Bill but mostly of the dragon that lived at the edge of the world. Which is another story . . . which you will find in Box 6.3.

BOX 6.3   The Dragon Who Lived at the Edge of the World

Once upon a time there was a beautiful baby dragon called Sam. He had shiny green scales, big eyes and a fine pointed tail. His parents were pleased with him, and took every opportunity to show him off. 'Look at his beautiful nose,' said his mother. 'Such fine nostrils. Just right for breathing fire. And his lovely little wings – so elegant and strong.'

In time, Sam went to school. Now, as you know, dragons are quite uncommon things, so he was the only dragon there. The other children were quite a mixture – some human girls and boys, a giant (they're quite small until they're about ten), two centaurs and a troll called Tod. Sam ran and played with the other children, flapping his wings to give a nice breeze on hot days, and was very popular.

Then, one day, something happened. He was playing as usual

when suddenly he felt a rumbling in his belly and a tingling in his nose. Smoke curled up from his nostril and, the next thing he knew, a lick of flame came out. Sam was delighted. Now see how his fine nostrils and beautiful nose were really working! The children clapped and shouted, and Sam's parents were very proud of their 'proper little dragon'.

Until the day, that is, when Sam sent out a particularly fierce flame that hit the ground with such force that it singed Tod's shoes. The children ran away, scared. Sam tried to stop, but he couldn't. Everyone shouted at him and teased him. And the more they shouted and teased, the more he breathed fire, and the more upset he felt. He got so upset that he discovered he could send a ten-metre flame right across the playground whenever he wanted to. So he did – quite often. After all, what did it matter if nobody would play with him any more?

Now, Sam was eleven by this time, which is quite grown-up for dragons. And because he was bothering everybody with his fire, his parents packed him off on the train to a town at the edge of the world where he wouldn't be such a nuisance. And there he stayed. How unfair, he thought. One minute he was being praised for his beautiful nose and fine nostrils; the next he was sent away because he couldn't help but use them.

At least one useful thing happened while he was away. He found that if he paid attention, he could notice the rumble in his tummy almost before it started, and only breathe fire when he wanted to. He breathed fire very hard when he saw somebody coming to steal his treasure (all dragons have treasure, of course), and he breathed quite hard into the central heating system when winter came. But he stopped singeing the gateposts by mistake when he was in a bad mood, and the birds came back to sing in the trees just as soon as the branches grew back.

And then, of course, you can guess what happened next. The people back at home found out why it would be good to have him around – their magic flame at the bakery turned out not to be magic after all, and went out so nobody could make any bread or pizza. Sam the dragon with his exceptional fire-breathing was just what was needed.

So Sam came back. He joined school again, didn't singe anybody at all, and was much admired for his amazing fiery skills.

> Where are your organisational dragons? Are the reasons for being afraid of them out of date? What would be a better role for them?

Uncertainty

Tommy Sprigett utters a stream of curses as he leaves a meeting of the Sigma project team at AutoCorp's Birmingham DDC. Surely they could see that getting the chassis right was central to the design of a load-carrying vehicle. For God's sake, vans were meant to carry things. He could see the merits of design iteration, but this was crazy. Someone in Detroit had suddenly got scared by the zero-emissions noise coming out of California. Would the millions of vehicles in the whole state, all put together, really have to emit less greenhouse gas than the animals in the San Diego zoo? AutoCorp should ignore this rubbish and get on with bringing out a cracking product. But no. The Sigma has got to be adaptable to take hybrid power, fuel cell power and a whole load of other possible power sources. What a mess! And just when the lads had come up with a really nifty solution to the variable loads problem.

The next morning, Tommy talks to his chassis design team. 'You all know that Marco gave us a "bellisimo" for our work on variable loads. I told you we'd made our big contribution to the project and could spend the next few months working on the details. Well, I was wrong. Detroit now say that since the Sigma platform will have to last at least until 2015 it will have to be able to take all kinds of new power sources. Next week they'll tell us what they mean by this. It will probably be far too vague. Whatever they say, it'll mean we've got to start all over again.'

'How did Marco react?' asks someone. 'Optimistic as usual,' replies Tommy. ' "Not a problem. We are real smart".' Hal, a newly joined engineer, pipes up. 'Once I was sent on a course. You'll never believe this – it was a course on story-telling! Any rate, they told a story about this Greek guy, Sisyphus. He was punished by the Gods, for smoking in the toilets or something. He had to roll a huge boulder up a hill, but the moment he got it to the top it rolled back down and he had to start again. That's the original story. But the blokes on the course re-told the story. In the new story Sisyphus was a fitness freak. He enjoyed pushing rocks around. Developed his muscles, got him out in the fresh air, had a lovely view from the top of the hill etcetera, etcetera. He kept complaining of course, in case the Gods shifted him to other work, but he really loved the job.'

Tommy turns to Hal. 'You're not suggesting we like scrapping our work and starting again?' 'Why not? We enjoy designing vehicles. The more tricky the problem, the more fun it is to find a solution.' There is an amazed silence. The old habit of moaning about Detroit suddenly seems a bit petty. 'Suppose you could be right,' says Tommy slowly. 'Yes, come to think about it, different engine configurations is much the same problem as variable loads. We could use our new approach. Lot of work, though.'

This is an example of 're-framing', a well-known technique borrowed from psychology. In stories, things often turn out to be different from how they appeared to be at first sight. That's why stories help in re-framing. The new way of looking at things doesn't actually remove the uncertainty about what kinds of engine the Sigma van will have, but it allows the design engineers to enjoy solving the problem, rather than moaning about it.

There are many reasons why uncertainty can make it hard to think or act. There may be individual reasons, for instance stemming from someone's childhood experiences that link uncertainty, helplessness and pain. Story-telling could help here, just as fairy-tales allow children to come to terms with their fears, but more structured counselling may be needed. Another possible reason for crippling uncertainty is an over-reliance on logic. If you believe that deduction from unchallenged axioms is the way to find a logically correct course of action, then in most practical situations you will be disappointed, because this kind of certainty is usually unattainable. And it is harder to work out what to do when things are uncertain. Most of us have experienced the relief that definite news – even when it is bad news – can bring. At least you know the worst.

 Sprigett's design team might have learnt from an example given by Charles Hampden-Turner in his book *Corporate Culture: From Vicious to Virtuous Circles* (1990). This example is of a company that designs integrated circuits. In this company there always seemed to be a fight between designers and planners. Designers wanted freedom so they could come up with creative solutions, while planners wanted tight schedules so that products got to market on time. Hampden-Turner suggests that these fights will continue unless a new mental model is adopted by everyone. The model will be neither that of the designer (a brilliant design) nor that of the planner (project completion on time and within budget). The first step in finding a better model is to recognise that both the designer's and the planner's present models have merit. The fact that both have merit is what generates a dilemma, and once you see this you can try and find a model that resolves the dilemma.

In the case of the integrated circuit company, the dilemma was resolved by adopting the model of 'pulling products towards a rendezvous with the strategies of customers'. The customer's needs are more important than the elegance of the engineering or than sticking to the project schedule. So if the chassis design team at AutoCorp were to use Charles Hampden-Turner's model of a rendezvous with the customer's strategy, they might respond constructively to the challenge posed by California's possible future anti-pollution laws. Hal's telling of the new Sisyphus story, in which pushing stones around is equated with keeping fit rather than with constant frustration, led to a similar reorientation in the chassis design team's view of their tasks. Pride in their engineering skills and a drive to do things on time remained, but became secondary to the customer's needs.

In Act II of Shakespeare's *The Merchant of Venice*, lots of young men want to marry the clever, beautiful and wealthy Portia. Before his death Portia's father had prepared three caskets, one of which held Portia's portrait. By the terms of her father's will, her suitors had to choose one of these caskets. The suitor who chose the right casket – the one containing the portrait – could marry her. Other suitors who chose wrongly could never see her again.

The first casket was made of gold and bore an inscription: 'Who chooseth me shall gain what many men desire'. The second was of silver and promised: 'Who chooseth me shall get as much as he deserves'. The third was of lead and carried the blunt warning: 'Who chooseth me must give and hazard all that he hath'.

The first suitor chooses the gold casket, opens it and finds, not Portia's picture, but a note that starts: 'All that glisters is not gold . . .' This tells him he has failed. The second suitor chooses the silver casket and finds inside a portrait of a 'blinking idiot', who has been distracted by the shine of silver. Once more the suitor has got it wrong.

The third suitor, of humbler estate but very attractive, is Bassanio. Portia begs him to wait a few days before making his choice among the caskets. If he chooses the wrong one, he will have to leave immediately and she rather likes his company. But Bassanio cannot bear uncertainty – he would rather pick a casket right away, in spite of Portia's pleadings and the risk he will get it wrong. He chooses, judging not by the outward appearance of the casket but rather expressing his willingness to hazard everything he has to win the woman he loves. He decides on the lead casket, which is of course the one with the portrait – and a rhyme that ends: 'Turn you where your lady is/And claim her with a loving kiss.'

The stories of Sisyphus, integrated circuit design and the three caskets illustrate different ways of coping with uncertainty. The first way is to re-frame the situation, in order to understand it more constructively. Looking at the situation through new eyes is an important part of the solution and this is where story-telling can help, with its appeal to tacit knowledge and to the emotions. The second way is to understand the dilemma, in this case through a deeper understanding of the customer's strategic needs. The third way is to accept that a choice has to be made, and to connect with your own core values when making that choice. You have to choose one of the three caskets, and you take a course of action you can be proud of, even if it turns out to be wrong. By putting the choice into a wider frame, that of your authentic value system, you at least have a good chance of learning something from the outcome, even if you fail. A choice guided by values is not simply a gamble, however uncertain the outcome. Leadership is today often seen as a response to uncertainty that inspires confidence in others. If a leader's values are clear, lived in practice and shared by others, a bold course of action will be supported and followed, even if the outcome is uncertain.

You might say that the 're-framing' and 'dilemmas' approaches force you to think clearly, and often radically, about the situation that you face. The 'values' approach forces you to think clearly about what is really important to you. All three approaches stop you wishing for an impossible definitive solution. Chapter 7, where we investigate the technique of scenarios, also has lessons for coping with uncertainty, by being prepared for a range of eventualities. So uncertainty is often present, but that does not mean you have to be paralysed by it.

Ambiguity

Ambiguity is a particular kind of uncertainty. It is uncertainty about the meaning of a word or a phrase, of a picture or a situation. It is not about how the dice will roll, but about the number of spots on the face of one of the dice. Sometimes ambiguity can be resolved by asking for an explanation, or by looking more carefully at a situation. But this is not always so. Sometimes there is no one around who is able to explain a doubtful text or provide the background for a cloudy situation.

Ambiguity may be intentional. The 'double entendre' delivered by a comedian like Benny Hill is deliberate, fitting the dictionary definition of the term: 'a phrase with two meanings, one usually indecent' (Shorter Oxford Dictionary). (The term itself carries some deliberate obscurity – it is not only in French, but in obsolete French.) So ambiguity may be there to be enjoyed, perhaps through its polite concealment that confuses no one.

In politics and in marketing, deliberate ambiguity is common. Words like 'opportunity' or 'modernisation' can be chosen because they mean different things to different people. When they are spoken by a smiling face, the listener picks up whichever meaning she would like to hear. Nevertheless, as humans, we are not particularly keen on uncertainty or ambiguity, because our brains like to resolve such circumstances into a singular coherent explanation. Visual ambiguity is a prime example of this. We start to make sense of what we are seeing, and we make a picture. It feels quite odd to have our sensemaking disconfirmed, as it can be by the well-known pictures like the duck/rabbit, the vase/profiles or the beauty/hag.

Jokes can be funny for similar reasons. A 1990s advertisement campaign for a national newspaper featured a businessman apparently being attacked by a youth. Then the camera panned back to give us a new view, seeing that the youth was actually saving the man from being hit by an object falling from a building. The advertisement worked because the new view was a surprise – a different 'sense' from the one we had already made. Encouraging ourselves not to reach early resolutions and stick to them is one way in which we can open possibilities. Stories about first appearances being deceptive have been told for generations; such as *Little Red Riding Hood*, where the girl at first thought the wolf was her grandmother.

By the same token, this tendency to resolve things, to seek closure and completeness, means that if we set ourselves up in an ambiguous situation, we will readily engage in changing it (assuming we believe ourselves able to do so). We will start to self-organise from the 'bottom up' rather than having to follow prescriptions from on high, which may not work. This is why ambiguity can favour self-organisation.

Nonaka and Takeuchi (1995, pp. 11–14) discuss the way the Honda company, in 1978, set about designing a new car, the Honda City. Top management started the process with a slogan – 'Let's gamble' – reflecting their view that Honda's existing cars were too conventional. They appointed an experienced head of design and development, but staffed his team with young designers. The team's average age was 27. Top management gave the team just two instructions:

1. The product concept must be fundamentally different from anything the company had done before.
2. The car must be inexpensive, but not cheap.

Nonaka and Takeuchi suggest that such cleverly framed, partly ambiguous instructions work in three ways. First, because they express the inexpressible through figurative language (inexpensive, but not cheap). Second, because they depend on shared tacit knowledge. And third because they have some redundancy – things are said in more than one way. The ambiguity of instructions like these is usually kept within a boundary. In the case of the Honda City, the instruction about fundamental novelty ruled out the adaptation of an existing design, like a smaller version of the Honda Civic, and stopped the design team from thinking conventionally.

William Empson's book *Seven Types of Ambiguity* is a work of literary criticism. Two of his seven types are particularly worth noting. One is the pun, the use of a word that has more than one meaning, or which sounds the same as a different word. From its association with unfunny jokes, the pun has got itself a bad name, but it is a straightforward example of how ambiguity can raise in the mind a connection between two distinct ideas. Another type of ambiguity discussed by Empson is the contradiction that forces the reader or listener to invent interpretations that make sense of a phrase. 'Inexpensive but not cheap' is a good example. Some English words carry their contradictions around all the time. For instance, 'quite' can mean very ('Quite, quite marvellous, my dear!') and also not very ('Well, it's quite good, I suppose.') And to 'sanction' means both to permit and to punish.

Sarcasm is a rather cheap use of ambiguity – you say something in a tone of voice that indicates you mean the opposite of what you say. And someone's powerful rejection of an idea gives a clue that it might actually attract that person ('methinks she doth protest too much'). Empson writes: '"Ambiguity" itself can mean an indecision as to what you mean, an intention to mean several things, a probability that one or other or both of two things has been meant, and the fact that a statement has several meanings' (p. 5).

If nothing else, these examples of word play show that ambiguity is widespread in our speech. The listener's or reader's imagination is stimulated by an ambiguous joke, an ambiguous phrase in a poem, or an ambiguous instruction to a design team. The connection Honda found between ambiguity and creativity is not confined to automobile design. But is it helpful to advocate ambiguity as part of organisational change? Surely the right way to manage change is to go for maximum clarity and certainty. Isn't change stressful enough without added worry about what a certain statement means?

Well, ambiguity due to evasiveness or laziness on the part of senior people is certainly not what we advocate. 'Weasel words' that disguise someone's real intentions, making a painful change temporarily less obvious, are dishonest and damaging. But if the intent is to stimulate self-organising change, that is different. Then ambiguity encourages innovation, providing the boundaries within which self-organisation can function are clear. So ambiguity is different from uncertainty, because it can be used constructively. Clever stories are often ambiguous, and the ambiguity may never be resolved even by the end of the story. Was Anna Karenina a tragic figure, driven to death by a hypocritical society, or simply selfish, or both?

Self-Organising Change at AutoCorp

Chuck Mascone of AutoCorp frequently uses the slogan 'change must be rationed'. He says that no organisation can cope with an overload of changes, even if all are beneficial. And with many changes, you don't know whether they are beneficial or not until you try them. He says that change is generally good, but you can have too much of a good thing. Mascone argues that the dangers of change overload are obvious to most people, but in practice the dangers are often ignored. Why is this? Well, it is always hard to overcome established practices and attitudes, so when an opportunity for change presents itself, managers tend to grab it. Chuck Mascone's remedy for change overload is self-organising change.

Chuck has plenty of stories about self-organising change. One concerns a large aircraft manufacturing company that introduced a computerised system for allocating space during the design of a new plane.

Once the external shape of a major part of the plane, such as the wing, had been fixed, the system split up the interior of the wing into a 3D grid. Designers of components, like fuel tanks, that were housed in the wing could bid for space within the grid. Once a claim had been staked by one group of designers, other groups who tried to use that space would be told by the system that the space was taken. The system also reported which of the other design groups had claimed the space in question. A practice rapidly grew up among designers of deliberately making tentative space claims around their area of interest. The purpose was not actually to claim space for themselves but to discover which other design groups were working on areas close to theirs. Once the system had given them the information, designers would then start talking directly to other groups. So the system didn't resolve conflict, but it did alert people to the need to work together. It was therefore a system that promoted self-organisation.

Another of Chuck's stories is about the way Japanese automobile companies used sports analogies for the design process in the 1980s and early 1990s.

The first analogy was for traditional practice, and that was the relay race. In the old days of vehicle design, the first phase was a development phase. When that was complete, the baton was passed to manufacturing who decided how they would produce the new vehicle. Only when manufacturing plans were complete was the baton passed to marketing, who then had to decide how the car would be sold. Each phase was virtually complete before the next phase started.

Several Japanese companies realised that this was a slow way to design a car and began to work on a new approach. The analogy for the new way was rugby. Here the ball is passed backwards and forwards between players as they run towards their opponent's touch-line. Passing the ball is a decision made by an individual player, and other players have to be ready all the time to receive a pass. The various departments – development, design, manufacturing and marketing – were all involved from the start, and they communicated continuously about the progress of the project, passing the ball between them in a spontaneous way.

By the 1990s, Japanese companies were operating internationally and this made the rugby analogy out of date. When much of manu-facturing and marketing took place outside Japan, frequent face-to-face meetings were unfeasible. The team couldn't pass the ball around in the flexible way needed for the rugby model. A switch was thus made to another analogy – that of American football. In this sport, detailed plays are worked out before the game, and players take time out during the game for consultations on tactics. The American football model involved neither the sequential baton-passing of the relay race, nor the free flow of the rugby game, but instead introduced a series of strategic and tactical co-ordinators who guided co-operation within the design team. A lot of self-organisation remained, but various boundaries were drawn during the course of the project that broke up self-organisation into manageable chunks. Chuck believes that sports analogies made the various types of organisation easy to remember and to talk about.

Mascone is often asked why he travels so much. If, as he claims, self-organisation makes life easier for him, why does he visit all parts of AutoCorp so frequently? Does he actually like airport lounges? Chuck's answer is given with a wry smile. 'I said it made my life *easier*. I didn't say it was *easy*. Unless I talk to people all the time, they don't believe self-organisation is possible. Instead they wait for someone to tell them what to do. So I go round reminding them they're in charge, asking them what they plan to do, encouraging them to talk to other AutoCorp people. I don't organise them, I get them to organise them-selves.'

And he says the best route to self-organisation is story-telling. Take the impact of market research on design. Market researchers like questions that produce statistical information. For instance, people could be asked how much more they would pay for a car with four doors than one with two doors: £50, £100, £200? If the median answer was £150, then designers would have a target: find a way to add two more doors to a two-door car that adds no more than £150 to the sale price. Mascone thought that this left out a lot of important information. Why did people like a four-door car anyway? Was it simply that they were used to having four doors? Was it because four doors made shopping easier? Was it for travelling with children or elderly parents? Did they associate four doors with dignity and comfort? And, incidentally, did they associate two doors with sport and youth?

Mascone organises and facilitates ideas workshops. He gets participants to tell stories about the use of the vehicle they are designing. He says these stories have to be of an everyday kind, not the fantasies of advertisements where the car is just a prop in a story about sexy, affluent people travelling through beautiful countryside. Instead they have to be realistic tales about heavy loads of shopping and fractious children, or collecting your parents for a Christmas lunch, of bad weather, traffic jams, dark winter mornings. The practicalities and the symbolism of using the car they are dreaming about come out in the stories the designers tell.

An Experiment in Self-Organisation

Chuck Mascone can't force people to organise themselves – that would be a contradiction in terms. In any case, he isn't the designers' boss. So he works by giving broad descriptions of design objectives, by encouraging pattern recognition, by stimulating story-telling. He tells stories himself. For instance, about the discovery of Lyme disease by two mothers in Connecticut, who noticed their children had a similar pattern of rashes and fevers, and who finally got doctors to recognise that this pattern might be the symptom of a hitherto unknown disease.

Self-organisation is built on faith. Not on blind faith that ignores human weakness, but on a reasonable expectation that people really like working together to achieve common goals. Mascone encourages people to work out their own rules for collective action, rules that they keep because they are committed to the group's purposes, not because the rules are imposed by someone outside the group. The dangers of free-riding have to be faced – free riders only pretend to go along with the rules, and hope they will get away with it because the rules don't have any external back-up. He encourages people to define carefully the boundaries of their self-organisation: 'Don't think you can self-organise the whole world'.

Chuck asks people to look for low-cost ways to achieve agreement on collective action; simple and quick forms for discussion and resolving disputes, so that problems don't fester and resentment doesn't have time to grow. He tries to find key people who have the energy and confidence to get things going, to show that self-organisation is perfectly possible. He suggests that they look for lessons from other fields, like the self-organised systems for managing scarce natural resources described by Elinor Ostrom in her book *Governing the Commons* (1990).

During a visit to the Birmingham DDC for review of the Sigma project, Chuck gets permission from Marco Belli, the chief designer, to hold three workshops on successive evenings for everyone on the project. He starts the workshops by asking participants to form groups of three or four, and gives each group a picture of a different vehicle in AutoCorp's current range. He then asks the groups to work out what animal their vehicle most closely resembles – lion, ox, rat, monkey, or whatever – and to justify their choice to the whole workshop by telling a story about a day in the life of the animal.

On the day following the last of Chuck's workshops, Belli gets the whole design team together. 'We gotta be much, much faster – much, much more creative. And don't ask me for certainty. You are not gonna get it. With his crazy exercises, Chuck has made you think. Now you go away and work out what you're going to do. In two weeks' time I want you back here with loads of ideas. Small ideas, big ideas. But your own ideas, not things you've thought up to please your Italian boss.'

Old hands like Tommy can't believe that big-ego Marco is handing over control like this. 'He must be really worried,' says Tommy. Even the old guys feel excited. The young ones are over the moon. The place is buzzing. That evening, senior design people are invited for a farewell drink with Mascone. After a couple of gin and tonics, Tommy goes up to Chuck and says: 'Admire your guts. But this won't fly. They'll stop Marco listening to you about self-organisation.' 'That may be correct, Mr Sprigett,' replies Chuck, 'but if we don't try we'll never know.'

When Mascone gets back to Detroit, he is told to attend a budget meeting. AutoCorp's CEO has issued a cost-saving edict: all staff groups have a 25% budget cut. 'Use more imagination and less money,' they are told. A family friend, who is a venture capitalist, has for years been urging Chuck to leave AutoCorp and set up on his own. 'You'll get plenty of work. The big corporations will hand you things they can't deal with. And a clever guy like you will be less threatening if you aren't part of the organisation.' So, acting on the CEO's instructions, Chuck uses his imagination. He resigns from AutoCorp, taking a couple of colleagues with him, and starts his own firm. After a year, AutoCorp is paying his firm twice as much in fees than the budget of his old unit, and he has won business from other companies as well.

Conclusion

In this chapter we have suggested that self-organisation is the best response to complexity. We have described how story-telling helps to put in place an enabling infrastructure from which a self-organised order may emerge. This happens when the organisation's skill-base is strong enough – when a high proportion of the organisation's members have the skills and the self-confidence to act autonomously. They will then be able to use story-telling as a regular practice. The power of the tale will generate capabilities for sensemaking and relationship-building, leading to effective collective action.

In the next chapter we give the history of a small organisation, but one which has to deal with real complexity because of its city-wide and worldwide connections.

7

LIFT – Stories for Innovation

What shall we tell you?
Tales, marvellous tales
Of ships and stars and
Isles where good men rest.

James Elroy Flecker

This chapter is about innovation. It shows how story-telling can
keep innovation bubbling while an organisation grows and matures.
It tells the history of a remarkably innovative organisation – the
London International Festival of Theatre (LIFT).

We will not start this chapter with LIFT, but with another innovative
organisation. One day in 1976 Bob Swanson, a young venture capitalist, read a news item in the *San Francisco Chronicle*. The item reported
the discovery at the University of California's San Francisco campus
of a technique for the manipulation of genes. The report speculated
that this technique might be the basis for making a wholly new range
of medical treatments for almost every kind of disease, from diabetes
to heart attacks to cancer.

Swanson worked for the now well-known venture capital firm
Kleiner Perkins. He had recently come to the conclusion that pharmaceuticals could be the next big field for venture investment, following
on from microelectronics. Reading the *Chronicle* article made him

think that the discovery it reported might be the trigger for a wave of investment in new, start-up pharmaceutical companies. The gene manipulation technique, known as recombinant DNA, had the potential to make many new medicines. The pharmaceuticals industry was then almost entirely made up of large, established firms. Would this new technology end the dominance of the giants, allowing the growth of dynamic newcomers, as new technologies from Silicon Valley had done in the electronics business?

Swanson tracked down Herb Boyer, one of the two inventors of the recombinant-DNA technique, and persuaded Boyer to see him. Boyer was working very hard on the basic scientific research opportunities the technique had opened up. He couldn't see why meeting someone from a bank could possibly be of interest to him, but Swanson told a good story. As he put it later: '. . . the strategy from the very beginning was to be able to make and sell our own products. Therefore, we needed not only to generate the products but to manufacture them and build the marketing force to sell them' (McKelvey, 1996, p. 101). For a scientist struggling to produce a microgram of a material, it was exciting to be approached by someone who was thinking in terms of kilograms.

So Boyer promised to meet Swanson in a bar close to his lab, consoling himself with the thought that after half an hour with this mad banker he would soon be back at work. He was wrong. Hours after they met, they were still talking. By then Boyer and Swanson had agreed that a start-up company would be a marvellous way to develop this novel science, as well as to make their fortunes. Together Swanson and Boyer founded Genentech, the first true research-based biotechnology company. When Genentech had its Initial Public Offering on NASDAQ in 1980 its stock price tripled overnight, setting off a boom in biotech stocks. Genentech pioneered the production of insulin, human growth hormone and a life-saving treatment for blood clots. It also pioneered new kinds of research collaboration between academia and industry. It became a company respected as much for its science as for its commercial success. Bob Swanson's meeting with Boyer is a legend in the industry and led to him appearing on the cover of *Time* magazine.

Swanson's and Boyer's vision of a highly creative company, skilled in the most up-to-date biological techniques and readily able to work with academic scientists, some of them Nobel prize-winners, was very innovative. Over the last twenty-five years, their vision has influenced most of the world's biology-based industries and the biological research community. For instance, the reading of the human genome turned out to be an extraordinary interaction between publicly funded research labs and private business, notably with a company called Celera Genomics. Swanson's imagination was the visionary starting point for this new kind of company.

The Swanson/Boyer vision generated a story about the role of start-up companies in leading edge innovation. This story travelled round the world and changed the course of important research endeavours and substantial industries. For example, the formation of Celltech, the first start-up company in the UK to work on recombinant DNA, was influenced by the story of Genentech. The example of Genentech helped to convince both academic collaborators and financiers of the potential viability of the Celltech venture.

The London International Festival of Theatre

In 1980 two recent university graduates, both with an intense interest in theatre, shared a vision. Like the vision of Swanson and Boyer, it was a joint vision, this time the brainchild of Rose Fenton and Lucy Neal. Their vision was stimulated by what they saw as an odd phenomenon. The British were very good at exporting their own theatre but were rudely ignorant of the theatre blooming in the rest of the world. Human experience was reflected in a multitude of different styles of theatre around the world, but in London little was on offer outside the proscenium-arch tradition of well-made plays performed by well-trained actors in old-fashioned theatres. Even theatres outside the West End mostly presented plays heavily reliant on text.

Neither Rose nor Lucy had any experience in theatre management. In spite of this inexperience (or perhaps because of it) they resolved to bring inspiring international theatre to London. They would search the world for performances which pushed theatre in new directions, were popular in their own countries and had a chance of being successful in London. They would bring these shows to London for an international festival, to be held every other year. Thus the London International Festival of Theatre (LIFT) was conceived.

For their first year Rose and Lucy managed to borrow a flat as their base. Their office equipment was two clipboards. Their transport was two bicycles. They gathered some financial support, but a critical application for funding was turned down a few months before the first festival was due to start in the summer of 1981. Most of the performers they were bringing to London had never been outside their own countries and certainly couldn't afford to stay in hotels. The expected grant would have paid for their accommodation. Would the loss of the grant be the death of LIFT before they'd had a single festival? Lucy and Rose bundled themselves up against the cold, propped their clipboards on their knees and began counting all the spare beds they could find among their families and friends. In the end, all the performers had a place to sleep, the festival flourished and LIFT's tradition of improvising and fighting against the odds had started.

This first festival brought six shows to London from four countries with a budget of £180 000. In 1999, LIFT's festival had a budget ten times as large, twenty-two performances (in addition to a regular schedule of Daily Dialogues between performers and the public), a shipboard cafe and club moored in the Thames and an education programme involving over a thousand young people. A further eighteen young performers had come from South Africa to work with young people in London in putting on a show. Over the four weeks of the 1999 festival LIFT's audiences added up to nearly 100 000 people.

LIFT was a pioneer in internationalism. By linking up with other festivals in the UK and the rest of Europe, Rose, Lucy and their colleagues found ways to move theatre troupes, sets and props across the world more economically. They found new sources of sponsorship from overseas businesses and governments. The international nature of their work led to other innovations. Many of the theatre forms LIFT presented used mime, music, dance and symbols to engage their audiences. British theatre artists found they could learn a lot from these shows. Styles of performance that did not depend on a set text were fostered by LIFT's internationalism. The frontiers between theatre and the visual arts and between theatre and music are blurred in cultures outside northern Europe; these unfamilar connections brought new inspiration to UK artists, releasing astounding creativity.

Mounting a festival with productions of different forms meant that most of London's traditional theatre spaces were inappropriate. LIFT had to pioneer the use of unconventional spaces, many of them well outside the theatreland of central London. Again necessity was the mother of invention, and site-specific theatre became a regular feature of LIFT. In the 1999 festival, one show was a 24-hour-a-day performance in a shop window in South-West London and another, in this case directed by a leading theatre director, Deborah Warner, was presented in unoccupied offices in a tower block. The location of these productions was determined by the imagination of the artists, but they probably would not have been put on by anyone but LIFT.

From the start, Rose and Lucy insisted that artistic creativity had to be top priority in all that LIFT did. Perhaps there is an analogy here with Swanson and Boyer's insistence on scientific creativity at Genentech. A guiding question for LIFT was, and still is, where is the passion?

Lucy Neal and Rose Fenton had a vision. They were able to tell good stories about that vision: stories that persuaded artists to come to London and work under unfamilar and sometimes difficult conditions; stories that persuaded funders and sponsors to provide money for risky experiments; stories that got audiences to travel to parts of London they had never seen before, to see shows they would have to work hard to understand. LIFT has changed the theatrical scene in London. Audiences now expect to see more than text-based shows in traditional venues. They expect performances that overlap with music or art. They expect to see shows from all around the world. Ambitious theatrical producers in South Africa, Latin America and India hope that by attracting LIFT's attention and getting their shows to London, they will achieve international recognition. A number of companies have already had their fortunes transformed by being part of LIFT. So, LIFT has had a wide influence – it has led to a flowering of international theatre across the UK.

Imagination, Vision and Stories

'Why didn't I think of that?' This is a question most of us must have asked ourselves at some time in our lives. Why didn't I have that great idea? It could be an idea that in retrospect seems obvious, although no one had yet thought of it. You might have got there first, but you didn't. Perhaps you did have a similar vague idea, but didn't express it clearly, couldn't get anyone interested in it, or never did anything about it.

The world of dotcoms, where fortunes have been made and lost so quickly, has many optimistic ideas. In some cases the idea really is great. Someone spots a possible connection between a technological capability and a market opportunity and builds a business on that idea. In other cases, it seemed a great idea, but . . . only a big corporation had the muscle to make it happen, or the world wasn't ready for it, or somehow it fizzled out.

The business entrepreneur, the social entrepreneur, the artist and the politician all hope to come up with a really good new idea. They all want to create something that excites people. You could say that creativity depends on talented people and leave it at that; but innovation in business, in society, in the arts or in politics needs more than creativity. You have to get people to believe in the new idea, whether they are your boss, a fellow member of your organisation, an outside funder, the media or a customer. To gain support from people like these you need to tell the story of your idea, tell it well and tell it over and over again – just as Bob Swanson, Herb Boyer, Rose Fenton and Lucy Neal had to do.

You may have the most inventive ideas, but if you cannot tell good stories about them, they will probably remain as ideas. For an idea to make a difference in the world, it has to be coupled with a story people want to listen to. An idea whose time has come is an idea that has a compelling story attached to it. What we hope to do in this chapter is to show how to find good stories at every stage of the process of innovation – from vision to reality to renewal.

In fact, a vision is a story – a compelling one, one that inspires its author as well as its audience. A foggy vision is like a rambling story: both result in people getting lost. Visions, being stories, should be expressed as vividly as possible. They should draw on all the skills of the story-teller's trade, including using images: 'the world's theatre brought to your doorstep'; metaphors: 'a delicious feast of world theatre'; and similes: 'LIFT's programme is like a pile of beautifully wrapped birthday presents'. The language describing an original vision should be clear and fresh. The way the description is structured should mirror the aspiration of the vision. The story and the project should unfold in a similar manner. Some mystery can be combined with the clarity: 'the example of Genentech may eventually transform the whole relationship between academic research and industrial practice.'

Yes, you do have to have imagination – the creative faculty of the mind. Yes, you do have to use this imagination to create a vision – a thing seen in the imagination. But how can we stimulate the imagination, get our creative juices flowing? How can we distinguish an idle dream from an inspiring vision? Where do we find those visions that can be turned into reality? How do we tell that the right time for an idea has come?

The first step is to get your imagination working. The key to this step is creativity. We will not describe here well-known techniques like brainstorming, spider diagrams, the ideas wall and laddering. These work by avoiding the early dismissal of options and by provoking lateral thinking, and they can be very effective. Try them and see if they work for you. Even if they do, please remember that reading or listening to stories is a superb way of getting your imagination going. The stories you read or hear can be directly relevant to the problem you are thinking about. Or they can be stories that simply clarify your thinking – epic poetry can do this, with its combination of rhythm and narrative. Or they can be stories about the process of imagination – like Jim Watson's account of a critical point in his discovery, with Francis Crick, of the structure of DNA. An extract from Watson's story is given in Box 7.1.

BOX 7.1 The Double Helix

By March 1953, Watson and Crick had spent months thinking intensely about the structure of DNA. They now hoped they had picked a plausible structure from the myriad possibilities; but the details had to be exact, and getting them right was proving quite difficult.

> The metal [models of bases], needed for systematically checking all the conceivable hydrogen-bonding possibilities, had not been finished on time. At least two more days were needed before they would be in our hands. This was much too long even for me to remain in limbo, so I spent the rest of the afternoon cutting accurate representations of the bases out of stiff cardboard. But by the time they were ready I realised that the answer must be put off till the following day. After dinner I was to join a group . . . at the theatre.
>
> When I got to our still empty office the following morning, I quickly cleared away the papers from my desk top so that I would have a large, flat surface on which to form pairs of bases held together by hydrogen bonds.

Although I initially went back to my like-with-like prejudices, I saw all too well that they led nowhere. When Jerry came in I looked up, saw that it was not Francis [Crick], and began shifting the bases in and out of various other pairing possibilities. Suddenly I became aware that an adenine–thymine pair held together by two hydrogen bonds was identical in shape to a guanine–cytosine pair held together by at least two hydrogen bonds. All the hydrogen bonds seemed to form naturally; no fudging was required to make the two types of base pairs identical in shape.

Upon his arrival Francis did not get more than halfway through the door before I let loose that the answer to everything was in our hands. However, we both knew that we would not be home until a complete model was built in which all the stereo-chemical contacts were satisfactory . . . Thus I felt slightly queasy when at lunch Francis winged into the Eagle to tell everyone within hearing distance that we had found the secret of life.

(Watson 1968, pp. 194–197)

Important as creativity is for innovation, it is by no means the whole story. Genius has been called 5% inspiration and 95% perspiration. Innovation is much the same. To turn the original idea into something useful requires a lot of hard work.

The rest of this chapter will show how story-telling can help innovation at every stage, from the first gleam of a new vision to the stage of renewal, needed when an innovation starts to get stale. We will start with tales that stimulate the imagination through vivid glimpses of unfamiliar territory, by giving insights into novel areas of life, then we will tell you some stories about the need to connect with other people, because most innovation comes from connection between different disciplines, by connecting technology with human need, system with purpose, the prose with the passion.

Then we will explore ways of finding the right images and metaphors for your tales and how you can best choose the occasions and places to tell them. We will go on to describe the use of narrative in spanning the boundaries with other organisations. Next we will use the example of LIFT to show how stories help in building an organisation around your vision and in expanding your vision into new fields. Finally, we will talk about renewal, about finding a new vision that keeps the best of the old one and adds to it the spark of something absolutely new.

The stages of innovation listed in Box 7.2 are fairly obvious ones. The first four steps go from the original idea, to the initial small team, to deciding how to tell the tale and then to attracting backers. There is usually iteration between these steps. For example, the original idea may not become fully developed until the small team has been together for a while, and working out how to tell the tale may make you change the original idea. The last three steps build on the success achieved in the first steps. The last three steps are: building an organisation, expanding into nearby territory and, when necessary, renewing the original vision. Our choice of these steps is validated by experience in organisations of all kinds – high-tech start-ups in Silicon Valley and both Cambridges (in the UK and the USA), biotechnology companies like Genentech and Celltech, arts festivals like LIFT and the Edinburgh Festival and educational innovations like the Open University. They are also validated by research – see Boxes 7.3 and 7.4 later in this chapter.

BOX 7.2   The Stages of Innovation

The stage	A story in this chapter
1. Stimulating your imagination	Easy and Rich
2. Making connections	Blue Tits and Red Robins
3. The right images, spaces and occasions	The Nerd and the Frog
4. Spanning boundaries	The Girder and the Joist
5. Building an organisation	Each performance is a rehearsal for the next show
6. Expanding your vision	Project Phakama
7. Renewing the vision	What I see in the mirror

Stimulating your Imagination

In their book *The Knowledge-Creating Company* Ikujiro Nonaka and Hirotaka Takeuchi (1995, pp. 29–30 and 95–123) discuss the Japanese belief that knowledge comes only from direct experience. Nishida, the philosopher who in the nineteenth century first articulated Zen experience in theoretical terms, said that only such occasions as a person scaling a cliff and holding on for dear life, or a musician playing a composition he has fully mastered, lead to deep learning. It is this acquisition of fact from pure experience, from action in the world, that characterises Zen, and also much of the Japanese style of innovation.

Hearing a well-told tale goes some way towards having this kind of direct experience, and can be quicker than spending seven years in a Zen Buddhist monastery. Nonaka and Takeuchi tell lots of stories in their book. One of them is about an innovation in home baking which came from the Matsushita company.

One part of Matsushita was the cooking appliances division. This division had done a lot of consumer research. They saw that changing job patterns in Japan, particularly for women, meant that people had more money but less time. They wanted, and could afford, delicious and nutritious food but no longer had the time to prepare food in traditional ways. Was junk food the only alternative? People in Matsushita thought not. They believed that appliances producing high-quality food without a lot of work would meet an important social need and would sell well. This concept was encapsulated in a story they called 'Easy and Rich', which we repeat here.

The story was simple: good food depended on good ingredients and skilled cooking. A machine that brought into the home the skills of a master chef would, when used with good ingredients, make food that deserved to be called 'rich'. A machine that was reliable and simple to operate would deserve to be called 'easy'. One of Matsushita's technologists, Ikuko Tanaka, was a member of the team that set out to invent a home bakery. The tale of Easy and Rich inspired him to spend weeks with a master baker. He learned the difficult task of kneading the dough to make bread with the right taste and texture. The master baker's knowlege was tacit. Tanaka first had to find out how to make this knowledge explicit and, second, how to put the knowledge into a machine. He managed to do this with the aid of a mental image that he called 'twisting stretch' which guided the design of the propellor that mixed the dough and the shape of the mixing chamber. The prototype design made excellent bread. This innovation's first step had been successful. To succeed Tanaka had to have lots of technical understanding, he had to concentrate on the fine details of the task and he had to have a good imagination. To organise and inspire his work he also needed a good story. Without Easy and Rich he would not have got anywhere.

BOX 7.3   What is Innovation?

Michael West (2000) writes:

> At the root of the development of our species from our primitive beginnings to the recent stunning advances in technology, communication and social complexity, has been innovation – the development and implementation of improved processes, products or procedures. Yet despite the fascination with individual creativity, innovation is not a solitary activity which results from the vigorous championing of an idea by one individual. It is more usually the result of concerted activities of groups of people developing and implementing their ideas over a period of time, and then diffusing successful innovations throughout organizations or societies.
>
> However, the notion that group creativity and innovation are easy, positive, opportunistic, processes is inappropriate. Conflict is a common characteristic of innovation processes, observable principally in resistance to change. Innovation, by definition, represents a threat to the status quo. So for a group to successfully implement innovation, its members must manage conflict with the attendant emotional pain and difficulty; overcome resistance to change; and persist in ensuring the successful implementation of their innovative proposal.
>
> If creativity is the development of new ideas, innovation includes creativity as well as the process (and outcome) of putting creative ideas into practice – innovation in implementation. The biggest challenge for creative individuals or groups is persuading others to accept their ideas and to successfully implement them in the workplace. Innovation can then be defined as both the development of ideas for, and the introduction of, new and improved ways of doing things at work thus encompassing both creativity and innovation implementation. (pp. 460–464)

Making Connections

Arie de Geus (1997) tells a story about learning among songbirds. Apart from the primates, songbirds are nature's best social learners. They work out patterns of behaviour that help their survival and reproduction and they teach these patterns to subsequent generations. A study in Britain of the learning of two species of songbird – the blue tit and the robin (called the red robin, when de Geus tells the story) – looked at the interaction of bird behaviour and human behaviour. In the 1950s, aluminum seals were introduced for milk bottles, replacing the former cardboard seals. Songbirds, both tits and robins, had been able to lift up the old cardboard seals and drink the creamy top layer from the milk bottles delivered to people's doorsteps. But the birds could not remove the new aluminum seals. It looked as if they would lose a valuable source of food. Listen to Arie telling the tale:

And this indeed was what happened to the Red Robins. Except for the occasional isolated genius, no robin has ever learned how to peck through the shiny metal seals of today's milk bottles. For the Blue Tits it is different. Fanning out from various points, the art of pecking through the seals has now spread throughout the Blue Tit population. The occasional clever bird learned the trick, others observed and copied what they saw and others still copied them. The difference between robins and tits is that robins are solitary birds, protecting their own territories, while tits flock together, travelling around in groups. Tits have plenty of opportunities to watch each other's behaviour. Robins have few. The moral of the story is: birds that flock are birds that learn. (Adapted from de Geus, 1997 p. 134)

When he tells the story of the blue tits and the red robins, de Geus usually embeds it within another story. This is the story of how the Royal Dutch/Shell Group of companies decided to try to improve its capability for organisational learning. De Geus was head of planning for the Shell Group and in the 1980s there was less understanding of organisation learning than there is today.

Arie became convinced that planning is actually a process of learning. So better planning must come from better organisation learning. He visited a range of people who were studying learning. It was at the University of California at Berkeley that he heard the story of the Blue Tits and the Red Robins. He quickly realised the implications for human learning. Flocking, or in human terms continuing conversation, is essential for collective learning in groups. Humans who act like robins, defending their own solitary territories, are much less likely to learn than those who flock with others, as the tits do.

The story of the tits and the robins is thus a carefully planned one. De Geus has told it many times, to small groups and large ones, and in his book *The Living Company*. It is a well-prepared set-piece, a designed rather than an emergent story, but an individual one, since the key analogy between bird flocking and human conversation was his. The metaphor of 'flocking' is powerful, but it is not precise, which may be a good thing, since that makes people consider just what is involved in collective learning. Organisations could stimulate the telling of stories by asking that formal studies, like Shell's study on ways of learning, include in their final reports both an account of how useful lessons emerged from the study (in other words, a learning history), and some imaginative stories illustrating the studies' conclusions.

As a type of learning, innovation depends on flocking. Innovation usually depends on the combination of ideas and understandings in the heads of different people. Ikuko Tanaka's mental image of a twisting stretch in the bread dough had to be combined with other novel ideas before Matsushita's home bakery became reality. For instance, while the dough is being kneaded the yeast in it is fermenting. The kind of yeast and the way it is added to the dough affect the quality of the bread. Other people's knowledge of fermentation had to be linked to Tanaka's ideas. Flocking was how this happened. Good story-telling was how the flock shared their visions and their knowledge.

Making connections is necessary for innovation. The connections can be with other disciplines, with other kinds of knowledge, whether tacit or explicit, with other cultures or with other generations. Making connections is why immigration is so valuable for the country that receives the immigrants. It is why innovation tends to come from clusters of diverse, but strongly connected activities. Silicon Valley is a flocking phenomenon.

Much of this chapter is about LIFT. Why have we told you so much of LIFT's story in a chapter about the use of story-telling in innovation? First, because LIFT is international, multi-ethnic, multi-locational and multimedia. LIFT gives people the opportunity to appreciate cultures other than their own. People and organisations that are able to understand a range of diverse cultures have a big advantage when it comes to innovation. And story-telling is easily the best route to awareness of less familar cultures. The lesson is: listen to stories about unfamilar things and you'll be a better innovator. The second reason why LIFT is such a valuable resource for this chapter is that the theatre is a story-telling medium. Those involved in the theatre – writers, directors, designers and actors – are all professional story-tellers. Their skills are deployed in telling a tale. Narrative is what holds a show together, what makes it theatre rather than just noise or spectacle. The lesson is: for the implementation of innovation you must tell a good story, and watching professionals at work can teach you a thing or two about story-telling. The third reason is that LIFT is, of course, an organisation – an unusual one, but an organisation nonetheless. It has found various solutions to the problem of keeping an organisation innovative. We will tell you stories about those solutions. The lesson is: if you want to make your organisation more innovative, listen to stories about other innovative organisations. The fourth reason is that, despite its modest size, there is a lot of complexity around LIFT. As it aims always to be innovative, it has to keep making more and more connections, across the world, across the places and spaces of London, across London's communities, between artistic disciplines, with sponsors of all kinds. The story of LIFT is partly a story about coping with complexity.

The Right Space to Tell the Tale

Julia Rowntree is director of LIFT's business education programme: the LIFT Forum. This brings artists together with people from business and the public sector to attend performances and participate in workshops. The aim is to inspire new approaches in the workplace. One workshop was held in April 2000 and lasted a full day. Its themes were change, continuity and succession, and it was sparked off by *Departures*, a show in the 1999 LIFT Festival. *Departures* was a collaboration between artists from India and the UK and explored how, when forced to move on, people decide what to take with them and what to leave behind. Appropriately, the workshop took place at the Royal Court Theatre in Sloane Square, an institution that has recently been through a long process of physical and structural change.

The night before, Forum members had been to the theatre, to see *Hard Fruit*, a new play by Jim Cartwright, a Royal Court stalwart. The play had explored the themes that would be taken up by the next day's workshop. The central character was an old man, hiding from the world and from what he feels about himself and others (particularly men), behind the wall of his back yard, where he builds fighting machines out of junk, and endlessly works through the routines of his wrestling exercises, while secretly dying of cancer.

The workshop opened with a presentation by Steve Tompkins, the architect responsible for the Royal Court's recent transformation, followed by a tour of the building guided by Steve. He described the challenge of creating a building that, while relevant to the present, takes into account the theatre's past, finding a balance between the forces of continuity and those of change. Steve explained how he and his colleagues had assimilated the theatre's physical and cultural context in a poetic way; searching for the intangible, subjective and intuitive. He described the building as marinaded in history, and as a coral reef formed from the accretions of hundreds of plays. The architects realised they needed to avoid strong contrasts between the old fabric and the new, because the real dialectic ought to be between the place and the work performed there.

The workshop moved on to talk about the previous night's play. The main character, Choke, has made a conscious decision not to embrace the present, but refuses to contemplate or accept his own past. He is stuck in a state of limbo, so obsessed with control and the old routines that he fails to live his life.

The next speaker was Richard Claughton, HR director at the Economist Intelligence Unit, which is going through a period of intense change, transforming itself from a print organisation to an electronic one. Richard said that the organisation may appear be changing beyond recognition, but at its heart it stays the same: the core of the company will always be its economists, and its values of quality, independence, integrity and people-orientation.

The workshop's final story was from Gerard Fairtlough, who twenty years earlier had founded the biotechnology company Celltech. Gerard emphasised that you should do everything you can to attract the very best people to an organisation, and that you should develop their talents to the full. When the time came to find a successor to his position of CEO at Celltech, he was determined not to make the classic mistake of the founder who can't let go. So he was delighted to have at his side an apparently ideal replacement – his current deputy. This chap, called Peter for the purposes of the story, was a brilliant salesman, with whom Gerard got on excellently. Peter was very keen to take over from Gerard. However, the non-executive chairman, a man with whom Gerard had never had a particularly close relationship, was non-committal about the idea. The board decided that Peter wouldn't get the job and that they would recruit externally, and Peter resigned. Gerard was asked to stay on as a non-executive director but, in the light of what had happened, he refused. His retirement date grew near and no replacement had been found. Things looked bleak for Celltech. Then, suddenly, a senior person from the pharmaceutical industry expressed interest. The board had little choice but to agree to his appointment, but in fact the new CEO did a fantastic job.

Gerard told the group that he now knows, a decade later, that it was a mistake to get involved in the succession. He recognises that in trying to choose his successor he was hanging on to his creation. He concealed from himself that he didn't want to let go of his baby. The human truths of the theatre might be more useful in such situations than management textbooks. The longest discussion of the day explored the effects of change upon organisations, with particular reference to arrival and departure. After hearing Gerard's story, no one could think of an example of an entirely painless transition. Is this because there is always an emotional investment in change?

The day ended with an exploration of ritual as a way of easing change. In many academic institutions people make a ritual of going for a chat at the bar after a formal seminar. This marks the transition from the official story to a range of unofficial ones. At the end of a workshop on succession, it was natural to think about the role of ritual in helping people deal with loss and departure and in facilitating the inclusion of newcomers into a group. Farewell parties are one ritual that helps with departure, by celebrating closure alongside new beginnings. Perhaps we should try to make sure that clever story-tellers are always on hand for a farewell party — for transmitting shared knowledge to newcomers.

The Royal Court Theatre was a superb place in which to tell tales. Images from *Hard Fruit* were easily called up throughout the day of the workshop. The building itself was redolent of both continuity and change, being both an historic site for the British theatre and a place of radical experimentation. The modernisation of the building respected its past but did not turn any part of it into a museum — old and new blended seamlessly. The workshop itself alternated between a series of narratives and discussions of their implications for the participants' current work and lives. The images, spaces and rhythms of the day nourished each other. Participants gained a strong sense of the contribution that spaces and occasions make to innovation.

Human values also contribute to innovation, but less so when they are expressed too solemnly. A funny story told at another LIFT Forum workshop illustrates this.

A software designer was so obsessed with his work that he ate and slept at his workplace. One day a frog hopped onto his desk and said: 'If you kiss me, I'll turn into the most beautiful woman you've ever met. I'll make love to you and be your girlfriend.' 'Shut up,' replied the nerd, 'I'm busy.'

The frog waited patiently for a couple of hours and then asked: 'Don't you want a gorgeous girlfriend?' The nerd said nothing. But he did pick up the frog and put her in his pocket. 'Why did you do that?' she asked. 'I've no time for a girlfriend,' said the nerd, 'but a talking frog is kinda cool.'

Boundary Spanning

Most innovations need external resources for their development. Heroic stories are told about artists in garrets or computer-makers in garages who have no help with their innovations. Sometimes these stories are true; but more often the innovator has to obtain resources from others. The artist wants a gallery to represent her and sell her work. The author needs an agent and then a publisher. The instrument designer seeks a venture capitalist or a bank to finance his production of prototypes. Gallery owners, agents and venture capitalists are busy people, who are bombarded with requests for help or money. Even when they are willing to respond, they seldom read more than a couple of pages of a script or a business plan, and seldom give more than half an hour for an initial interview. Successful innovation thus often depends on getting attention, which often means successfully spanning a boundary into an organisation of some kind.

Boundary spanning is therefore a necessary skill for innovators and innovative organisations. It is different from selling a product or service, where the product or service is usually well defined and where selling depends on convincing customers that the product or service will solve their problems or make life easier for them. The innovator, on the other hand, will initially make life harder for the agent or venture capitalist. Yes, there should be a reward in the long run, but there will be no instant gratification. Selling the idea therefore needs a very good story. The innovation may be complex, but the story will have to be simple, in order to gain the attention of busy listeners. However, in making the story simple its truth must not be corrupted. This is not an easy task. Once more, skill in telling the tale is an essential part of the process of innovation.

Part of the skill is in understanding the listener to, or reader of, the tale. 'Know and respect your audience' is lesson number one. And if your audience is in an organisation, you should understand that organisation's way of doing things, its values, its myths, its culture. A young entrepreneur in the high-technology field will often know little about the culture of venture capital firms or banks. She may have been taught to despise the people working for financial services organisations, probably thinking of them as 'suits'. Yet this entrepreneur has to frame a story, in the shape of a business plan or a slide presentation, about the wonderful investment opportunity her idea provides, and do so in a way that will attract at least one source of finance.

A social entrepreneur, with a great idea for improving the lot of inner-city kids, will usually be looking for support from a foundation or other charitable organisation. He may not have much understanding of the history, objectives and ethos of the body he is approaching. If the business entrepreneur or the social entrepreneur is to successfully span the boundary into the bank or the foundation, he will have a lot of learning to do. Listening to stories, rather than telling them, should therefore be the first step: get the venture capitalist or the foundation executive to talk about the founder of that institution, about its successes, about its occasional failures, and about its present heroes. That will make the institution come alive and should inspire the entrepreneur in telling his own tale.

Humour can be a great ally in boundary spanning. Ted Cohen, a philosopher who loves jokes, has written a wonderful book about them. Few of the jokes are new, but they are so well told and so sympathetically analysed that you long to find all your old favourites as you turn the pages. One old favourite, the story of the Girder and the Joist, can be found in Box 7.4. This story, along with many other jokes, depends on the demolition of a stereotype. Boundary spanning likewise benefits from the recognition of the stereotypical assumptions that suppound the boundary, which are then questioned and partly demolished.

Building an Organisation

Lucy Neal and Rose Fenton believe that LIFT's continuing innovation is greatly helped by its particular rhythm. LIFT festivals are only held every other year. During festival years, a team of over eighty artists, volunteers and freelance staff gather to do all the critical tasks that make the festival function. Then, when the festival is over, they disappear and LIFT undergoes a rapid metamorphosis. Things slow

> **BOX 7.4   The Girder and the Joist**
>
> An out of work Irishman went walking around London until he
> found a building site that was hiring workers. When he applied for
> the job, it was his bad luck that the site foreman was an Englishman
> who held the stereotypical view that the Irish were ignorant.
> 'Paddy, do you know anything about building?' asked the foreman.
> 'Sure,' said the Irishman 'Test me.'
> 'Then, tell me the difference between a girder and a joist.'
> 'That's easy,' said the Irishman. 'The first lived in Wiemar and
> wrote *Faust,* and the second lived in Dublin and wrote *Ulysses.*'
>
> Adapted from Cohen (1999). Cohen points out that this is an
> English joke as well as an Irish one.

down; a period of exhaustion and reflection sets in. This is sabbatical
time, when Lucy and Rose can choose to take some time out, travelling, reading, seeing more of their families. But activity soon resumes
and innovation hots up. In the LIFT office the cycle begins again.
'We've never knowingly done the same thing twice,' says Lucy.
Instead, the festival is a collection of performances that 'flower and
collapse; flower and collapse' every other year. Is that an innovative
process other organisations could copy?

LIFT's relationship between it, London and the rest of the world is
complex, involving many different kinds of partnership. There is a
risk, as the biennial searches for artists, ideas, venues and finance criss-
cross each other, that LIFT will spin out of control. But LIFT has
learned to manage this risk with a few simple, practical skills.

Naming the values was the first step, taken during a two-day meeting in 1994 – LIFT's first strategy review. Like many organisations
founded and run by charismatic individuals, much of LIFT's purpose
was carried in its two founders' minds. Naming the values made these
explicit, handing them over to others and enabling them to make
their own decisions. Because things get 'very complex, very quickly'
these values function like a 'hymn sheet' allowing people in LIFT to
test whether a proposal is consistent with what the organisation is
trying to do. The values become 'a well anyone can use'. The values
are also communicated by story-telling. Newcomers to LIFT hear

stories about the triumphs and disasters of earlier festivals that demon-strate these values in action. Remember that LIFT recreates a large part of itself every two years, and you will recognise why these stories have to be told.

Even with clear values, a structure is needed. At LIFT it is simple. Employment is very formal, with clear contracts and regular apprais-als. But individuals generally work in a way that suits them, arranging autonomously what they need to do with others. A very few routine meetings are, however, sacrosanct. These are on Tuesdays, when LIFT reviews its progress in a predictable agenda of subjects. No outside meetings are allowed that day.

Rituals are important at LIFT. Within the open-plan office on one floor of a loft in Clerkenwell, there is a Friday five o'clock bell. One new person was working when the Friday bell rang, and she said she was too busy to stop and attend this meeting. 'Too busy,' she was told, was not acceptable – everyone who is in the office at five o'clock on Friday stops when the bell rings. Sometimes there is nothing to discuss – it's just a party. Sometimes it is simply the opportunity to wish someone in the organisation a happy birthday. Sometimes more diffi-cult issues are raised and handled. Sometimes there is a story or two about the arts world. In short, Friday at five is an open time when things that need to come out are raised.

Many stories live inside the LIFT organisation. In fact, LIFT's management style is not articulated by formal values, instead, people tell stories. Here is one of them.

The story begins when LIFT arranged for Christophe Berthonneau to work with three or four London artists and a group of school-children in their early teens. Christophe is a pyro-technician – his theatrical medium is fire. This project was called 'The Factory of Dreams'. Together, over the course of six months, Christophe, the London artists, the schoolchildren and their teachers developed the show, which was performed in a South London park during the summer of 1996. The show was a gamble. The mixture of fireworks, school arts projects and international performers blended uneasily with the usual school routines, upsetting old habits and revealing new possibilities. But the show was also a great success. Schoolchildren who were at an age to mistrust themselves and the world at large became proud par-ticipants, their large back-lit sculptures providing the setting for Christophe's fireworks in Brockwell Park, and delighting thousands of people. Educationally it was a success, encouraging students and teachers to communicate across disciplines, thus extending their potentials.

A year after 'The Factory of Dreams', the opening event of LIFT's 1997 festival was an even better display of Christophe's fireworks. And two and a half years later still, on Millennium Eve, Christophe was responsible for the fireworks from the Eiffel Tower in Paris. He provided the centrepiece for all France's celebrations. LIFT, he says, had been his place of experiment. It gave him opportunities no one else had ever given him, helping him build up to his midnight success in Paris. Lucy Neal tells the story of Christophe's progress from humble beginnings to the grandeur of a national spectacle. Christophe had been asked, 'How do you rehearse a fireworks show?' Clearly it would be impossible to test something on the Eiffel Tower or the River Thames before the performance itself. 'Each performance,' answered Christophe, 'is a rehearsal for the next show.'

Expanding the Vision

LIFT Education

The first word in LIFT's name is London. London is a city of extremes. In some parts it is very rich – a world financial centre, a city of historic and beautiful buildings, great art galleries and museums, thriving theatre – but in other parts, it is poor and harrassed, with high levels of unemployment, illiteracy and ill-health. In 1991, LIFT began experimenting with ways in which the festival might involve young people from parts of the city that had little arts provision. Tony Fegan joined LIFT's tiny band of permanent employees as head of education.

The purpose of the education programme is to link LIFT performers with young people in London schools and out-of-school, youth arts groups. 'Tony's work,' say Rose and Lucy, 'has become completely crucial. The prism of Tony's work is now in everything.' LIFT began to put education at the centre of their thinking. As the experiment of putting young people together with international artists bore fruit, the role of LIFT began to change. 'When we began, the festival was a celebration, one in which "The World Comes to London". Now the festival is a resource, developing long-term relationships between London and the rest of the world.'

One such project is of cultural exchange between young people in South Africa and London, also linking arts educators working in both countries. Project Phakama (pronounced pakkarma and meaning 'lift up' or 'rise up' in Zulu) has, for five years, been exploring the power of performance to tell young people's own stories via the development of their creative and performance skills.

Project Phakama was initiated by LIFT with Sibikwa Community Theatre, Johannesburg in 1995. LIFT had had a long association with South Africa through presenting theatre productions in the festival. Following the end of apartheid, LIFT was interested in collaborating with an emerging generation of artists and in helping to initiate a venture which could help build creative skills among young people in both South Africa and London. From the outset, there was an assumption that the venture would help young people develop a voice and creative responsibility in their communities, and importantly, also help some of these young people forge a route to economic survival in an era when routes to long-term employment can be hard to find, both in Johannesburg and inner city London.

The format of Phakama residencies is now well established. Individual groups research and create pieces of theatre and performance in their own regions. Representatives of these groups are then selected by their peers to participate in an international residency with tutors and young people coming from many different regions. Over a nine-day period a new piece of work is created out of the regional pieces. The finished piece emerges from individual stories which then become everyone's and can be communicated to the public. The performance often takes place outside a conventional theatre and is created for a specific location in the fabric of the city. In this way, art and life are merged and a link forged between the act of creation and daily life. This helps all those involved to maintain a creative approach to other aspects of their lives, rather than keeping their imaginations in the box called 'art'.

Phakama is a place to explore urgent issues. One of the residencies focused on the theme of womens' lives. Members of the regional groups, aged mainly between 11 and 25, made performances based on the life stories of their mothers, aunts, grandmothers and sisters. The resulting performances, many of which were performed by young men, raised questions of great urgency touching on issues of violence and traditional gender roles. Too often, young people need to tackle these questions and their own direct experience before they are able to begin a connection with more conventional education. They are rarely invited to address such issues elsewhere, let alone address them in a creative way that enables them to develop confident, shared responses. The arts educators involved were convinced that the most remarkable educational results emerged from young people in out-of-school activities focused on the stories of young people themselves. As the formal curriculum has gathered momentum in both countries, there has been an increasing emphasis on literacy and numeracy skills, with an ensuing erosion of the possibilities of group learning and shared critique which the arts educators observed emerging so vividly in these other settings. Part of their draw for young people is that these settings offer a different ambience from the status quo; and yet it is often here that the big questions of society are being examined, where efforts are made at turning people's lives around. Box 7.5 discusses another arts organisation.

BOX 7.5   The Arts and Young People

LIFT isn't the only arts organisation reaching out to young people in deprived communities. Shirley Brice Heath is Professor of English, Education, Linguistics and Anthropology at Stanford University in California, USA. She and Laura Smythe wrote about the profound educational benefit of young people's involvement in out-of-school arts activities.

The most effective of these non-school opportunities [for instance, in sport and the arts] come through sustained involvement in an entity for which one feels some responsibility . . . In these organisations **roles, rules and risks** in thousands of interwoven patterns link structural organisation with the minutiae of everyday interactions. Effective community organisations operate from an ethos that leaves no doubt that youth members constitute essential resources for setting and achieving group and individual goals.

The structure of such community organisations ensures that young people play meaningful **roles** that matter to the life of the group. Experience and reliable performance over time determine how far and how fast individuals move into and through roles, but the real possibility of working one's way up as well as laterally in the organisation has to be present.

Rules spring from group philosophy, and they change as situations create occasions to rethink older organisational practices. Broad 'rules' come out as assertions: 'everyone's got work to do here' or 'we've got good things going'. The upbeat can-do spirit of community organisations that rely on young people rests not on a simple idea of having fun, but on complex interactions of demonstrating, explaining, modeling, critiquing, and extending.

It is in the need for extending and reaching that **risks** come. Essential for attracting and retaining young people, risks put them 'on stage', 'out there', 'in front', 'on the edge' – terms heard often to describe adrenaline-producing thrills of pursuits that can bring harm. Community organisations generate risks in safe places where adult support and guidance place young people at the centre of ample opportunities to try, fail, regroup and reach again . . . Risk taking by the group and not by individuals thus offers the attractive challenge. (Heath and Smythe 1999, p. 8)

LIFT's Business/Arts Forum

The LIFT Business/Arts Forum started a few years after the educational work, was designed to connect LIFT to the world of organisations. Julia Rowntree had for many years been raising money for LIFT from London's business community. However, she had become increasingly dissatisfied with her role as a supplicant holding out the arts begging-bowl to the lords of the corporate world. She had begun to think about a different relationship, based on mutual learning, between business people and people from LIFT. Her thinking attracted a variety of business advisors, including Charles Handy, Arie de Geus and two of the authors of this book, Gerard Fairtlough and Barbara Heinzen, whom she'd met when they were speaking at a meeting of the London chapter of the Global Business Network. The result was LIFT's Business/Arts Forum, held in parallel with the festival. The first Forum, sponsored by *The Financial Times*, was held in 1995.

The third Forum, held in 1999, began with a day-long meeting in May at *The Financial Times* offices. The founders of LIFT, Lucy Neal and Rose Fenton, introduced the performances on offer. Arie de Geus talked about organisational learning and the role of the theatre. Barbara Heinzen introduced LIFT as an organisation that had much to teach other organisations about the 'art of invention'. Forum participants came from all over – banking, the media, Britain's National Health Service and arts administration. Each attended at least four LIFT performances, and then joined in a day-long session for a structured exploration of what they had learned from the festival and how they would apply the lessons back in their own organisations.

At the end of the third Forum, participants' feedback was analysed. Most had learned a lot from the festival and from the Forum meetings. Why did this mode of learning work so well? These were some of the reasons:

- The arts create a fairly safe way of removing boundaries to powerful new experiences. The most disturbing play is only a play. If it all gets too much, participants can walk out or close their eyes. Further-more, LIFT has learned how to create a trusting environment within the Forum, which allows people to discuss what they have experienced without a lot of fear.

  It is this combination of trust and safety that allows people to let go of their preconceptions and inhibitions – to lose their fear of challenging convention, or to let go a working pattern they're unhappy with. It allows people to go on a journey together. It allows openness and acceptance of vulnerability that is sometimes the first stage of learning. It allows the music to play itself.

  Removing boundaries in a way that people find safe allows all kinds of learning to take place; learning from the performances, from other participants and from the places we visit. We can learn from people different from ourselves, and from ways of doing things that are strange to us. We can connect our feelings with our work. We can embrace error.
- The theatre can teach us how to structure a presentation or tell a story. The arts have to entice people into theatres to see shows, and they can only do that if their presentations are striking and their tales are gripping. People from the world of organisations can learn a lot about presentation and story-telling from professionals in the arts, providing they open their minds a little.
- Team building. Creative people like actors and artists can, with the rest of humanity, have big egos, but they learn how to contain them in the interest of the performance and the idea behind the show. This is mostly self-discipline, in contrast to the usual way within organisations, where discipline is imposed. The organisation of LIFT itself is a wonderful example of team building; very few organisations can match this capability.

Renewing the Vision

In 2000 LIFT was twenty years old. Over those years its youthful vitality had given lots of people pleasure and made London's theatre more adventurous. But was its job now done? Should LIFT settle down and join the establishment? Should it pack its bags and go off to seduce some other city? Or should it use its creative powers to reinvent itself? These were the questions Rose Fenton and Lucy Neal started to ask themselves as the anniversary approached.

'Mirroring' is a research methodology similar to 'grounded theory'. Like research based on grounded theory, it is based on data gathering through interviews and observations, all of which are carefully recorded. Any statement made or conclusion drawn must be traceable back to interview or observation data. Each statement must be backed by at least two relevant pieces of data. This is how results can be 'grounded' in spoken and behavioural evidence.

Arie de Geus assembled a team of three facilitators – himself, Barbara Heinzen and Gerard Fairtlough – to conduct a series of interviews with people connected in one way or another with LIFT. Their stories would provide a 'mirror' in which LIFT could see itself. Arie's past experience was that a careful look in a non-distorting mirror made an organisation see its current state and its future possibilities far more clearly. It might be a shock, but it was usually worth it. The facilitating team met senior LIFT staff and a couple of board members to tell them the story of what they'd seen in the mirror. Out of all this came a radically new vision. The two-year cycle will give way to a five-year plan. Many shows will be presented over these five years and will culminate in an extra-large event in 2005. Alongside the continuing festival will be LIFT's vital educational work, plus a new theme: an investigation into the long-term future of the art of the theatre and its role in society. It promises to be an exciting five years.

Conclusion

Innovators need to gather support by spanning the boundaries of other organisations. They need their own organisations to turn ideas into reality; and their organisations often have to be built alongside the innovation. A successful original vision can often be expanded into other fields. The time will probably come when the vision has to be renewed. Innovation depends on connections, particularly across scientific disciplines, between different cultures, across generations, and between varied ways of seeing the world. Box 7.6 contains tips for innovators to improve their story-telling.

BOX 7.6   Tips for Innovators

1. Creative writing teachers tell you: 'I can't teach creative writing. You learn it by doing it. All I can do is to encourage you to write, write, write.' So dream your dreams. And constantly practice making stories from them, stories you tell and stories you write. Remember – a vision *is* a story.

2. Birds that flock are birds that learn. You need people to listen to your narratives; then you will find out which bits of the story work and which don't. Listening, in turn, to others' stories may then add the missing piece that makes an interesting tale a compelling one.

3. Watch how others tell their tales. When you read the newspaper or a novel, when you see a play or a film, if you join a convivial set of story-tellers, see how it is done. The real masters are so good it is sometimes hard to see how they do it. So learn from people whose story-telling powers are just a little better than yours.

4. Pay attention to metaphors and similes, to symbols and slogans. See how others use them.

5. Find good places to tell stories: a building whose whole history is innovation; somewhere novel and exciting; a comfortable space where listeners and speakers can easily see and hear one another. Also, the right music, pictures and lighting often help.

6. Use open questions to provoke people into telling imaginative stories. The mirroring technique described above is a good example.

As inter-connectedness grows, so does complexity. This is why a small, constantly innovative organisation like LIFT, with connections all over the world and to many areas of London, must be just as capable of handling complexity as a large organisation. In our history of LIFT we have given several examples of handling complexity through story-telling. Here is a reminder of a few of them:

- Arie de Geus presents his key insight about flocking and learning in the form of an engaging and memorable story – Blue Tits and Red Robins.
- The stories of Swanson and Boyer and of Watson and Crick are about innovation in biology. They illustrate the parallels between scientific and artistic creation.
- The history of LIFT tells of an organisation that partly recreates itself every two years, through rapid bursts of self-organisation and story-telling. The stories are emergent and designed, individual and collective. We have told a few of them in this chapter.

The next chapter presents the last of our seven histories. It deals with a complex situation – that of a whole country.

8

Kenya – Scenarios for a Country's Future

It is easier to live with alternative versions of a story than with alternative premises in a 'scientific' account . . . We know from our own experience in telling consequential stories about ourselves that there is an ineluctably 'human' side to making sense. And we are prepared to accept another version as 'only human'.

Jerome Bruner

This is a chapter about a country, Kenya, and about a particular way of using stories: scenario planning.

The word 'scenario' is used not only for film scripts but also for stories that organisations use to think about the future. Because the future is unknown, scenarios should come in sets, usually sets of two to four. Each scenario tells a different story about the future context within which the organisation will have to live – the political, social, economic, technological and environmental context. Typically each scenario tells a story of what could happen over the next ten years. Later in this chapter we will discuss how scenarios are constructed and why they are so useful, but first we tell a story about one particular use of scenarios – the Mont Fleur scenario exercise, undertaken in South Africa during 1991/92.

The Mont Fleur Scenarios

The Mont Fleur exercise, so named because its main meetings were held at the Mont Fleur conference centre outside Cape Town, was one of the first uses of the scenario technique in a political setting. It took place during the critical time between February 1990, when Nelson Mandela was released from prison, and South Africa's first all-race elections, held in April 1994. During this period dozens of all-race forums were held to discuss education, housing, economic policy, the country's future constitution and other matters. Mont Fleur was the only one that used the scenario technique, and it brought together for three workshops, each lasting three days, twenty-two prominent South Africans – politicians, activists, academics and business people – with widely differing views.

The twenty-two people – let's call them the scenario team – considered many different stories about the coming ten years in South Africa, including stories of revolution, economic growth, right-wing revolts and free-market utopias. They finally agreed on four scenarios, which all members of the team thought were plausible and relevant. As is always the case when the scenario technique is used, there are no blueprints for action, just coherent, well thought-out stories of possible outcomes. Debating these allows people to discuss the future, with the benefit of the comprehensive thinking and shared language thrashed out during the workshops. The scenarios were named after different kinds of birds (in one case, after a person pretending to be a bird) and were published in a South African newspaper, *The Weekly Mail and The Guardian Weekly*, in July 1992.

The first scenario was called Ostrich. It is the story of a white minority government that sticks its head in the sand. It makes enough concessions to black liberation movements to avoid international sanctions, but not enough to prevent an escalating cycle of violence and repression and a poor climate for economic development. Eventually the parties are forced to negotiate, but under worse economic and social conditions than before. As a single story, the scenario team would probably have rejected Ostrich, but as one of a set of stories it was plausible enough to be accepted.

The second scenario, Lame Duck, tells the story of slow and uncertain progress to majority rule. Both the government and the liberation movements are sincere in trying to build confidence and to agree on a fair form of government, but both are afraid to take risks, and a weak and indecisive coalition results, leading to faltering economic growth. The consequence of this long and uncertain transition is, ironically, a loss of confidence in the future.

The third scenario, Icarus, foresees the election of a fully democratic government. With the noblest of motives, the government tries to achieve too much, too quickly. It initiates massive investment, and heavily subsidises food and housing. Initially there is spectacular economic growth, and real social progress, but after a year or two the budget deficit grows rapidly, inflation increases and there is a serious currency crisis. The government has to appeal to the International Monetary Fund (IMF), which imposes severe economic cutbacks. The noble intentions are left in ruins. In devising this scenario, the team noted the experience of several countries in Latin America. There, rapid expansion followed by a massive reversal has led to authoritarian regimes. An outcome like this was part of the Icarus scenario.

The final scenario is called the Flight of the Flamingoes. Flamingoes characteristically take off slowly, fly high and fly together. A decisive political settlement, followed by good government, generates a steady and sustainable economic and social progress. Well-targeted social investments give people confidence that social needs will eventually be met, even though they are slow in coming at first. Health and schooling have top priority. Local and international business confidence in the South African economy steadily increases. Although the Flight of the Flamingoes is an optimistic story, the team recognised that it had to include some setbacks. Flamingoes don't always have a smooth flight.

A few years after the Mont Fleur exercise, one of the participants, Adam Kahane, looked back on the results from the project (Kahane 1996). First, it was clear that the scenarios had sent some definitive messages to South Africans. The message of Ostrich was that a non-negotiated outcome would not be sustainable. After hearing about the team's work, the National Party leader, F.W. de Klerk was quoted as saying 'I am not an Ostrich.' Likewise, the message of Lame Duck was that a weak coalition could achieve little. Icarus warned of the dangers of a Latin American-style, populist economic policy. And the Flight of the Flamingoes showed that a positive outcome, while not certain, was not impossible.

Another result was the creation of informal networks among those who had participated in the workshops, which continued for years afterwards. However, Kahane suggests that the most important result was an intangible change in the way the participants thought about the issues facing the country. The diverse group of participants was able to tell the stories to many different audiences, and the stories became well known in political circles. Kahane says that the vivid, concise names for the scenarios helped to spread their ideas widely. We would add that the general characteristics of stories – they are memorable and economical, they encourage creativity, they help in handling emotion and they stimulate wider thinking – must also have played an important part in their wide dissemination.

To be of any value, scenarios must be plausible. Kahane says that this generally means they have to be logical. In a political context, the scenario process thus encourages logical thinking, and discourages people from taking a fixed position or closing their minds to other views. Since scenarios are 'only' stories, people can discuss almost anything, even previously taboo subjects. People become accustomed to multiple perspectives, and are then more ready to listen to unfamiliar and unpalatable viewpoints. Finally, Kahane says, the process is constructive, turning people's thoughts towards building a common future rather than agonising about the past.

In this case the quality of the scenario team was critical; and the team represented all but one of the important interest groups in South Africa. Kahane's conclusion is, 'The Mont Fleur exercise demonstrated the informal, indirect scenario approach to be an innovative and productive method for a society in conflict to approach the future. This approach is different from and complementary to negotiation. As this project demonstrates, it is a promising tool for future attempts to reach public consensus.' Box 8.1 explains the scenario planning approach that was used in the Mont Fleur exercise, while Box 8.2 discusses mental models, and how these can be changed by scenario planning.

BOX 8.1   How Scenario Planning was Born

In France, to be called an intellectual is not an insult. There, logical thought is admired, especially if it is connected to first principles and is followed by articulate exposition. To be named as a Cartesian, a follower of that supremely clear thinker René

Descartes, is real praise. Pierre Wack was a Cartesian. He was also a mystic. He studied garden design in Japan, which there depends on intense observation of details. He practised meditation, once a year visiting a teacher in India. In 1971 Wack went to work in Shell's central office in London in the Group Planning division. His task was to equip Shell to cope better with an uncertain future. He had a supportive boss, who knew that a French mystic and intellectual would need protection in the Shell Group, said to be run by Dutch engineers and Scottish accountants. Working with his colleagues, Wack developed close contacts with think-tanks in the USA, like the Hudson Institute in New York State. Herman Kahn, head of the Hudson Institute, was famous for being willing to 'think the unthinkable'. He was Stanley Kubrick's model for the character of Dr Strangelove. Kahn used the term 'scenario' to describe a picture of a possible future. Scenarios were not predictions, but were credible possibilities.

Wack called elements of the future 'predetermined' when they related to events that had already occurred but whose conse-quences had not yet unfolded. He gave the example of heavy monsoon rains falling in the upper part of the Ganges river basin. Once that rain has fallen, you then know that a week later there will be floods downriver at Benares. The floods are predetermined. But not everything is. Wack believed that critical uncertainties were as important as the predetermined elements. Critical uncer-tainties called for imagination and out-of-the-box thinking. Perhaps only a personality like Pierre Wack's, both Cartesian and mystical, could have foreseen the need to combine analysis with imagination.

Wack's second big insight concerned the psychology of decision-making. It proved to be the way to bridge the gap between under-standing and action. Wack (1985) later wrote:

> Every manager has a mental model of the world in which he or she acts based on experience and knowledge. When a manager must make a decision, he or she thinks of behavior alternatives within this mental model. When a decision is good, others will say the manager has good judgment. In fact, what has really happened is that his or her mental map matches the fundamentals of the real world. (p. 84)

Wack realised that strongly-held mental models had to change if people were to see the world differently – but how could this be done? The answer was: through story-telling. As we keep saying, stories are memorable and connect with the emotions. Wack's scenarios were stories. They proved to be memorable and in many cases were effective in altering the mental models of a wide range of people.

Earlier, Wack and his team had tried to tell stories that sounded good (and later might look good when compared with what actually happened). Now they tried to tell stories that made managers question their own models of reality. Uncertainty was something which managers in Shell were already able to live with. In exploring for oil it is uncertain what you will find when you start to drill, and in research it is uncertain which of innumerable possible combinations of chemicals will give you a good catalyst. But in oil exploration or catalyst research people have mental models that allow them to cope. Wack wanted Shell's managers to construct new mental models to help them cope with the political, economic and social uncertainties affecting their work. (For more on mental models, see Box 8.2.)

By 1973 Wack and his colleagues were changing mental models across the whole of the Shell group. Scenarios were making friends and influencing people. In Wack's words:

> We hit planning pay dirt with the 1973 scenarios because they met the deepest concerns of managers. If any managers were not fully convinced, the events of October [the oil shock] soon made them believers. Only when the oil embargo began could we appreciate the power of scenarios – power that becomes apparent when the world overturns, power that has immense and immediate value in a large, decentralized organization. When the world changes, managers need to share some common view of the new world. Otherwise, decentralized strategic decisions will result in management anarchy. Scenarios express and communicate this common view, a shared understanding of the new realities, to all parts of the organization. Decentralized management in worldwide operating companies can adapt and use that view for strategic decisions appropriate to its varied circumstances. Its initiative is not limited by instructions from the center but facilitated and freed by a broad framework; all will speak the same language in adapting their operations to a new business environment. (p. 89)

BOX 8.2   Mental Models

In order to make sense of the world and to survive in it, we all have to know about the functioning of things. For instance, to drive a car safely in a city we need to know what it means when the traffic lights turn from red to amber to green. Actually, we need to know more than the formal sequence of lights we learn in driving school. We also need to know about the behaviour of drivers in that particular city. Do drivers regard traffic lights as purely 'advisory'? What do drivers do when a set of lights appears to be malfunctioning? Do drivers behave differently when a police officer is nearby? Indeed, we need to know what counts as a road and what as an area for pedestrians, and much else besides.

From our training and our experience, we build for ourselves, or partly borrow from others, a picture of how traffic lights operate and how drivers behave around them. Such pictures become unconscious, internalised parts of our knowledge. When necessary – if we are telling a newcomer how to drive safely in this city – we can make explicit parts of this tacit knowledge. It is this under-standing, or picture, or map, or story of how things work in the world that we call a mental model.

In the 1960s and the early 1970s, most managers in the oil industry in Europe shared a broadly similar mental model of what determined the price of crude oil. Most people's models probably stemmed from the model of supply and demand in economics textbooks. But it was powerfully reinforced by the way prices actually behaved throughout the decades following World War II. Managers knew that when there was an unexpectedly cold winter, prices went up, and when a large, new source of crude oil came on-stream in the Middle East prices fell. All over the industry, people's mental models of crude oil price determination were most likely limited to this.

Shell's early scenario work introduced an alternative mental model – of an oil-producing state that preferred to leave its oil under the ground if it didn't like the price that the old supply-and-demand model produced. For the alternative model to be credible, several oil-rich states would have to believe that in the long term oil prices would increase. These states would need enough cash resources to sit out a period in which they might have little or no revenue from oil sales. They would also have to believe they could withstand the political pressure from oil-importing countries that a suspension of oil supplies would undoubtedly provoke. And the oil states would have to be willing to trust each other in applying a joint policy of suspending oil supplies.

None of these assumptions was certain in the early 1970s. However, Wack and his colleagues were able to construct a scenario that involved a number of oil-producing countries working together to cut off supplies until the price had risen several-fold. They did not claim that this scenario would come to pass – just that it was sufficiently likely to be worth taking seriously. They wanted Shell's managers to absorb this new mental model, not to replace their old model (which might well go on being useful) but to be there as part of managers' thinking.

Some people don't like the term 'mental model', because they feel it implies an unwarranted view about the workings of the human brain. They prefer terms like 'conceptual system', 'habitual way of thinking', 'picture of the world' or 'theory in use'. So we should make it clear that our use of 'mental model', a usage taken over from the originators of scenario thinking, does not imply anything more than these other terms do. What we are saying is that mental models help us make sense of the world and talk about it with others.

The culture of an organisation is made up of its practices, mental models, values, symbols and so on. As an organisation embraces the practice of scenario-building, its members develop their understanding of the practice. They find good ways of involving people in the process of building scenarios, of encouraging strategic conversation in the organisation and of using scenarios to influence its decision-making. They also learn more and more about the relationship between the organisation and the outside world. After several years of serious and widespead use of scenarios, the culture of an organisation can change profoundly; so the use of scenarios as an ongoing practice has very different effects from a once-off exercise.

When we turn from an organisation to a nation – from Shell to South Africa, for instance – the effects of a practice of scenario-building are less easy to describe. The political culture of a nation takes a long time to change. The particular mental models, conversations or decisions that the practice could modify are less easy to identify. Nevertheless, we believe the two examples from Africa that we discuss in this chapter indicate that scenarios can influence mental models on a national scale.

The Benefits of Scenarios

The Mont Fleur exercise used scenarios to think about the future of a nation. However, the organisation, not the nation, was the theatre in which scenario thinking was first developed and today most of the use of this story-telling approach remains within organisations. In this section we will look at the various ways organisations benefit by following the discipline of scenario thinking, and particularly how the discipline encourages strategic debate.

Once Pierre Wack had distinguished between the predetermined aspects of the future and the uncertain aspects, and had realised that both are vitally important, story-telling became essential. This is because story-telling is the best way to weave together analysis of the predetermined with imagination about the uncertain. Stories are the way to make the link between planning and dreaming. They also provide other links. In a large organisation which is serious about its future, there will be masses of future-orientated work going on in many different departments. Planners here will be trying to connect with dreamers there. Shorter-term preoccupations have to be connected with longer-term goals. The scenario discipline provides the ideal language for making these connections, and produces these benefits:

- The organisation has to tell coherent stories about possible futures. Because stories are memorable and economical, the result is the spread of a shared vocabulary across the organisation. When de Klerk said 'I am not an Ostrich,' he was using part of a new vocabulary which had spread not just within an organisation but within the South African nation.
- People's stocks of mental models are expanded, leading to better thinking about the future.
- There is a better interpretation of information about the world. With a variety of stories about the future in their minds, organisa-

tion members are able to spot the relevance of a tangential piece of news, which otherwise might pass unnoticed. Events can be seen as part of a series of possible patterns. Early signals can be more easily picked up, signals that suggest a particular vision of the future is worth careful attention. One way of describing this benefit is to say that scenarios give people 'a memory of the future'.

- Decision-making becomes more robust — meaning that decisions turn out well in a wide variety of different conditions. They provide a 'wind tunnel' in which decisions can be tested.

We have used the Shell group as an example of good decisions. But it can also provide examples of bad ones. The disposal of the Brent Spar offshore oil storage tank is a bad one. Shell's scenario planning didn't work this time, as it failed to anticipate a possible public reaction to the decision to dump the tank in deep water in the Atlantic. Shell had carefully considered several alternative methods of disposal, had consulted several experts, and after much discussion had got the approval of the UK government. But the decision was not a robust one, as it had ignored the protests of Greenpeace and other environmental pressure groups.

Shell would undoubtedly have made a different decision about Brent Spar had its 'wind tunnel' included the ways that public opinion about the environment might unfold. This would have avoided a huge public relations disaster. This is so regardless of whether or not there would have been significant ecological damage resulting from deep-sea dumping. Shell thought they had done everything possible to assess this risk, and that it was a negligable one. Another factor raised at the time was whether Greenpeace used false information in their campaign against Shell. But, false or not, the information was believed by the public.

- Scenarios and other forms of story-telling spread vision and values and nourish a vigorous debate on strategy in autonomy-rich organisations, creating the right context for decision-making. The context is partly made by the example of senior peoples' behaviour, and partly by a shared vision of the organisation's purpose — why it exists — and by the set of values that ought to guide everything that it does. But to a great extent the context for decentralised decisions is set by the mental models shared by the organisation's members.

The best process of scenario generation is one that leads to these new models being widely shared.

Scenarios are, of course, stories in themselves. But story-telling has a part to play throughout the scenario process. Stories help to create good scenarios. To show how this can happen, we devote the rest of this chapter to an actual scenario project – scenarios for the future of Kenya.

Kenya

Kenya is a country whose population has quadrupled over the past forty years. Most people still work on the land, tending herds and growing crops, but many of the traditional ways of working cannot support the larger population while still maintaining the environment's resilience. The four-fold increase in the number of mouths to feed has thus put an end to the old simplicity of pastoral and village-based production. It is not possible to colonise new lands, as two-thirds of the country's land is arid or semi-arid. Without water, there are also limits to expansion of intensive agriculture. All of this has put a strain on the political organisation, which grew out of earlier, simpler times. The double strain on the economic system and the political system means that Kenya is today facing an unprecedented set of challenges. The country manages to feed itself most years, but if the population increases further, food imports will become a regular necessity.

Kenya's borders were drawn as a result of nineteenth-century colonial rivalries. English and Kiswahili are the common languages. Nairobi, the capital, is a sophisticated city, but Kenya has forty-five different peoples, each with their own language and with differing traditions of government, and different practices for farming, industry and commerce. Patron–client government is the style of government that grew out of the simpler economies of the past, and this is the kind that comes most naturally to many Kenyans. There is a big man, the patron, who dispenses favours to the rest, who are the clients. To his family and others close to him he gives special favours. To distant clients, the favours are more general, but are constructed so as to emphasise the big man's role in providing them. The patron's aim is that everyone should feel indebted to him. Kenya is formally a parliamentary democracy but this does not inhibit the patron–client system, which extends from villages through districts and provinces to the country as a whole, with patrons at every level. The system pervades politics, the civil service and parts of business. Corruption is universal and merges seamlessly with friendship and mutual obligation.

Here is a story about the origins of Africa's political conflicts.

'My theory,' said the Westerner, 'is that when a colonial power is in place, people are not allowed to take responsibility for themselves and lose the habit of it because they can always blame the colonisers for trouble. When the colonial power leaves, they have no habit of responsibility but also no one to blame, so they begin to blame their neighbours instead whenever anything goes wrong.'

'No, no,' said the African. 'That is not the way it happened at all. It is like this: in an African village decisions were always taken by a consultation of the elders who discussed the matter and decided what to do. They then handed the decision to the chief who could not be questioned after that. In this way, the chief had authority, but no power because the decision was actually made by the elders. In your system, your chiefs have a great deal of power, but they can always be questioned, by Parliament, by Congress, by the press. President Clinton had to face the threat of impeachment. But what we have in Africa today is the unfortunate offspring of both systems: a chief with great power who can never be questioned.'

In the last decade Kenya has had to face three further challenges. The first comes from globalisation and the growth of information technology. There are good opportunities for developing countries to participate in world trade, but they can only do this successfully if they have sufficient proficiency in information technology and the management skills to provide the ever-increasing levels of service demanded by international businesses. If a country like Kenya lacks such skills, there are other low-wage countries in Asia, Latin America and elsewhere in Africa that have them. Tourism, high-value agricultural exports, and export-orientated industrial production will only generate income for Kenya if its people have skills of these kinds.

The second challenge is the environment. When Kenya had a sparse population and its agriculture and industries were fairly simple, environmental issues were relatively unimportant. Now, with four

times the population of 1960, many more city-dwellers, plus height-
ened awareness of the risks of ecological degradation, new industrial
and agricultural developments will have to take account of the environment and foreign aid will come with ecological strings attached. In the
old days, it was possible to move away from an ecological problem, to
find somewhere else to operate. But now there is nowhere to move to
and industries must find sustainable solutions. Unfortunately the
Western industrial model is not helpful, as it is just as unsustainable.

The last, and most serious, challenge is AIDS. It is a human tragedy
and also an economic one. The disease has an incubation period of ten
to fifteen years, so AIDS tends to kill people in their early 30s, hitting
the most productive section of the population, and wasting their
education and training. At least a quarter of young adults in Kenya are
at serious risk. Furthermore, a lot of resource goes into treating the sick
and looking after the orphans of AIDS. This would be a big burden in
any country; in Kenya it is a catastrophic one. With all these problems
it is not surprising that many Kenyans, and concerned outsiders, are
pessimistic about the future of the country.

In 1998, a Non-Governmental Organisation (NGO) decided to do
something to help Kenya, perhaps confounding the pessimists. It was
the Society for International Development (SID), which is based in
Rome. SID has 3000 individual members, and 55 institutional members. It aims to support innovative development work in order to
combat poverty and injustice at local, national and global levels. It
wants to develop a community of committed individuals, to connect
theory with practice, and to connect experts with the general public,
usually by helping local initiatives. Its director of organisation
development is Arthur Muliro.

Arthur Muliro had the idea of using the scenario technique as a
way of introducing new thinking into the Kenyan situation. From
working in South Africa, he knew the Mont Fleur scenarios and their
influence on South Africa's transition from the apartheid regime, and
had met Adam Kahane. Arthur needed a local partner in Kenya, and
approached the Institute of Economic Affairs (IEA). Based in Nairobi,
this is a small think-tank, and its director is Betty Maina. The IEA was
formed in 1994 and has since carved itself a niche in Kenya as a
credible non-partisan policy forum. The task of the IEA is to stimulate
and inform public debate on issues of importance to Kenya, bringing
civil society into areas previously seen to be the province of govern-

ment. The Institute has built up a reputation as a source of reliable infomation. Betty agreed to work with SID and agreed that the scenario approach might be helpful in Kenya. Arthur found Barbara Heinzen's e-mail address on a paper of hers that Kahane had given him. This paper, 'Political Experiments of the 1990s', was published by the Global Business Network, and described several instances of the use of the scenario technique in national settings. Barbara has worked in several African countries, has been involved in scenario planning for many years, and is an experienced facilitator of scenario workshops.

Arthur arranged for Barbara, Betty and himself to meet in London to design the process for a Kenya scenario project. Betty and Arthur then raised the money needed for the project from a combination of US, UK and Scandinavian sources. It was therefore SID's network that made possible the contacts between Betty, Arthur and Barbara.

The project took place over a two-year period during 1998, 1999 and 2000, with five workshops and many other meetings in various locations. Twenty senior Kenyan figures agreed to act as trustees, over-seeing the project. A core team of about twenty-five shared the research and scenario-building work. In all, about eighty Kenyans of all ages and affiliations were involved. This was an elite group, composed mainly of Nairobi-based intellectuals. But most of the group had roots in the villages, connecting them to much of Kenya's ethnic diversity. By and large, it was a confident group, whose members could find work in other countries if things got really bad in Kenya; but no one wanted this to happen. The group was strongly committed to finding a good future for their country.

It was probably the first scenario exercise that looked at Kenya as a whole and brought in diverse groups and representatives of different stakeholders. The aim was to build a new spirit – one that challenged conventional ideas, made dialogue an essential part of national life, enabled Kenyans to discuss the undiscussable, and altered the 'paralysis of passivity' that seemed to be a major feature of Kenyan life.

Story-Telling and Scenarios

The process for creating a set of scenarios is now highly developed and involves more than story-telling, but story-telling is a crucial part, not only in writing the scenarios themselves but also for the preparatory stages of the scenario process. This is not the place to discuss the process as a whole – rather, we will concentrate on areas where our experience has shown that stories make a valuable contribution. Box 8.3 summarises these areas, and the following sections of this chapter will explore each of these in more detail.

BOX 8.3   Stories for Scenarios

- Gather the stories stakeholders tell among themselves.
- Create stories to tell others about your research.
- Detoxify the mind by telling stories.
- Construct scenarios, making each scenario a lively story.
- Make the whole set of scenarios more than the sum of its parts.

Mount Kenya Safari Club

The first workshop in the project was held on the equator, on the slopes of Mount Kenya, in the comfortable surroundings of the Mount Kenya Safari Club. The climate was cool and the food was good, and the formal dress code of the club, which at first surprised some of the participants, proved to be a minor problem. Not a place typical of Kenyan life, but right for hard work.

The first workshop session began at 8.30 am with a welcome from Betty Maina and Arthur Muliro. Barbara Heinzen, as facilitator, then asked everyone to reveal his or her 'pet passion' – an issue about which he or she had some special knowledge and strong feelings. This proved to be a quick way of discovering the diverse interests and resources participants had brought to the meeting. The next step was to agree the rules of engagement for the whole meeting – things such as all ideas are welcome and everyone should respect whatever the group produces.

The main purpose of this workshop was to specify the research needed for the project. To do so, the aims of the project itself had to be debated, which was not straightforward. This was the point at which the African tradition of story-telling made its first appearance. Someone described a dance that used to be watched by all the villagers before men went out to hunt. The dance was a mock hunt, not done

by the hunters themselves but by mock hunters, whose dance symbolised the vital role hunting played in sustaining the village. The real
hunters then set off, while the mock hunters and the rest of the
villagers awaited their return. The point of the story was that the
politicians of Kenya mostly behaved like 'mock dancers', but unlike
the dancers in the villages, they did not support a real hunt. Instead,
they made a lot of noise, and no one brought back food to the village.
All the villagers could do was to look on. This story produced a
concept which proved to be important for the whole project: the
'paralysis of passivity' among Kenyans who simply wait for constructive change to be instigated by politicians. But the politicians are only
mock dancers, who pursue their own objectives, regardless of the
country's needs. Mock dancing means that politicians can't deliver,
and the paralysis of passivity means that no one challenges this situation. It was agreed that the project would be immensely worthwhile if
it could help Kenyans discuss the undiscussable and thereby reduce
the paralysis of their passivity.

As a first step, everyone was asked to imagine what a Kenyan might
face twenty years from now. Barbara asked people to put themselves in
the shoes of Kenyans of different ages and positions in society. What
might be important in twenty years' time to a baby born today? What
might people from groups not represented at the workshop have as a
twenty-year perspective? Doing this produced a range of questions
about the future, which were recorded on charts and reviewed in a
plenary session.

In another exercise, Barbara asked participants to write down on a
card something about Kenya they had noticed, but could not explain.
This had to be something they knew was important because it gave
them a shiver up the spine or some other physical reaction, which she
called the 'felt sense', a term she had learnt from Eugene Gendlin (see
pp. 229–230). After reading out these cards, one of the participants,
Oby Obyerodhyambo, suggested that they divide the cards into two
clusters and give them to two workshop groups. Each group was then
asked to write a story that illustrated all the cards in their cluster. The
stories were then shared. Both stories are clearly examples of emergent,
collective story creation. The first was about the sinking of the
passenger ship *Titanic*, and the second about a character called Mr
Mengich, a senior executive with a multi-national firm in Kenya. We
tell one of these – *Titanic* – in Box 8.4.

BOX 8.4   Titanic – A Story Illustrating the Unexplained

Once upon a time a powerful land produced a powerful ship. Its passengers were divided into three classes: first, second and third. Its captain demanded – and got – total obedience from his crew. It had an orchestra that entertained the first- and second-class passengers throughout the voyage. Among the first-class passengers were a prominent businessman, Zaccheus, plus the architect of the ship, who had not revealed to his fellow passengers that the *Titanic* had poor navigational aids and a weak hull.

As the ship continued on its journey it entered the cold northern regions and there it hit an iceberg and began to sink. There were only enough lifeboats for women and children from the first and second classes. The whole of the third class were locked in their crowded quarters by Afande, the head of security. To save himself, Zaccheus gave the captain a huge bribe. The captain accepted the bribe, but later returned the money, realising it was useless on a sinking ship. The lifeboats pulled away from the ship, which sank beneath the waves, drowning the captain, Zaccheus, Afande, the orchestra and all the third class. The orchestra played on until the ship sank.

After each group had told its story, the opposite group had to identify a number of questions raised by the story, which the story-tellers were asked to answer. *Titanic* was obviously a metaphor for Kenya. The weak hull represented Kenya's institutions, the orchestra represented the 'mock dancers' of the political world, and the three classes of passengers represented the economic classes of the country.

Questions raised by the story included:

- Why was the *Titanic* thought to be unsinkable?
- Why did the orchestra keep on playing until the end?
- Why did the captain accept a bribe?
- Why were the passengers divided into three classes?
- Why did the third class largely accept their fate?

After each question was answered, further questions were asked. For example, to 'Why did the captain take the bribe?' the answer was:

'That was normal.' This provoked another question: 'Why was it normal?', to which the answer was: 'He thought he'd never be punished.'

Everyone found the story-telling exciting and felt it had given them lots of insights. But the use of 'why' questions moved the workshop back to an analytical mode, which didn't work well for most people. Perhaps it would have been better to stick to story-telling and have faith that a good research agenda would emerge after overnight contemplation.

At any rate, the following day was very hard work, as the workshop tried to convert the insights generated by analytical and metaphorical approaches into the research agenda. The agenda was important, because experience in scenario-building shows that good research leads to good scenarios. The task was made easier by agreeing on an overall question that the Kenya Scenarios Project would have to answer. The question was: How will Kenya's social, political, economic and cultural systems evolve over the next twenty years?

The Research Workshop

Six months later the research had generated a series of fairly conventional research reports, amounting in total to about 400 pages. The topics covered included:

- the education, health and skills of the Kenyan people;
- international influences, such as the growth of IT and the possibility of conflicts in East Africa that would affect Kenya;
- Kenya's natural resource base;
- Kenya's politics and public institutions.

It was time for another workshop, one at which the research would be discussed between the people who had done all this work. This was held in April 1999 at the Aberdare Country Club, Nyeri, which is on the drier, lower slopes of the highlands, overlooking the plains. As a first step, participants agreed to present their work to each other. One research team told the story of its research to a partner team, and then listened to the other team's story. This paired peer presentation (PPP) was between teams chosen for their differing intellectual backgrounds. The partner teams acted as test clients for each other.

After three hours of PPP, the paired teams reported jointly to the whole workshop. They were asked to say which area they had disagreed on the most, or the most emotional discussion they had had, and also to report on areas which they both felt were important but could not precisely say why. The object was to tap into the 'felt sense' among participants, so as to capture perceptions that were hard to formulate clearly but could nevertheless be vital for the project.

Aidan Eyakuze was a member of the economics team which was paired with the cultural team which included Oby Obyerodhyambo. Oby, as a theatre director, was passionately committed to uncovering the hidden strengths of African culture. Aidan argued for the role of global forces. Their discussion was one of the most passionate, yet it produced some of the best stories and insights of the session.

The workshop then discussed the process they'd used. Did PPP work? Some objected that it meant that no one could hear about all the research that had been done; but most people felt that the depth of their learning more than compensated for its lack of breadth. Furthermore, by emphasising mutual learning, PPP had influenced the dynamics of the project as a whole. It had made process important as well as content. For those whose background was academic, this was a shock. A well-constructed research report was a proper conclusion for months of work. The process of a meeting, even a good one, seemed much less satisfying. Story-telling was the exception – that was emotionally fulfilling.

Trying to understand this difficulty, someone drew on a flip-chart. An upward-sloping blue line represented analytical thinking, which aimed to produce solutions. It would generate a work plan, 'our' answer to the problems, a statement of where Kenya should go. This language was likely to gain a hearing from powerful people and a high profile for the project. A horizontal green line on the chart represented a process of shared learning, from which new ideas would be created – new solutions, new insights. As 'green line' thinkers, the workshop participants would run the risk that their work would look uncontrolled or unfinished. In short, the group was facing a dilemma: was the process or the solution more important? While most believed there were few clear solutions and the process was critical, they kept

the desire for solutions in mind and thereby learned to float between
the horns of this dilemma.

Detoxifying the Mind

The work on the following day aimed to free people from their usual
assumptions about the future of Kenya. Difference in viewpoint, like
that between Aidan and Oby, highlighted to participants how hard it
was to let go of their firmly entrenched ideas. So, when the workshop
facilitators organised people into three groups and asked them to play
the 'detoxification game', people realised why this was necessary. The
detox game involved each group imagining a different future for
Kenya. One goal was to force people to think about the future of
Kenya along lines that differed both from the thinking behind the
research and from the viewpoint each participant brought to the
workshop. That was the process of 'detoxifying' the mind – admitting
that one's mental models might have to change. The other goal of the
game was to give everyone a taste of scenario writing, of transforming
analytical research into compelling stories.

The first of the three groups was asked to consider how the country
might evolve into a society based upon international trade and information technology. This picture of globalisation was not a forecast of
where Kenya was heading, nor was it a particularly desirable future;
rather, it was a possible picture derived from two principles – international trade and information technology. The second group was
asked to use different principles as their starting point – ecological
awareness and biodiversity. The third group used the principles of
Afro-centric institutions and of self-reliance – life without Western
political models and without aid from Western donors.

It is always tough to put your preconceptions on one side and work
from different principles, and this was indeed how people experienced
the detox game. There was also the problem that the principles they
were asked to adopt were unfamiliar to many participants. Perhaps the
Afro-centric group had the hardest task, since no one knew of any previous attempt to adopt such principles in thinking about the future.
The Ecology group also had to move into an area that was unfamiliar to
many. The principles the Globalisation group was using were better

known, but were hard to reconcile with Kenya's present reality. These are the stories the groups invented:

The story told by the Globalisation group starts with a decade of decline as Kenya's existing institutions fail to adapt to a world of international trade and extensive use of information technology. A variety of new initiatives starts to emerge. These are as yet too small to have much impact but do act as a nursery for social and economic entrepreneurs. After 2010, when the formal state and large commercial organisations are largely discredited, home-grown entrepreneurial organisations, both social and economic, begin to grow in number and diversity. By the year 2020, these new institutions take Kenya into the world system as a respected equal player.

The Ecology group's story also started with a decade of decline, leading to violent conflict, ethnic polarisation within the country and the collapse of formal systems. The outcome is a new institutional structure, with a national land-use programme and an emphasis on finding local solutions to local needs.

In contrast, the Afro-centric story starts with the steady and spontaneous growth of local solutions to problems like the spread of AIDS. By building on African traditions, social norms evolve that lead to safer sexual practices, better care for AIDS orphans and less damaging use of natural resources. Regional trade grows at the expense of trade with the rest of the world. Gradually a new paradigm of social and economic organisation is defined by the people of Kenya.

The stories told by the three groups in the detox game did not meet all the criteria for good scenario stories: they were not always internally consistent, nor were they particularly plausible and their internal dynamics weren't very credible. But the stories seemed to be relevant to the future of Kenya. And the stories were certainly challenging – conventional thinking had been overthrown, at least while the stories were being told.

Furthermore, the workshop as a whole, and the detox game in particular, had enabled participants, many for the first time, to learn about the new style of thinking needed for scenario work. The familiar old blue line style of research involves researchers in carrying out studies which they pass on to decision-makers in government or commerce. The decision-makers seek agreement for their decisions, which are passed on for implementation to a third set of people. Thus the old style separates those who think, those who agree and decide, and those who do. The new green line research style associated with scenario thinking gives each person three responsibilities: to think, to agree and to do. Everyone should go through a series of cycles: act, learn and re-perceive – act, learn and re-perceive – and so on.

Further Workshops – Lake Baringo, Mombasa and Amboseli

Three months after the workshop at the Aberdare Country Club came a series of workshops at monthly intervals. It is not necessary to say much about the three end-stage workshops, because the important stories to come out of them are the scenarios themselves, described in a later section. But below are some highlights from these workshops.

At Lake Baringo a key task was to identify clearly the most critical questions about the future of Kenya. Several story-telling sessions were held. The best story-telling came from asking people for their earliest political memory as children. Many stories involved disappearances or assassinations of political leaders. They threw an uncomfortable light on the accepted picture of Kenya as a generally peaceful country.

Eventually agreement crystallised around two interacting uncertainties:

1. When and how will economic recovery come?
2. When and how will Kenya determine how it shall be governed, and what shall be the basis for political legitimacy?

At the Lake Baringo workshop, Barbara Heinzen told a story about a walk she had taken with a group of scenario planners in California. After a couple of hours the group had to decide how to get back to their cars. They studied their map and chose a path down into a valley which they thought would lead to the car park. An hour later they found they were in a different valley from the one they were aiming for. How had they gone wrong? Their mistake came from the early part of the walk when they were not paying much attention to their route. When they decided to take the valley path, they thought they were standing at one point on the map, but were actually somewhere else entirely. Barbara's story showed workshop members that to describe possible futures it was essential to have a clear view of the present. This led to a determined effort to paint the clearest possible 'picture of now'. The remainder of the time at Lake Baringo was devoted to this task.

On the first day of the Mombasa workshop, participants were asked to recall traditional Kenyan fables which might have some connection to the scenarios they were starting to construct. Three fables were told, involving ogres, hyenas and other creatures, but they did not immediately seem to make good analogies with Kenya's situation today or how it might unfold. So this use of story-telling did not produce the hoped-for results. Perhaps with more time there might have been a better outcome, but people were impatient to get on with scenario-building. The lesson may be not to use story-telling when there is a clear task ahead: it works better when a group gets stuck and doesn't know what to do next.

Mombasa was where everyone had to face up to the demanding job of actually constructing scenarios. It was the longest of the workshops and all of five days was needed to work out a set of plausible, credible and compelling tales about possible futures. In spite of careful preparation and a lot of energy within the team, by the end of the second day Barbara Heinzen, as facilitator and as the person with the most experience of scenario work, was dismayed to find that the whole team was trapped by images of 'good' and 'bad' futures – based on the hopes and fears of this group of individuals. It was easy to imagine futures that were better or worse, but hard to imagine those that were radically different. Barbara feared that some of the creative forces at work within Kenya were being overlooked and that the potential for novel ideas might be lost. This struggle between the emergence of new ideas and people's deep, personal worries made this workshop very difficult – intellectually, emotionally and socially.

In the end a choice was made. Perhaps a choice was forced by the stalemate – it may have been the only choice everyone could accept. The workshop went back to the two major uncertainties identified at Lake Baringo. The combination of these led to four possible scenarios. Once these were identified and named, the work of fleshing them out became a lot easier and by the end of the Mombasa event, four good scenarios were in place. The early bad tempers may have been caused by the sound of crashing dreams.

The Amboseli workshop had a simpler job to do. It was about the mode of presentation of the scenarios and about attracting good audiences for them. However, one participant reflected, 'This workshop is a microcosm of Kenyan society. The trouble we've had with the scenario process reflects the difficulties others will have in accepting our results.'

The most entertaining exercise at Amboseli came from a role-playing game in which the four scenarios were acted out to various imagined audiences.

The Scenarios

The team described (Maina and Muliro 2000) four possible roads down which the country could go:

- If both economic and political reform are thwarted, tension will heighten and by 2020 Kenya will fracture into ethnic districts, each with separate systems of government. This is the *El Niño* scenario. If Kenya takes this road, ethnic animosity erupts, corruption continues and unemployment grows. The security forces rebel, plunging the country into civil war. The elite flee the country, while the majority of Kenyans retreat into their ethnic groups, headed by dictatorial tribal chiefs. Eventually, people grow so weary of conflict that some kind of peace emerges, with some hope of reconstruction.

- If the country concentrates on economic reform, there will be initial gains, but the inequality and instability this generates will lead to major difficulties at the end of the scenario period. This scenario is called *Maendelo,* a Kiswahili word meaning 'progress'. The government invests in infrastructure, especially railways, and privatises many government enterprises. Spending on health and education is increased. Great efforts are made to shift the economy to knowledge-based service industries, high-value agriculture and tourism. However, there is no reform of political institutions. Economic growth makes the rich richer, but the poor are little better off. So towards the end of the twenty-year scenario period, demand for change re-emerges. If politics is reformed, a path to a better Kenya could be possible.

- A transformation of politics leading to democratic and locally accountable institutions would be possible without economic reform. This scenario is labelled *Katiba*, which means 'constitution'. At the start of this scenario, unemployment is high and discontent increases. Violence spreads and everyone fears the disintegration of the country. At the brink, the country demands the resignation of the government, new elections and a new constitution. To the surprise of many, the government concedes all this. Kenya's ethnic diversity is recognised as a key asset, which leads to the creation of a House of Tribes, ensuring that no region of Kenya is economically or politically dominant over the others. However, economic progress is slow. Towards the year 2020, growing confidence in political institutions leads to a slow economic revival, but Kenya is still a poor country.

- If all actors engage in political and economic transformation, Kenya can achieve inclusive democracy and economic growth. This is the scenario of *Flying Geese*. In this scenario, politics becomes much more open, with town hall meetings, radio debates involving senior politicians, and trips to all parts of the country by new leaders. Economic reform is given equal priority, but the transition to high-value agricultural production and knowledge-based industry is fraught with problems. There are not enough skilled people and AIDS kills many of these. The unskilled feel that reform will bring only trouble for them. But a continued effort to keep government open, honest and keen to listen pays off, making the majority of people willing to give reform a chance. Foreign donors increase aid to Kenya and foreign investors move in. Kenyans living abroad return to the country, bringing skills and some capital. After twenty years, Kenya has a vibrant democracy and a steadily growing economy.

Influence of the Scenario Project

In the year and a half after the scenarios were completed, Betty Maina and her colleagues at the Institute of Economic Affairs have made vigorous efforts to tell these stories to a wide range of people in Kenya. At the last count, presentations had been given in 128 towns. Ten thousand copies of the booklet *Kenya at the Crossroads* have already been distributed, and it is now being reprinted. The Kenya Council of

Churches is arranging for the booklet to be translated into Kikuyu. The Army Chief of Staff has asked the National Defence College to incorporate the scenarios into its curriculum. The civil service is taking notice, through its College of Public Policy. An Institute for Leadership is being discussed.

Media comment has brought the stories to the attention of many more members of society. A garage owner recently rang Betty Maina and insisted on having a presentation of the four scenarios for his staff. There are already signs that the 'paralysis of passivity' has started to change. A similar project is being organised for the neighbouring country of Tanzania. The project is definitely making its mark.

Conclusion

We hope that in this chapter we have demonstrated that the role of story-telling in scenario projects goes beyond the writing of the scenarios themselves. Story-telling brings out stakeholders' hopes and fears and provides the best link between the factual analysis of research and the imaginative exploration of possible futures.

The most difficult phase of a scenario project is usually the middle one. For real thinking outside the box a blizzard of information and emotion is indispensible, but handling it constructively is a struggle. There are various well-tested practices for helping a scenario team through this tricky middle phase. The first is the use of people who bring unusual insights to the process – those termed by Pierre Wack as 'remarkable people'. For Wack, the archetypal remarkable person was a Zen master, but he knew that poets and musicians are equally good sources of insight, as are those who are very close to nature and those who can weave intellectual patterns of clarity and novelty.

Another valuable practice for the middle phase of a scenario project is the learning journey. Members of the scenario team go to visit places that seem likely to be relevant to the futures the team is trying to imagine. The very sight of the ultra-clean environment of a factory making silicon chips, or of the rundown houses left over from a failed experiment in social planning, or of a watercourse dried up through over-extraction, can make a big impact. A good learning journey draws on factual research but its biggest influence may be on the imagination.

The third practice is story-telling. Stories can come from stake-holders, researchers and perhaps even from interested bystanders. At critical moments, the job of process facilitators is to encourage the telling of tales.

The Kenya project was a temporary organisation that proved able to commission a good deal of research, arrange five large workshops and publish a lot of material. The core team of Betty Maina, Arthur Muliro and Barbara Heinzen stuck closely together throughout the project. The difficulties encountered during the project were partly due to the fact that the scenarios were for a whole country, and were partly those faced by any serious scenario exercise. Working in Africa had the advantage that story-telling is a more integral part of life than it is in the West. In any organisation, unless it has a long history of scenario work, the multiple roles of the participants and the need for repeated iterations have to be learned on the job. It is hard to integrate process and content, to combine 'blue line' and 'green line' thinking. The Kenya project was no exception, but the team got there in the end.

9

Thinking about Stories

In Act I, Scene ii of The Tempest, *Prospero tells his daughter Miranda why they left Milan. After his tale, he asks his daughter if she has understood the reasons.*

Prospero: Doest thou hear?
Miranda: Your tale, sir, would cure deafness.

Shakespeare, The Tempest

This chapter relates story-telling to a number of areas in the social sciences. It is therefore more explicitly theoretical than the other chapters in this book. The chapter has four main sections: story characteristics, learning through stories, stories and organisations, and finally stories and society. We explore these topics through accounts of thinkers whose work we have found particularly relevant, rather than making a general survey of an area.

Story Characteristics

Spoken and Written Stories – Ong

According to Walter Ong, author of *Orality and Literacy*, our ability to write is only 6000 years old (p. 6), but it has transformed the way literate people think. Stories are a bridge between the world of literacy and the world of orality – the world where nothing is written down and there is nothing to read. Much of the success of stories therefore derives from their roots in orality rather than literacy. In his Chapter 3, 'Some psychodynamics of orality', Ong explores the nature of culture, communications and thought among people who have never learned to read or write. His discussion helps us to understand why stories are important in today's world. He identifies two important character-istics of cultures based on sound, rather than writing. First, sound vanishes. It only exists at the moment it is created and needs a voice or instrument powered by the action of a body to create the sound. Second, knowledge which is not repeated aloud soon vanishes (p. 41). One can only know what one can recall. These two qualities are linked to many of the special characteristics Walter Ong associates with oral societies, which can be described here under two headings: memory and participation.

Because knowledge only exists as an act of memory (there is no library outside of people's recall), oral societies use language, speech and stories to aid recall. These share a number of characteristics. There is, for example, a lot of redundancy where the same information is repeated in many different ways. Because sound vanishes, one cannot go back to check what has been heard. Instead, the checking takes place in the repetition of the idea or fact.

Repetition is not the only aide-memoire. Memory is also helped by the use of rhyme, rhythm, alliteration and metaphor. These tricks of image and sound are further backed up by the use of clichés, formulas and well-known clusters of words which make it easier to remember what has been said. For that reason, an oak will be a sturdy oak. The literate person might ask, 'Why is the oak sturdy?', but to the oral person the sturdiness of the oak is an important and memorable part of the story. Similarly, characters in stories are not the subtle, rounded and finely nuanced personalities one finds in great novels. Instead, the characters that appear in oral societies are often larger than life: more heroic, more bizarre and more beautiful than anyone ever found in the everyday world. To the modern ear, these characters can seem to be little more than stereotypes. Ong, however, calls them 'heavy' figures because their deeds are monumental, memorable and public. As he rightly points out, the fact the cyclops is a one-eyed monster is much more memorable than any ordinary monster with two eyes. Finally, he adds another quality to oral societies. In an oral world, the body is always engaged in producing speech. The Orthodox Jew, he notes, will rock backwards and forwards while saying his prayers. This is sound as action and action as the production of sound, with the action – in this case – reinforcing the memory of the sounds.

The need to remember the knowledge held in vanishing sounds is one important force in oral societies. However, oral societies are also societies of participation, because knowledge only exists when it is recalled, and it is only recalled when it is useful or shared. One result of this is that there is very little objective distance or categorical abstraction in the knowledge base of oral societies; rather, all knowledge is related to people and situations.

One of the best illustrations of this situational quality comes from research done in the early 1930s in Uzbekistan and Kyrgyzstan when they were part of the former Soviet Union. In this research, subjects were presented with drawings of four objects, three of which belonged to one category, while the fourth belonged to another – in this case a hammer, saw, log, and hatchet. While a literate person would immediately conclude that the odd one out was the log because it is not a tool, one of the illiterate peasants who was shown the drawings said simply, 'They're all alike. The saw will saw the log and the hatchet will chop it into small pieces. If one of these has to go, I'd throw out the hatchet. It doesn't do as good a job as a saw.' Told that the hammer, saw and hatchet are all tools, he discounts the categorical class and persists in situational thinking, 'Yes, but even if we have tools, we still need wood – otherwise we can't build anything' (p. 51; Luria 1976).

Because the oral world is always close to people and situations, the stories that are used to trap knowledge are often expressed in polemical or combative terms: struggles with other men, with the elements or with monsters. This quality, which Walter Ong calls 'agonistic', is not just based on the need to make knowledge memorable. It also reflects that fact that speech and orality exist when there is both a teller and a listener who are close enough to each other to hear and respond to what is being said. This situation can be unifying, but might also be one of antagonism and argument, flaring up in the close-knit groups which form around the spoken word. Another quality of orality, however, is that because stories exist in a constant state of dialogue, they are constantly being adapted to their listeners and the situation in which they are told. For that reason, stories evolve over time, shifting and adapting to the new needs and understandings of their listeners.

In short, oral cultures prize and develop memory. They use tales to unify people and to struggle with them; they live vividly in immediate situations, working with concepts that are not grounded in logical abstractions but in the situations around them and the human inter- actions that are involved. These elements from our pre-literate lives are relevant today because they remain in our thought processes – particularly when emotions are involved.

Metaphor – Lakoff and Johnson

In their book *Metaphors We Live By*, George Lakoff and Mark Johnson (1980) argue that human thought processes are largely metaphorical. They claim that nearly everything we think and say has some kind of metaphorical structure. Some metaphors are so deeply embedded in our thought processes that we rarely notice they are metaphors. For instance, we say that car theft in the city is up, meaning it has increased. Everyone knows that more is 'up' and less is 'down'. There is a physical basis behind this pair of metaphors: for example, if you add more sand to a pile, the top of the pile goes up. Because our thought is so metaphorical, good metaphors seem real and true. They become a guide to actions: 'Such actions will of course fit the metaphor. This will, in turn, reinforce the power of the metaphor to make experiences coherent. In this sense metaphors become self-fufilling prophecies' (p. 156).

To create striking phrases, we usually have to use new metaphors. Those that have become part of conventional conceptual schemes and part of our language, such as 'up is more', no longer have the power to make us take notice of them. New metaphors 'can give new meaning to our pasts, to our daily activity, and to what we know and believe'. Lakoff and Johnson give, as an example of a new metaphor, one they created: 'Love is a collaborative work of art' (pp. 139–143). There are many things one can say about a collaborative work of art – 'it requires co-operation', 'it requires dedication', and 'it is unique in every instance' are only a few of them. If the metaphor is a good one, it will make sense to say the same things about love – 'love requires co-operation and dedication and is unique in every instance.'

Using a particular metaphor highlights certain factors while sup- pressing others. Imagining love as a work of art emphasises the active aspect of being in love. Of course, there are alternative metaphors. For instance, 'love is madness', a central metaphor of romanticism, is now everywhere in popular culture, as with 'I'm crazy about her'. Just as 'love is a collaborative work of art' stresses collaboration, hard work and creativity, so the madness metaphor stresses the lack of control you experience when you fall in love.

Metaphors guide action. If you believe that love is madness, there is nothing you can do but endure its agony and revel in its ecstasy. But if it is a collaborative work of art, then collaboration and imagination are called for. It is more prosaic, but more likely to endure. The chosen metaphor influences our actions, and our actions make the metaphor seem appropriate, in a feedback loop.

Peter Fryer was CEO of the Humberside Training and Enterprise Council (TEC). He believed that his organisation needed radical change. But he had seen in other places how harmful the imposition of rapid change could be. He had seen other CEOs place a Trojan horse in the organisation, from which armed men emerged to enforce the CEO's ideas. Peter wanted change, but less destructively, so he came up with the idea of Trojan mice. He planted small ideas for change in every part of the organisation. Many of these ideas never flourished, but some of them ran around and bred and crept into unexpected areas. In the end, the changes generated by his Trojan mice were much greater than those a Trojan horse could have achieved.

Eric S. Raymond's book *The Cathedral and the Bazaar* (1999) describes two different styles of software development. On one hand is the cathedral, the model used by a tightly-managed group of developers in big firms like Microsoft, who work towards a defined goal. Everything must fit together; if not, the whole edifice can come crashing down. On the other hand, there is the bazaar. The key example is Linux, developed with no planning by thousands of volunteer programmers collaborating over the Internet, each eager to show the others how smart he is. The double, contrasting metaphors of the cathedral and the bazaar are memorable, and they make sense of complex phenomena.

Bettelheim, Gardner and Harris

Bruno Bettelheim was born in Vienna in 1903 and became a well-known psychoanalyst. In particular, he is known for his work concerning the value of stories and story-telling in children's lives, and his work has provided a seminal strand of theory and practice in this area. In his book *The Uses of Enchantment* (1991; first published in 1976), Bettelheim criticises what he saw as the shallow and vacuous nature of much children's literature and forwards the view that the 'folk fairy-tale' has far more to offer. In Chapter 1 we quoted his view that 'these tales are the purveyors of deep insights . . .'. Bettelheim argues that the prettified versions of tales that are usually presented to children, perhaps through film and television, are doing them a disservice. He does not extend this censure to happy endings, which he believes teach children that by going out into the world and forming satisfying relationships they can safely separate from their parents.

In *Storytelling in Psychotherapy with Children* (1993) Richard Gardner puts forward a different view: that fantasy '. . . engenders unreal expectations about living which may contribute to life-long feelings of dissatisfaction and frustration' (p. 243). To counter this, Gardner adapted traditional tales. 'The Ugly Duck' doesn't become a swan, but finds a good way of living with what he is. 'Cinderelma' isn't rescued by a prince, but nonetheless overcomes her circumstances and lives happily until the end of her days (which do not last forever).

Gardner developed a psychotherapy approach he called mutual story-telling, which involved telling stories back to a child, based on a story the child had created earlier in the session. He found that this was engaging and interesting for the child, the more so because a pre-selected story will not be relevant to every listener. Gardner added drama to story-telling, bringing in images and movement. He also believed that having animals as characters reduced the threat presented to a child by a story about dangerous happenings. He speculated that because stories are so useful only those early societies which could tell good stories survived.

Paul Harris's *The Work of the Imagination* (2000) reports on empirical research carried out into child behaviour. The carefully designed studies show that even two- and three-year-olds know very well how to distinguish between the real and the imaginary. Their play is often about imaginary events, but this is not because children confuse their pretended companions with real animals or people. Harris believes that children are natural story-tellers. They, like adults, easily slip into the construction of narratives. Why might this be so? Harris suggests that language naturally takes on a narrative form, and that as children start to acquire language, they need to practise it constantly. What better way is there to do this than by telling stories?

Jung

Carl Jung and Sigmund Freud probably are the best-known figures in child psychology. Jung's ideas about archetypes and the collective unconscious have influenced everyday language and thought. The 'collective unconscious' represents a predisposition, shared by all humankind, to produce myths and visions (some of them religious) containing a series of 'archetypes'. Fordham (1991) notes Jung's view that we are not capable of fully comprehending the archetypes because it was not our thoughts that created them:

> Nevertheless it has been possible to isolate various figures, which recur in dreams and fantasy series, which appear to have a typical significance for human beings, and which can be correlated with historical parallels and myths from all over the world; these Jung, after much careful research work, has described as some of the principal archetypes affecting human thought and behaviour, and has named the *persona*, the *shadow*, the *anima* and *animus*, the *old wise man*, the *earth mother*, and the *self*. (p. 28)

Says Jung in his *Memories, Dreams, Reflections* (1995):

> I was never able to agree with Freud that the dream is a 'façade' behind which its meaning lies hidden – a meaning already known but maliciously, so to speak, withheld from consciousness. To me, dreams are a part of nature, which harbours no intention to deceive, but expresses something as best it can. (p. 185)

The archetypes and images that emerge in dreams (and through stories) are thus a creative source of self-knowledge.

Berne

Eric Berne developed transactional analysis (TA), which emphasised the 'ego states' of parent, adult and child. During a particular inter-action with another person, one or other of these states or roles is usually in play. He believed people lived their lives by following 'scripts' which defined their behaviour, and playing out 'games', which involved certain roles and pay-offs to the participants. In *What do You Say After You Say Hello?* (1975) Berne addresses a variety of common scripts including Cinderella, the Dragon Slayer and Little Miss Muffet. He also explains the means by which our scripts turn into full-blown dramas through a series of 'switches' summarised by Karpman's drama triangle (1968):

> Each hero in drama or in life (the protagonist) starts off in one of three main roles: Rescuer, Persecutor, or Victim, with the other principal player (the antagonist) in one of the other roles. When the crisis occurs, the two players move around the triangle, thus switching roles. (Berne, p. 186)

There are links here with Aristotle's view of a story being something in which the status quo is changed, producing emotional satisfaction. Berne continues:

> Fairy tales, treated as dramas, show exactly this feature. Little Red Riding Hood, for example, is a victim of the persecuting wolf until the hunter rescues her, when she suddenly becomes the persecutor, putting stones in the belly of the now victimized wolf: (p. 187)

Gestalt

Among the many viewpoints on psychology is an approach (and philosophy) known as Gestalt. Many people know of this through the saying, 'the whole is greater than the sum of the parts', to indicate that an entity can't really be fully described or explained by analysing the components because much more is created through the various inter-actions between the components. Gestalt concerns itself with addressing the way in which we perceive the world, including how we make sense of the information coming in through our senses to make 'wholes', or coherent stories, from generally incomplete information.

Among the tricks of the story-teller is the appreciation of our drive to 'make sense', to complete an incomplete picture, to achieve some sort of outcome, resolution or closure. With this in mind, a story can engage the attention through causing the listener or reader to specu-late on outcomes, to try to fit the pieces together, until a resolution is arrived at or provided by the story-teller. We can't help but make sense of things for ourselves.

Fritz Perls, the originator of Gestalt therapy, was influenced by psychodrama and by Zen, with its drive to aid enlightenment through 'attention, attention, attention' and circumventing over-reliance on our logic-analytical capacities. It is therefore not surprising to discover that a variety of 'experiments' aimed at assisting us to attend fully to our senses can be found among the Gestalt literature, examples of which have been included in Chapter 10 of this book.

Communicative Competence – Habermas

To co-operate effectively, groups of people have to reach agreement about their situation and about what they are going to do to improve it. But is an unreflective consensus enough? Jürgen Habermas (1994) argues that really effective agreement needs proper debate, with unconstrained and skilful communication or, in other words, with a high level of communicative competence. According to Habermas, a proper debate should be along the following lines. First, all those involved have to be ready to discuss matters of fact in a way which follows scientific practice. They have to use arguments based on practical investigation and tested theory. This does not mean bowing to the expert. In fact, no experts need be involved, just people who have taken the trouble to investigate the situation and to think about it carefully. As in science, if theory fails to match observation it must be rejected and if simpler theories, or theories which provide better predictions, come along they should replace the previous theories. This need not be a complicated process, since sometimes theorising and the testing of theories can be done in a few minutes. What counts is the willingness of the group to accept new evidence and to stringently test new theories.

Second, members of the group have to be ready to discuss matters of right and wrong by reference to universal norms: what is right for one person has in principle to be right for another, what is right on Monday has in principle to be right on Tuesday, what is sauce for the goose has to be sauce for the gander. As well as being tested for consistency, the norms themselves are open to challenge. Response to a challenge has to be similar to the response on factual matters: careful thought, a willingness to listen and a willingness to abandon norms that fail to convince.

Third, the feelings of individuals are to be taken into account, even if these are apparently no more than subjective preferences. The value of gut feelings is recognised. But the consistency and authenticity of feelings and the sincerity of their expression are open to question in much the same way as factual or ethical matters. Again, the test is the consensus of those who have taken the trouble to consider the consistency and coherence of individual expressions of feeling.

Communicative competence therefore means being open to criticism, being ready to seek shared definitions of the situation and actively seeking the agreement of everyone, not just hoping for passive assent. In modern societies, agreement is often sought only about matters of fact. But ethics and feelings have to be brought in as well. Obviously, it is hard to get agreement on all these things all the time, so the search for complete communicative competence is a search for an unattainable ideal. But the ideal is nevertheless a great guide for practice.

Stories in Organisations

The Three Imperatives – Kleiner

Art Kleiner (2001) writes about constructing oral histories of organisational change. He often encounters a clash of loyalties in his stories. Do they aim to report the facts accurately? To please their sponsors and audience? Or to tell a good story? This goes to the core of the story-telling process, both written and oral. Kleiner has found three imperatives to be equally important in a story-telling project. They are:

1. Rigorous study of observable activity (research imperative).
2. Compelling recounting of the organisation's heroism, trials, tribulations and destiny (mythic imperative).
3. Respect for the readiness of the organisation and its members to learn and develop (pragmatic imperative).

The research imperative embodies a commitment to search out and tell the truth. It relies on the methods of 'grounded theory' – a process rigorously based on interview transcripts and observation notes. Kleiner says about the mythic imperative:

> Our challenge, as artists, is to find the most powerful of those stories *as they rise out of the material*. We want, with all our intellect and intuition, to get to the heart of the matter. We look for tragedy and grief; for joy and aspiration. We look for soul. (original author's emphasis)

The pragmatic imperative makes us ask: How can the story be designed so that the people who are written about accept it – but not simply respond complacently? How can the history help an organisation grow in a beneficial way? How will it meet an audience's potential needs? Kleiner describes how he and his associates go about the task of telling a story while continuously keeping in mind all three imperatives. Repeated iteration is the key, and to achieve that you have to develop a plan for research and writing that constantly refers you to the three imperatives.

Gabriel

Yiannis Gabriel is the writer who has given us what is perhaps the most comprehensive account of story-telling in organisations. He writes mainly from the point of view of an organisational analyst, in contrast to the view in this book which is mainly that of participants. We drew on Gabriel's work for our typology of stories in Chapter 1. He is an energetic collector and analyst of stories. His book *Storytelling in Organizations* (2000) argues that stories are valuable as windows on the emotional, political and symbolic lives of organisations, to be used by academic researchers and by organisational participants as a means for understanding the culture and functioning of a particular organisation or of organisations in general. He emphasises the entertainment value of stories – they work because people enjoy them. They do all sorts of things – stimulate the imagination, offer reassurance, provide moral education, inform, advise and warn – but this does not happen unless people want to hear them. Folk tales have familar plots, but remain entertaining through variation in their telling. So story-telling is an art that '. . . re-enchants the disenchanted, introducing wit and invention, laughter and tears into the information iron cage' (p. 18).

Stories meet the psychological needs of organisation members. They do this by being heroic, tragic, comic or romantic, or as mixed forms such as tragi-comic. They are also linked to the socio-political structures of the organisation in which they are told. They can be, in Freudian terms, an outlet for the repressed or, in Marxian terms, a solace for the oppressed. They provide a means of management control, stimulating pride and loyalty through tales of the founding heroes. They can humanise power, in the manner of a court jester, who can laugh at powerful people without really challenging them. But in every organisation there is an 'unmanaged' terrain in which jokes, gossip, nicknames, cartoons and stories swirl around subversively. Unmanaged stories allow individuals to affirm themselves as independent agents and to cast others as villains, fools or tricksters, providing a type of communication that is often not available through officially approved practices. 'By highlighting the untypical, the critical and the extraordinary, stories give access to what lies behind the normal and mundane' (p. 240).

Boje, Snowden, Ward and Hollingsworth

David Boje's seminal article on 'The Storytelling Organization' (1991) suggests that the way a story is told is as important as the story itself. The tale can be more effective because it is terse, allowing listeners to fill in the gaps in order to make sense of it. Weaving a tale into an ongoing conversation is another device that binds the story to the listeners' lives. Deliberate mystification or ambiguity, so long as it isn't overdone and therefore annoying, can get listeners' minds working around the tale. Boje suggests that one might expect fuller texts to be told in newer organisations, where there is less shared experience. Terse texts work best when there is lots of shared experience.

Dave Snowden (2001) has worked extensively on organisation stories, particularly in the context of one large, well-known organisation. As European director of IBM's Institute for Knowledge Management (IKM) he successfully concentrated on the use of stories to communicate knowledge. Snowden sees much of an organisation's knowledge as incapable of meaningful codification in traditional text formats, and views stories as the best way to tap into this knowledge. An understanding of story-telling is a valuable management resource, which IBM can provide to its clients. He distinguishes between an anecdote (something arising spontaneously within an organisation) and a story (something created purposefully). Stories can be created by various people in an organisation, including trainers and management. Sometimes this happens in 'created environments' which are designed to elicit stories.

The IKM methodology developed by Snowden involves systematic collection of anecdotes using anthropological observation (often with naive observers), story circles (both actual and virtual) and pervasive, opportunistic capture of stories by tape recording or other means. The captured anecdotes are systematically deconstructed and indexed, using software specially designed to aid this task, producing generalised story sets, and what Snowden calls 'emergent archetypes', which are characters particularly representative of the organisation. (Snowden's use of the term 'archetype' is different from Jung's.) These characters can play parts in stories that are subsequently constructed, which reflect the culture discovered by the collection of anecdotes and seek to modify it in various ways. This story-telling can be done by senior members of staff or by hired actors, as well as by others throughout an organisation. The aim is to share learning and challenge received wisdom.

This methodology might become highly manipulative, so Snowden is keen to establish a strong ethical background to the work. One rule is that any anecdote collected covertly cannot be used until the teller voluntarily gives permission. Another is that all management stories must be rooted in genuine anecdotes, collected using proper ethnocultural methods. Further, everyone must know that a study is being conducted and questions about it must be honestly answered. For a big project, an independent ombudsman might be appointed to whom people could appeal in confidence.

Victoria Ward and her co-workers, known collectively as Sparknow, drawing on interesting work by Steve Denning and others (see Denning 2000), have for some years been using stories and drama as an organisation tool. One use is to explore the lessons learned from large projects, avoiding blame and giving time for reflection by careful story collection and presentation. In their booklet *Corporania (The Treasure Map)*, Sparkteam (2001) first tell a fable which was generated by the history of a large-scale project in an investment bank. They then annotate the fable, to illustrate the various story elements used, such as casting and character, beginnings and endings, journeys, maps, magic, mystery and surprise.

Sue Hollingsworth, Bernard Kelly and Ashley Ramsden are the group Story-telling in Organisations. Since 1995, their work has concerned the transformational power of stories to address issues at the heart of business. Ashley and Sue teach at the School of Story-telling at Emerson College which Ashley heads, whilst Bernard runs a story-telling venue in London. They explain their work with a story:

A group of bushmen once led some anthropologists to see some rock paintings. When they arrived, the anthropologists could see nothing. The bushmen laughed; throwing some water onto the rock, the images burst into life.

Our work involves the most ancient form of communication and paradoxically, the most modern. Howard Gardner in *Leading Minds* (1997) puts it like this: 'All successful leaders, political, military, religious, academic or industrial, are successful to the extent that they tell and embody persuasive stories about where the institutions they lead should be going and how they will get there.'

Stories speak directly to the imagination so that we can create our own pictures in our *own* mind's eye: personal images that arise out of our deepest memories and longings. Images that are far more intimately connected to us than any rousing presentation or launch could hope to be. Take the bushmen story. Here it is the experts who fail to find what they are looking for. It takes the ancient people of the bush, a people who have survived by modern standards on practically nothing, with their perspective, their laughter and their water, to bring the images to life. Stories are like water. They allow us to reflect, to playfully imagine, to become mobile in our thinking. They bring things back to life. They also demand that we engage our powers of listening to their fullest extent. This level of alertness means not just paying attention but deeply engaging at all levels. The quality of listening good story-telling engenders is desperately needed in every sphere of industry today – listening to resolve conflict, listening to provide exceptional service, listening to make good sales, listening to understand employees' potential and how to release it.

In Australia the outback, dry, dusty and lifeless, stretches on for miles, but if you are there when the rain falls, the whole landscape starts to bloom before your very eyes. It's the bushman principle again. There are people around us who bring this kind of moisture, who open up new vistas, who transform the drudgery of a day-to-day desert into a colourful workplace. They appear to be drawing their energy from a different source. We call them story-tellers.

Spirit, ideas, emotions, these are intangible things. We can't pin them down but like it or not they are the invisible forces that fuel our existence, the source of our happiness or unhappiness, the centre of our creativity. This is the cutting edge for which the business world has currently very little vocabulary, but reach for a story and the language you're looking for is there. (personal communication)

Story-Telling and Power

Does story-telling support those in power or undermine them? Stories certainly can be supportive of power. Official stories do work sometimes, otherwise they would not be told. Heroic stories about an organisation's founders starting the business in a garage really are inspirational to some. The court jester is useful to the king and may survive for years if his stories are funny enough and if he is consistently good at judging the fine line between joke and insult. Much of what Snowden tells us is about stories that help those in power. He gives us a picture of management stories being mocked by anti-stories, of anti-stories being pre-empted by management spreading viral stories. Subversive stories are also widely told. They can be amusing to those who have to endure the pretensions of the office-holders who have been lucky enough to reach positions with some kind of power. They can give solace to the seriously oppressed. Gabriel says that stories slip furtively in and out of sight, evade censors and are hard to suppress (Gabriel 2000, p. 129). Rumour and scandal can upset a hierarchy, fairly or not. So a talent for story-telling, like other talents like creativity or charisma, can be used both to support power and to counter it, as seen with Radio Trottoir (p. 5).

There are situations where story-telling is mainly libertarian. This is the case when stories are used to cope with complexity. The virtuous circle described in Chapter 5, in which story-telling generates the capability for sensemaking in complex situations and strengthens interpersonal relationships, depends on the widespread development of individual talents and having the freedom to use them. Further, as effective communication about collective action must be unconstrained by imbalances of power, this is also a force for equality.

Stories and Learning

Individual Learning

Is all the world a stage? Do we live our lives as a story? Do we indeed make sense of our experience and create meaning for ourselves and others by story-telling? Making things memorable aids learning. Linking them with existing knowledge and experience aids learning. Making them look bright and making them 'touch' us aids learning. Engendering curiosity and engagement aids learning. There is evidence to support all these assertions.

Study of how the brain processes, retains and arranges recall of information coming in through the senses (e.g. Baddeley 1976) has helped us understand how to render things memorable. Attention to how we make sense of the world (e.g. Kelly 1955) has helped us address how we might be interpreting/creating and encoding our experience. Others have looked at our styles of attention and engagement (Kolb and Fry 1975; Kolb 1984; Honey and Mumford 1982) tailoring learning to greatest effect for each individual.

In his book *Experiential Learning* (1984), David Kolb not only reviews how learning might be defined, how individuals may learn in different ways from each other, and the value of using experience effectively to promote learning, he also tells an intriguing story of what he believes we are faced with:

> Our species long ago left the harmony of a nonreflective union with the 'natural' order to embark on an adaptive journey of its own choosing. With this choosing has come responsibility for a world that is increasingly of our own creation – a world paved in concrete, girded in steel, wrapped in plastic, and positively awash in symbolic communications. From those first few shards of clay recording inventories of ancient commerce has sprung a symbol store that is exploding at exponential rates, and that has been growing thus for hundreds of years. On paper, through wires and glass, on cables into our homes – even the invisible air around us is filled with songs and stories, news and commerce interlaced on precisely encoded radio waves and microwaves. (p. 1)

Learning in Small Groups

Robin Dunbar's ideas about gossip (1996) were discussed in Chapter 2. He considers interaction within groups of around 150 people, which is likely to be the size of group within which human psychology was formed during evolution. Most writers on organisations do not distinguish between smaller organisations, say of up to 200 people, and larger ones. But in these smaller organisations communication can be mainly face-to-face, which makes it easier to develop trust between their members. Dunbar's view of gossip about other group members being a means for group bonding only applies to groups small enough for everyone to know everyone else. So the effects of gossip create a further difference between large and small organisations.

Gerard Fairtlough's book *Creative Compartments* (1994) explores communication within smaller organisations, of up to 200 people. Openness of communication leads to a high degree of trust, engenders a strong commitment to the organisation's goals, and genuine feelings of empowerment. The ideal is to have no work-related secrets between organisation members. At this scale it is possible to keep information confidential within the organisation to a degree that would become impossible in a larger organisation. At this smaller scale, stories are less about remote, heroic figures or bureaucratic muddles and more about sensemaking between people committed to common purposes. Openness and trust grow together in a virtuous circle, as do commitment and empowerment. In this kind of culture stories about what is actually happening can be freely told, without fear. Constant sharing of knowledge, mutual help in problem-solving, interactive innovation, all these flourish in this 'creative compartment'.

Large Organisations – Seely-Brown and Duguid

It is more difficult to generate trust in a large organisation than in a small one. The general level of interaction between people is less, and much of the interaction is not face-to-face, or is too infrequent for individuals to get to know their colleagues well. John Seely-Brown and Paul Duguid's book *The Social Life of Information* (2000) is an excellent antidote to 'infohype' without being in any way anti-technological. One of the book's most powerful sections has stories about service engineering representatives at Xerox.

The service reps had a manual which was supposed to tell them how to deal with problematic photocopy machines. But the manual was never enough – the machines and the people who use them were too unpredictable. So the reps met regularly, for breakfast, lunch or for drinks, to share knowledge and experience. For reps who were part of such a group, the mutual support enabled them to function adequately. To provide for reps who didn't have frequent contact with their peers and to generally enhance interaction, a Web-based database of reps' knowledge was set up:

> . . . preserving over time and delivering over space resourceful ideas. It drew directly on the reps' own insights and their own sense of what they needed. The reps' tips are subject to peer review, drawing on those same lateral ties that make the reps [act as] resources for each other. A rep submits a tip, peers review it, and if it stands up to scrutiny – is original, is useful – then it is added to the database. There, other reps can find it over Web-based links. (p. 112)

> The talk made the work intelligible, and the work made the talk intelligible. As part of this common work-and-talk, creating, learning, sharing, and using knowledge appear almost indivisible. Conversely, talk without work, communication without practice is, if not unintelligible, at least unusable. Become a member of a community, engage in its practices, and you can acquire and make use of its knowledge and information. Remain an outsider, and these will remain indigestible. (pp. 125–126)

The Living Company – de Geus

Arie de Geus's book *The Living Company* (1997) is informed by his long career in the Royal Dutch/Shell group of companies. It is what we call a 'history', a setting for many stories about Shell. A study on the life cycles of large businesses made de Geus think about possible causes for the differences in longevity revealed by the study, and led to his book. He concluded that the prime purpose of a 'living company' is to perpetuate itself as an ongoing community. People join, and may remain with the community for many years, but in the end they leave, and others take their place. The community has rules that ensure its self-perpetuation and the most important of these rules are about people – defining membership, clarifying values, the process of recruitment, ways of developing, rewarding and honouring people.

A key question is, 'Who is us?' Who belongs to the community and who does not? Someone who is 'us' can be expected to share many of the values of the community. The process of recruitment to a living company is a rite of passage, testing the fit between the potential recruit and the community. It is a bit like becoming a doctor or a lawyer, and the recruits of today provide nearly all the top managers of thirty years' time. The living company has an implicit contract with its people: to try to develop everybody's potential to the full. Since this contract is largely fulfilled in practice, it builds a great deal of trust, rather like that in a well-functioning civil society, where commitment to common goals can generally be taken for granted.

In the past, the implicit contract meant lifelong employment for everyone – with a good pension at the end. This is less so today, but there is a definite possibility of a job for life and the certainty of help to find other work if the connection with the living company has to be broken. The age for retirement is well defined and relatively young, providing a flow of people through the management ranks. In his book, de Geus says that it takes many years to build a living company but only twelve months to destroy one. A business has to make money in order to survive, but if profit is ranked higher than people, it will cease to be a living company. Although de Geus's book is about businesses, and is modelled on Shell, other kinds of organisation have the characteristics of living companies. In some countries, the civil service and the military have these characteristics. The stories told in living companies reflect these defining characteristics. Sometimes the stories are about behaviour that doesn't meet its standards. At other times the stories are about extreme efforts to live up to these standards. But here is one story that could never be told in a true living company, because it is so far from the ethos of developing everyone's full potential. A young man, with a good university degree, was recruited by an organisation. He was set to work on a study of a particular market. After two months of hard work, the recruit submitted his report. Two days later he was called into the boss's office. Without saying a word, his boss held up the report, ripped it in half and threw it in the bin. 'You may go now,' said his boss.

The Learning Company

Mike Pedlar, in Burgoyne *et al.* (1994), writes: 'From a learning company perspective organizations are in a dynamic process of becoming; and *being* only in transition. The biographical metaphor with its births and deaths, ages and stages (events), periods and themes, lends itself well to this perspective' (p. 127). Pedlar uses this approach to look at organisational biography as theory and practice, noting, 'Organizational biography builds on the organismic metaphor which sees organizations as living systems, exchanging with a wider environment to satisfy their needs' (p. 128).

Dixon (1994) offers a warning about taking some stories of organisational life at face value, particularly as they relate to organisational cultures. She asks us to consider the nature of reality and truth; of time; of space (shared or private); of human nature; of human activity and of human relationships (including responsibility and authority). For her, organisational learning is collectively creating meaning and learning through acting (neither learn then act, nor act then learn, but do both together).

Communities of Practice – Wenger

Etienne Wenger's *Communities of Practice* (1998) is a powerful book. Much of its power comes from the ethnographic fieldwork that Wenger did in 1989–90 in the medical claims processing centre of a major US insurance company. Wenger's account of what happens in the centre is immediately recognisable – yet it is also novel. Wenger has found some wonderfully revealing ways to describe the practice of this community. His account is, in our terms, a history and one that includes many stories told by the people who work in the centre.

Wenger's theory of learning is a social one. Learning happens through a process of 'flocking'. He sees learning as produced by the interaction of meaning (the experience of the world as meaningful), practice (mutual engagement in action), community and personal identity. Communities of practice are everywhere – we just hadn't found a name for them before Wenger pointed them out. Participants in a community of practice develop a repertoire of capabilities that allow them to negotiate meaning with their fellow members. The repertoire develops over time through mutual engagement, and is ambiguous and adaptable. It includes vocabulary and gestures, stories and 'smileys', pictures and documents, concepts and routines. When people join a community they have to learn fast – particularly from old-timers. Wenger writes:

> As a community of practice, these old-timers deliver the past and offer the future, in the form of narratives and participation both. Each has a story to tell. In addition, the practice itself gives life to these stories, and the possibility of mutual engagement offers a way to enter these stories through one's own experience. (p. 156)

To belong to a community of practice you need to relate to it in three ways. The first is engagement – you actually take part in what the community does. The second is imagination, which is active evaluation of the practice and consideration of possibilities for it and for the community. The third is what Wenger calls alignment, which is reaction to the formal requirements of the task and the administrative demands of the organisation. Story-telling is particularly relevant to the imaginative way of belonging, as are story-like activities such as imagining possible worlds, playing games, making maps and devising models:

> Imagination, too, can be a way to appropriate meanings. Stories . . . allow us to enter the events, the characters and their plights by calling upon the imagination. Stories can transport our experience into the situations they relate and involve us in producing the meanings of these events as though we were participants. As a result, they can be integrated into our identities and remembered as personal experience, rather than as mere reification. It is this ability to enable negotiability through imagination that makes stories, parables, and fables powerful communication devices. (pp. 203–204)

One final point from Wenger's work: the unplanned emergence of communities of practice in many situations gives support to the concept of self-organisation.

Sensemaking in Organisations – Weick

In his *Sensemaking in Organizations* (1995), Karl Weick states: 'Although the word *sensemaking* may have an informal, poetic flavour, that should not mask the fact that it is literally just what it says it is' (p. 16). Although the aim of sensemaking is straightforward, the process is not. It is a multiform, partly unconscious activity, often rough-and-ready. Weick says: 'When you are lost, any old map will do' (p. 54), but that doesn't stop us from going on to look for a better map.

Sensemaking is a collective process. Weick says: 'Individual sensemaking is something of an oxymoron' (p. 80). One way of making sense of a confusing situation is to argue with others about it. This is a collective, analytical process. But another way is to tell stories about it, which is also collective, but not analytical. You gain support from others for the sense you are making of the experiences you are sharing with them. Weick lists a number of sensemaking principles. We cannot go into all of these here, but a key principle is that sensemaking usually comes after you've done or said something. Weick describes this retrospective justification of your actions as post-decision behaviour. He suggests that the retrospective nature of sensemaking is captured by the question: 'How can I know what I think until I see what I say?' Another principle is that, in sensemaking, plausibility is more important than accuracy. You need to know enough about what you think to get on with your projects – but no more.

Weick writes:

> Most models of organization are based on argumentation rather than narration. This means that people are often handicapped when they try to make sense of organizational life, because their skills at using narratives for interpretation are not tapped by structures designed for argumentation. (p. 127)

Weick emphasises that story-tellers do lots of editing. The events in a story are sorted into a clear-cut sequence before the story is told. But this is no surprise, given the retrospective nature of sensemaking. Nor should it be surprising that stories have a widespread power to order individuals' own thoughts and their communications with others. The influence of a story's order and clarity helps sensemaking in areas adjacent to the orginal story area.

Further functions of stories are to integrate the known with the conjectural, to suggest a causal order for events, to guide actions before routines are formulated and enrich routines once they have taken place, and to convey shared values and meanings. Stories allow us to cope better with threats, because threats can be imagined beforehand in story form. In doing so, stories interact with conceptual frameworks. Weick says: 'Stories that exemplify frames, and frames that imply stories, are two basic forms in which the substance of sensemaking becomes meaningful' (p. 131).

Stories and Society

The Nation-State

Benedict Anderson's book *Imagined Communities* (1991) is about stories that construct the nation-state. Note that the title of the book is not 'Imaginary Communities', for Anderson does not deny that national communities exist. His point is that these communities depend on their members' imaginations. It is impossible to know personally more than a tiny fraction of your fellow Englishmen, Americans, or Japanese, so it is by imagining the lives of your compatriots that you develop feelings of solidarity with them. You construct part of your own identity by thinking of yourself as belonging to a particular nation; and some of your sense of what constitutes Britishness or Frenchness comes from imagining a typical British man or French woman.

Story-telling is the main means of constructing imagined communities. You do not learn much about a typical Briton from a list of his characteristics. The stories he appears in are much more revealing, whether these are written by Charles Dickens, Sir Walter Scott or told in countless local gossip sessions. Anderson and other writers (e.g. Hobsbawm and Ranger 1992) investigate the history of national myth-making. For example, the myth of Scottishness was carefully constructed early in the nineteenth century. National dress – kilts, sporrans and tam o'shanters – played a part, but Scott's stories were central to this work.

Arendt

Hannah Arendt thought that everyone should be involved in public debate and decision. She believed that speaking and acting together develops and expresses a vital aspect of humanity. In her view, the curse of modernity is that shared public politics is no longer considered to be the most important and the most enjoyable of our activities. Arendt held that direct political activity was required for human fulfilment and that public happiness:

> ... consisted in the citizen's right of access to the public realm, in his share in public power – to be a participant in the government of affairs, in Jefferson's telling phrase – as distinct from the generally recognised rights of subjects to be protected by the government in the pursuit of private happiness (1973, p. 127)

For Arendt, politics had to be public; it was necessary to be involved and to be seen to be involved: 'This is also why the theater is the political art par excellence; only there is the political sphere of human life transposed into art. By the same token, it is the only art whose sole subject is man in his relationship to others' (1958, p. 188). Arendt thus sees politics as discourse, as open, public debate. Politics cannot be left to others – politics must necessarily be participatory. And stories told during the debate, as theatre or around the table, enthuse the participants and enable them to put their arguments in a compelling way. Arendt's view of politics is similar to the concept of politics as active learning. Participatory politics needs openness and a willingness to listen actively to the views of others. Such direct democracy must be about convincing people that your ideas will lead to a better result for everyone, and about being ready to be convinced by others' ideas. Learning within a group also needs openness and a willingness to listen to others' ideas. If people's minds are closed, they fail to contemplate new ways of looking at the world, and no learning takes place. Thus, politics as happiness is necessary for politics as learning.

Michael

Don Michael first published *Learning to Plan – and Planning to Learn* in 1973. The world, he argued, is becoming more complex. We have more information than ever before, things change more quickly, and we are beginning to realise that the environmental consequences of what we do are creating an unpredictable situation. As this happens, we become more and more aware that we are living in a time when we don't even know what we don't know.

This state of blind and irreducible ignorance was the biggest challenge Michael thought we faced. In managing it, he argued that we use stories to interpret the mysterious world around us, creating mythologies that can be our guide through the unknown while also forming the basis of our shared social lives. However, he also argued that the increased availability of information has led to some of the great unifying myths – like the myth of progress – breaking down into multiple stories. An article he wrote with Walter Truett Anderson, entitled 'Norms in Conflict and Confusion: Six Stories in Search of an Author' (1987) named six of the stories circulating in various parts of the world at that time. There was the progress story, the story of Christian values, the Islamic story and the classic Marxist story, as well as the Green story, which rejected progress, and the New Paradigm story, which foresaw a brave new world of technological achievements. These stories were the way that people made sense of the confusing world around them. But the stories were contending with each other, destroying the ability of society to agree on important issues of the day. For that reason, Michael and Anderson also believed that if governments were to be effective, they needed to help their societies create a shared story – and the story he most wanted governments and societies to create was the story of learning.

Michael's interest in stories, planning and learning combined in his support for the use of scenarios. His view of these stories about the future was closer to Walter Ong's description of the personal, participatory world of oral society than to the rational, logical world of economic analysts. In Michael's view, futurists who wrote stories about the future should not pretend that their predictions are the rational, analytical products of reasoning minds. Instead, he argued, scenarios are always personal, emotional and moral.

> A worthy and well-told story implies a moral, and stories about the future are especially well suited to convey some crucial morals. One moral meriting emphasis is, that the nature of the future world will be an expression of emotions at least as much as rational deliberations, programs and practices. Emotions are critical to what happens, both those emotions driving creativity

and reasons, aspiration, power seeking, greed, and the will to control; and those emotions responding to the existential questions of being human (1985, p. 83)

Gendlin

Eugene Gendlin has been working since the early 1960s on a philosophy of experiencing or 'focusing', which explores the 'supra-logical' order we can sense in our physical reactions to confusing situations, but not easily articulate. Where Michael talks about complexity, Gendlin has been exploring the experience of intricacy. In a 1991 essay titled 'Thinking beyond patterns: body, language and situations', he notes:

> Today the social forms fall short of guiding what we do. Every day we must improvise and create more intricate ways to act in many situations. We do it not by just inventing, but from our sense that an unclear situation is *more intricate* than the known roles and concepts. Now the social forms seem primitive and simplistic.

Starting with Wilhelm Reich in the 1940s (see Wahl forthcoming) several practitioners have introduced body-orientation into psycho-therapy, although this remains somewhat on the margin of the discipline, and requires clear ethical guidelines. Following this tradition, Gendlin believes it is possible to identify a physical sensa-tion connected to an unclear and intricate personal situation. Gend-lin is fascinated by two qualities in particular: first the confusion, the inarticulate, 'pre-logical' sense of a situation, which he identifies in his essay as a visual symbol: '....'. To illustrate the meaning of this symbol, he tells stories about individuals exploring the physical sensa-tions that are associated with their own inarticulate knowledge of '....'. As they focus on that '....', the individual talks to a partner who listens and repeats what is said about this feeling. In focusing on the experience of this inarticulate feeling, new images, metaphors and relationships may be described. Dreams may be recalled or histories of things long forgotten. New connections are often made to current events that had previously seemed absurdly irrelevant. In this way, the focusing itself becomes a kind of journey that is often later told as a story of insight and change.

Gendlin uses the expression a 'felt sense' to describe the physical sensation of this inarticulate space symbolised by '....'. However, his philosophy of intricacy is attempting to understand the non-rational, non-empirical dimensions of knowledge. He therefore uses physical sensations – the felt sense – as well as the unconscious symbols of our dreams and metaphors as part of an expanded toolkit of understanding which works with rational and empirical knowledge to help us grasp intricate situations we might not otherwise be able to understand.

This all brings us back to stories. Stories are the sharing of intricate knowledge. They often provoke physical and emotional reactions. They have a reasonableness that is often not rational, but clear and easy to communicate. They help us to work through complex situations in ways that may be based on logic, but may also be based on experience, emotion, metaphor and allegory. They are, in that sense, the perfect tool for the age of intricacy we live in, where our once-reliable social forms seem primitive and incomplete. That stories also draw on the reservoir of human experience from before the age of script may also be important. After all, our confusion now may be at least as great as the confusion once faced by *homo sapiens* just beginning to understand the world they called home, and our rational tools may in fact be only the latest invention of humankind.

Bohm and Bruner

In his *Wholeness and the Implicate Order* (1983) and in other works, David Bohm distinguishes between dialogue and discussion. In discussion, people present their own views, not listening to the views of others except to score points. Dialogue, on the other hand, is a free flow of meaning between people. The first step is to understand clearly what others are talking about. 'When you listen to someone else, whether you like it or not, what they say becomes part of you' – Bohm believes that simply listening to other people will bring a certain order into social relations.

Society cannot work, according to Bohm, unless there is a good degree of shared meaning, and society's present ills are due to a lack of shared meaning. With shared meaning we could experience the wholeness of the world, not the fragmented individual views that we presently know.

Bohm says little about dialogue – only that participants must suspend their assumptions and preconceptions and really listen to what others people say. He suggests that dialogue be conducted without an agenda and without a leader, and preferably in groups of twenty or more people who meet regularly over a lengthy period. Bohm doesn't offer organisations a quick fix. In Chapter 2 we told a story in which dialogue was carefully introduced into an organisation (M4) that already had habits of open communication and listening to the stories of others.

Nancy Dixon's book *Dialogue at Work* (1998) draws on the work of Bohm and other writers to develop practical guidelines for dialogue. She writes: 'When Bohm eschewed agendas it was an attempt to avoid the instrumental relationships that agendas typically precipitate.' But she recognises that a manager's job is, by definition, instrumental – to get work done through others. Thus there is a tension, which will never completely disappear, which makes it hard to use dialogue in organisations. Her simple, but thoughtful, book provides a good starting point for tackling this task.

Jerome Bruner in *Acts of Meaning* (1990) makes the case that the narrative form is intrinsic to human thinking. He believes that our minds are hard-wired to organise experience as narratives. Bruner uses his own and others' research into how children acquire language, concluding that narratives are not only used by children to develop their language skills, but they are also the way that children enter their native culture. An important narrative, for children and adults, is the autobiographical one, which forms our personal identities. (In this he is supported by Damasio's studies on the functioning of the brain; see Damasio 2000.) Stories have a plot and this is what makes them economical and memorable. Everything in a good story should move the plot forward. Another feature of narratives noted by Bruner is that they take account of the difference between the ordinary and the extraordinary. He says that we enjoy unexpected twists in stories because this distinction is an important one for our survival. If we do not notice the unexpected we might be in trouble. Active sense-making and searches for meaning are triggered by an extraordinary turn in the narrative. Our appraisal of something new is helped by including it in a story alongside the familar.

Once more, story-telling is found to be central to human existence.

Conclusions

In this chapter we have briefly described some of what anthropology, psychology, linguistics, organisation theory, social theory and philosophy can tell us about story-telling and its value to organisations. Four themes emerge from this variety:

- The centrality of metaphor and story in human life, as shown by their importance for pre-literate societies and for children.
- The close link between story-telling and sensemaking, as shown by the urge to complete a half-told tale, and the stimulus this gives to memory, learning and imagination.
- How easily stories bring together body with mind, emotion with rationality, purpose with ethics, entertainment and art.
- How stories can both support and subvert power.

10

Tools and Techniques for Story Use

What you can do,
Or dream you can do,
Begin it.
Boldness has genius,
Power and magic in it.

Goethe, *Faust*

This chapter suggests ways to engage with the power of the tale in organisational settings – tales that may be individual or collective, designed or emergent. Drawing on the stories in preceding chapters, this chapter gives practical information and starting points, from helping individuals and groups create, uncover and learn from their own stories, to developing and maintaining your own creative capacities.

A Note on Ethics

We believe that it is unethical for anybody to use stories for such probing unless they have the appropriate psychological training or sufficient experience to attend to boundaries and psychological safety. Even with the involvement of an appropriately skilled practitioner, there are many organisational circumstances that would render this kind of approach unethical.

The context of working in organisations generally raises many complex issues, and there is useful and growing attention being paid to ethical issues. As a small example, some organisations now request from suppliers of development-related services a statement of their ethical position and values. Themes around sustainability, servant leadership, social inclusion and so on increasingly require re-examination of business practices. Stories can be, and are, pressed into service in a range of ways, and it is because they are powerful that careful attention needs to be paid to the circumstances of their use.

Story-telling can be a safe and creative way for us to reflect on ourselves and on our organisational worlds. It provides information, aids sensemaking, and is appropriate to our ways of perceiving and navigating changing environments. It may be therapeutic. But we're not writing about therapy. We hope that you will use this chapter for ideas and options, but also to start or guide your thinking, to consider the skill sets required for different circumstances, and to review your own continuing development as a professional.

As the old joke about the plumber (or consultant or whatever) goes: it's £1 for tapping the piping; £199 for knowing where and how to tap it. All of us need to invest in knowing *where* and *how*.

Chapter Format

The preceding chapters showed how, as individuals or in groups, we can use stories in order to communicate effectively, learn, create community, deal with conflict, navigate complexity, support innovation and work towards new futures, among other activities. This chapter contains frameworks and exercises to support the use of story-telling in such endeavours, collated under three main headings. These are:

- **Story-telling frameworks and starting points** – examples of basic frameworks and options for starting a story process;
- **Workshop games and activities** – examples of exercises primarily with workshops in mind, although these may be adapted to suit a variety of uses;
- **Developing your own skills** – activities that address some of the underlying capabilities that support individual story-telling skills.

Sub-sections are arranged to:

- introduce an approach or exercise;
- provide an example and/or instructions;
- give tips, hints or suggested uses.

Finally, there is a note on story-telling and organisational research before the Conclusion to the chapter.

Story-Telling Frameworks and Starting Points

We discussed story characteristics and story types in Chapter 1, but it may be useful to highlight here some of the things that make stories work.

No one is going to listen properly to a story which is not engaging, which does not hold the attention. Things that help make a story engaging (and thus entertaining) are:

- movement – there is a progress of events, the resolution of a contradiction or a conflict;
- suspense – something unknown or unanswered until the story reaches a close;
- intriguing characters – people, places or organisations with something about them that is unique or individual, and/or with whom it is easy to identify;
- emotion – we can be touched by the characters or situations;
- relevance – the story is appropriate to its audience, even if it originated in a very different setting. You may have to translate some things, generalise others, identify stereotypes of character or situation;
- pace – depending on the context, take too long to tell the tale and people may be bored, tell it too quickly and no one understands;
- simplicity – overload it with details and a story can be confused and confusing; simplify a situation and the story can become more allegorical and have greater significance.

A Six-Part Story Framework

In his book *Creative Supervision* (1992), Mooli Lahad explains his methods for using story creation, among other expressive activities, in the continuing professional development (CPD) of a range of health professionals. His book explains a range of approaches that are probably most easily accessible by those with psychological or therapeutic training. However, the story-creating framework he uses, which draws on the common elements found in fairy-tales from across the globe, can be adapted for use in a very straightforward manner in other settings.

Instructions: To help individuals or groups structure a story in a simple way, use the six questions below. This is the framework adapted for use in creating the Chirpy and Dragon workshop stories of Chapter 6, AutoCorp – Evolving.

1. Who is the main character of the story (real, imaginative, single, few, animal, hero or heroine)?
2. What is the task or mission of that character?
3. Who or what can help in this task (if at all)?
4. What is the obstacle in the way? What prevents it from happening?
5. How does the main character go about it? How does he cope with the obstacle?
6. What is the outcome? The end? Or any possible continuity?

Box 10.1 shows one of a series of applications of this framework by Julie Allan.

Tip: Where time is short and people may not be used to writing or telling stories, providing a framework can be helpful.

Metaphor

Much of story-telling includes metaphor. Somebody can be a devil to deal with, a cowboy at work, a lion in battle. The interest lies in the comparison, and the transfer of qualities from one state or situation into another. Analogy and simile also enable this. Such use of language allows stories to highlight aspects of a situation, while thinking of metaphorical or analogous situations can be a prompt to new ideas

BOX 10.1   A Story-telling Exercise

StoryPower challenge

Your task . . .

➤ With the materials/props provided, create a five-minute story to tell to the other groups

➤ Your story includes how life is now and how you'd like it to be in future

➤ Remember to give it a title

➤ Here is a simple and effective story framework

1. Who (main character/s).
2. Where are we?
3. Problem/difficulty.
4. Who/what comes along?
5. What happens (helps/hinders)?
6. Outcome (resolution and the future).

Adapted from Lahad 2000

JOKER IN THE PACK:

If you take a gift-wrapped parcel from the props box, you must use it in some way!

and viewpoints as well as offering insight into current situations. In Chapter 2, Lorna used such approaches with M4.

Exercise: Just suppose

Instructions
1. Use starter questions, as in Chapter 2.
2. Individually, create a very short tale on the theme of one of the answers you gave, and share this with somebody else (in groups of twos and threes).

At M4, examples were:
'M4 is an adventurer. He travels the world with a bag of tricks and helps all those he meets. He tells stories about the people he has met and how they changed things.'
'When M4 chooses to tell stories, she always chooses a story about a journey into a wood, like Little Red Riding Hood or Baba Yaga. But instead of telling the whole story, she starts it off, then says what should happen later, but doesn't tell the bit in the middle.'

3. Then discuss these in the whole group. What themes are emerging? Where are there any confusions or conflicts?

Tip: This can work well in bringing together representatives of different work functions, agencies and so forth that need to work together. Each function can be asked to create a story about them at their 'best' and their 'worst', or a story that represents what the proposed project looks like from their perspective.

Useful starter questions include:

- If X were an animal, what animal would it be?
- If X were the main family in a spoof documentary or soap, what would they be like?
- In X, which departments are King, Queen, Joker, Thief?

All these starting points can provide the basis for a story, even though some answers to them will turn out to be stories in their own right.

Useful follow-up questions include:

- Create a story about how X will end.
- Describe a day in the life of X the animal.
- What happens if the King spends a day with the Joker? The Queen with the Thief?
- In the imaginary building that could represent X, what's in the secret room where nobody goes? What guards the door and why? How is it opened? By whom? What is the outcome?

Tip: With these stories, as with any other, a framework such as Lahad's (see above) could be offered if people would like to use it. But since no story is 'wrong', it's entirely optional.

Exercise: Morphological analysis

This is a long (and borrowed) name for a simple idea that encourages the use of stories about 'other' real and imagined situations to create options for moving forward. A morpheme is the smallest meaningful unit of language, and morphological analysis has been used with language and anatomical shapes (like brain scans). The idea in using it as a creative tool is to find small meaningful 'units' in one situation and apply them to another.

Instructions
1. Choose a comparison for the current situation. For example, to look at regenerating an inner-city area you might look at a success-

ful leisure facility (country park, golf course, sports centre), and an inner-city regeneration elsewhere.
2. Then, consider what makes a golf course, for example, successful. Tell a story about a day in the life of the club director, a golfer, a green keeper, the golf shop owner etc.
3. What information do the stories offer about how each person's day can be enjoyable and successful, and contribute to the success of the club? What difficulties are there? What is needed?
4. Review the success factors and challenges. How do they apply to the current situation? What would a project look like that built on all the success factors possible (leisure, atmosphere, bar, essential shopping) and attended to the difficulties (cost, dress code, green maintenance)? In some derelict docks in Liverpool, the answer was an angling centre and a water sports centre.

Traditional Tales

Traditional tales, like poetry, can provide a useful starting point to help groups and individuals think differently about a situation. They may be selected because their content reflects an issue identified for consideration, or they may be more metaphorical or allegorical in order to support divergent thinking. They may be chosen by a trainer or facilitator, or selected by the group or individual.

Instructions for a coaching exercise
1. Start with the real-life situation, using critical incident questioning and the Lahad six-part structure to create the story of an event (see Box 10.2).

BOX 10.2   Creating a Real-life Story

Opening question
Bring to mind a challenging incident or situation you faced or are facing at work.

Follow-on questions
1. Say something about the main people involved. (Real, invented or nicknames are fine. This should include the story owner).

2. What were/are you trying to do or achieve? And the other
   main characters?
3. Who or what is helping you/them?
4. What is getting in the way?
5. How have you been dealing with the obstacles? And the other
   main characters?
6. What is the outcome (so far)?

2. To continue into the use of traditional and other tales, ask: 'Now
   imagine the story as a fairy story or folk tale. You can use any typical
   fairy-tale characters you know, or ones you invent.'
   Follow-on story structure questions:

- Who would be the main characters in your story?
- What is the task?
- Who or what is helping?
- What is getting in the way?
- How does the main character get around this?
- What is the outcome or end?

   Follow-on story exploration questions:

- What are the most useful characteristics of the heroine in this
  situation?
- What other characteristics would be helpful?
- If you could give the heroine a magic skill or object, what would it
  be?
- What was a key turning point in this story?
- Do you associate any colours or sounds with the story?
- What is the effect of changing them?
- Can you think of alternative endings?
- How would these occur?

Tip: In group and individual use, consideration should be given to
cultural appropriateness because traditional tales are windows into the
sensemaking, values and cultures of their originators. Their origins are
important. In coaching, it is the coachee who chooses the story and
gives permission for this metaphorical style to be used. The coachee

remains in charge of her own interpretation and analysis. In Chapter 3, AutoCorp – Learning, when Leonora used a storying approach with Faye, what she *didn't* do was interpret the story she was hearing; what she *did* do was seek permission from her colleague to explore in this slightly unusual way.

Choosing and using ancient tales

Ashley Ramsden and Bernard Kelly of Storytelling in Organisations offer these thought-provoking words:

Remember

Be passionate about the story you're telling or else don't tell it
The silence you bring to a tale is just as important as the words
Stories are primarily about Magic and God
It's the listener that tells the tale
Stories are about consequences, not what's right or wrong
Use a story as propaganda, and it will poison you
Listen to everyone's unique understanding and interpretation of the story
The story is created in the space between people
Never say, 'The moral of this story is. . .' (unless you're joking!)
The stories are older and wiser than you are

The last point is a reminder of the pervasive nature over time of a variety of organisational themes. The stories – of Zeus, Prometheus, Coyote, kings, serpents, forbidden rooms – require no embellishment and can provide a stimulating window on organisational dynamics.

Objects and Creative Play

Creative materials can engender a playful approach and be used either as props or to make miniature settings in which the story takes place. The visual aspects of such creations frequently provide creative metaphors for key issues. As part of a story gathering or story-creating exercise, visuals can be included in a variety of ways, with individuals and with groups, including:

- an object representing an aspect of the tale, or its theme;
- an item for free association, as a starting point for creating a tale;
- crayons, paints and coloured paper, for workshop use with the focus on the colours of a story;
- drawing representational characters to caricature story themes;
- drawing, painting, collage etc. to create a journey landscape.

A play crate

Box 10.3 indicates a typical materials kit used by Julie Allan.

BOX 10.3   A Play Crate

Crate: a large plastic play crate with a lid and wheels. Contents are variable but may include: paper/card, A3 and A4 coloured thin card and paper or sugar paper, plus:

- crepe paper and tissue paper in a variety of colours;
- colouring tools: crayons and washable felt tips of various types;
- fixing tools: glue pens, tape, string, pegs;
- books: some small books on subjects including art, gardens, poetry;
- balls: juggling and other sorts of various sizes – all soft;
- characters: toy people, puppets, creatures;
- balloons and pump;
- modelling material;
- variety of curiosity items collected in passing;

Safety scissors are supplied separately – left- and right-handed options.

Such a crate is useful for workshop or working group purposes and can be used to support a wide range of activities, including the one in Box 10.1.

Tip: For many general story-telling purposes, it is fine and appropriate that individuals create and keep their own mental images and impressions. In organisational storying contexts it may also be useful to be able to share images and impressions, particularly those for which there may be no words (yet), or to create a focus or artefact around which a joint story may be engaged with.

Individual objects

These should be present as a selection on a table or tray. Practicalities generally dictate size and weight constraints, while the selection otherwise includes a requirement for variety, including symbolic potential. They should be generally decorative or pleasing to look at, touch and smell, since the intention is to engage the senses in a creative way.

Suggested options include:

- items with different textures and colours – for example, velvet and silk scarves;
- containers – for example, small trinket boxes in metal, wood, leather or soapstone, and bowl-like or cup-like items;
- everyday items 'with a twist' – for example, a ballpoint pen with an elaborate casing or a tassel attached, a gold-coloured pencil, a teaspoon with a decorative handle, an interesting paperweight;
- natural items – pebbles, shells, dried leaves, driftwood, fruit;
- chocolate (gold/silver) coins;
- ribbons, string, coloured thread;
- small soft toys or model animals.

Tip: If you are choosing an object as a prop for your own story-telling, or asking others to do so, ask yourself the following questions, or suggest that others do so if they are selecting the objects. The questions will help you to choose a suitable item and use it well.

- What do I feel about this object?
- What is most important about it to me?
- Who do I associate with it?
- Am I prepared to tell my audience the answers to the above questions?
- If other people don't like or understand this item, will that be OK?

Storyboards

This exercise is suitable for use with any size group, or with individuals, and helps visualise current and future situations.

Instructions
1. Supply images of various types that could make a frame or shot in a short film. Line drawings of individuals and groups (Margot Sunderland's book *Drawing on Your Emotions* (1993) can be photocopied once purchased), postcards of environments and buildings,

and a range of printed out copyright-free software icons would provide a useful mix.

2. Invite small groups to create a storyboard for a TV advertisement that conveys the main issues around their chosen topic, using characters in a small number of 'scenes'. Topics should be expressed in a couple of sentences that suit the purpose, from contemplation of a particular issue to exploring new product development.

Supply a guiding framework if needed, such as:

- an opening scene – who are the main characters, and where are they?
- a challenge scene – something is causing tension.
- a turning point scene – something makes a difference.
- a final scene – where are we now *or* what does the future look like?

You can have more than four scenes if you like, but include the above four.

3. When complete, lay the storyboards out on tabletops covered with flip-chart paper, or pin to screens/pinboards. Once displayed, groups should do a 'promenade' and a debrief will centre around issues including: What did the other groups think the storyboard depicted? What is interesting about each storyboard? Similarities and differences – and perhaps the facilitated construction of an agreed storyboard if appropriate.

Tip: In this, as in any other image-based exercise, you could also supply blank squares of paper and pens so that the storyboarders have the option to create some of their own 'frames'.

Theme Pictures

Instructions
1. Supply images of people or characters, of representative locations such as a shopfront, high street, garden, hospital, of animals and of various everyday objects.
2. Spread out all the materials in the available space and invite individuals to choose a number of cards of most interest to them

(either personally, or with a group focus, depending on the purpose of the story creation).

Options following from this beginning are many, and they include:

- Create a story that links the cards you have chosen. Introduce your choices to the rest of the group through telling this short story.
- Select the card you would most like to keep. Tell a story about that card as if you were the picture on it (including, if appropriate, the useful qualities it brings to the group situation).
- Join with a small group of others. Introduce your cards to them in a couple of sentences each. Then create a short story that includes them all and prepare to tell this to the other groups.

3. Debrief includes reflection of what was hard/easy about the exercise, what was enjoyable, were there any surprises, did any themes emerge, and thoughts/actions prompted by the themes for workplace application.

Workshop Games and Activities

Many of the above starting points make suitable workshop activities. The following selection includes simple story-based warm-up activities, some of which are also good personal development exercises for any story-teller.

Telling Half a Story

This is a particular approach to using role play, which can be adapted to a variety of issues including conflict, diversity, customer care, personal safety and so on. It was one of the options used by Themis in Chapter 4.

Instructions
1. Tell a story of your own but without its resolution/ending so that listeners are taken to the middle of the situation, generally just before what would be a turning point in the real tale.
2. At this point, use some role play or 'stepping into the shoes of' activity.

3. Debrief the information gained from this activity before completing the story as it happened at the time being recalled.

The following, taken from a Themis day, would be a suitable introduction, although this depends on the content of the story to follow. Box 10.4 draws out the important qualities for an introduction to such an exercise.

'I want to tell you a story. It's a horror story. And the horror is all the more potent because it's a true story.

'This happened to me, and it happened last July. So I have had time to think it all over. I've thought of every part and every angle, and so this story has great depth and significance for me. And I have learned a lot from it.

'I'd like to know what you would have done in my place.

'I'm going to tell you just half the tale to start with, then ask you to consider what you think is going on and the thoughts and feelings of particular people in the story. Then we will tell that part of the story from each of those perspectives, and create an outcome.

'When we have finished, I'll tell you how things turned out last July and we'll explore the implications for our own lives and work.'

BOX 10.4   Tips for Setting up a Role-play Story

- Use short impactful sentences.
- The 'rule of threes' – notice how the first paragraph has three short parts, each of which builds on the previous one.
- It should be personal to the teller.
- Emotion. The teller included her own reaction (depth, significance, learned a lot), conveyed in an appropriate tone of voice.
- It requires attention ('I'd like to know what you would have done in my place').
- It requires the audience to walk in the character's shoes in the middle of the telling.
- The promise that the audience would, in the end, find out what really happened. The teller has set up a situation in which people are expecting an eventual closure or resolution, and since humans tend to seek this, they will be motivated to engage.

Chinese Whispers

This exercise addresses the issue of truth and of control. These are common issues in using stories within organisational contexts, where questions arise about how to move between metaphor and practical application, from concrete to abstract, from creative to pragmatic (or any number of other, probably false, dichotomies that occur).

Instructions (the process is well known to most people):
1. The facilitator, or other person, thinks of a short message. For example, 'If I went out for a walk today I'm sure the change of scenery would do me good. How about you?'
2. This is passed from person to person, in a circle, by whispering the message in the next person's ear. You only get one go to pass on or hear the message.
3. When the message arrives back where it started (or at the person next to the person who started it) then the current version is spoken aloud, followed by the original version.

Once, with a group of twelve people, the message above came back as, 'I went out to a talk on change and almost got killed. Did you?' It was funny and thought-provoking, given what was going on in the organisation at the time.

Alternatives: Set more than one circle going with the same statement and then compare the outcomes; pass it round the circle twice – and see if anybody is tempted to bring it back in line with the message they first heard.

Consequences

This is a much underused story creation format that most people actually know well, if only they could remember it. Barbara Heinzen remembered it with the questions below; however, you can invent others.

Instructions
1. Each person is given a long strip of paper. Each person writes an answer to the first question at the top of the strip, folds it to cover the answer, and passes it to the person on their left.

2. Each person answers the second question on the sheet they received from their right, folds the paper over the answer, and again passes it to their left.
3. This continues until all questions are answered. The papers are then unfolded and the stories read out.
4. The debrief covers any issues that arose – what was recognised about the situations, any surprises and so on.

The questions are as follows.

There was a boy called . . .
And a girl called . . .
They met at/in . . .
He said to her . . .
She said to him . . .
The consequence was . . .
And the world said . . .

Tip: The boy and the girl could be different companies or departments, or it may be left more general to form something more allegorical. The boy and girl should *not* under most circumstances be named people in an organisation.

Titles Please

This is a warm-up exercise with words. You will need a selection of magazine articles.

Instructions
1. Read out the 'sell' paragraph from a magazine article (the first paragraph under the headline).
2. Get people to jot down as many headlines as they can think of in no more than a minute.
3. Repeat for three or four articles.
4. Have groups of three select their favourites for each and shout them out.
5. Reveal the actual articles. What groups come up with can often be at least as good as the original.

Noticing

Story-telling engages the emotions and the imagination. If we want to create and tell stories, or even listen fully to the stories of others, we can engage in a much more lively way if we simply use our five senses well. This exercise and the following two address aspects of this process.

Instructions
This exercise is from Perls *et al.* (1994, p. 64). It helps develop the ability to attend and observe, starting with consideration of an every-day object. In this case, a pencil. You can read it as it is or adapt it. Tell participants they will next go through the same procedure with objects of their spontaneous selection.

Notice first that the pencil is *this unique thing*. There are other pencils, to be sure, but not this very one. Say its name, "pencil", and realize vividly that *the thing is not the word*! The pencil as thing is *non-verbal*.

'Next, notice as many as you can of the qualities and properties that inhere in and constitute this thing – the cylinder of black graphite, the reddish wood, the weight, hardness, smoothness; the way it is sharpened, the yellow it is painted; the fact that its wood forms a hex-agonal prism; the trademark, the rubber eraser and the metal which crimps it to the wood.

'Next, review its functions and possible roles in the environment – for writing, for pointing out a passage, for wetting with one's tongue or biting on, for sale as a piece of merchandise. Also, think of its more 'accidental' roles – to burn if the house burns, to dig into a child's eye if he runs with it and falls; also, its more far-fetched and fantastic uses – to send to someone as a Christmas present or to feed hungry termites.

'As you abstract from this unique thing, *this* pencil, its many qualities and functions, note how in detail they go together or cohere as a structure – for example, the wood firmly holds and protects the graph-ite and is gripped by the writing hand.

'Now try this out on something of your own choosing.'

Tip: this exercise may be unusual in many contexts, so it is important to explain the purpose of getting the senses 'in training'. As presented here it may be a little too formal, so you should adapt it to suit your style while retaining the key features.

Awareness

This exercise is from Houston (1990, p. 8). It focuses very specifically on 'stating the obvious'. Often it's the ability to spot what should have been obvious but actually went unnoticed that can produce excellent stories which are memorable because the experience is so recognisable and because it has been finely observed.

Instructions
1. Explain the purpose of the exercise in accordance with the preceding paragraph.
2. Read the book extract below, or a version adapted to suit your style and purpose. You may like to give a two-sentence demonstration, such as 'Now I am aware of the blue colour of your shirt, now I am aware of feeling a little awkward. . .'
3. The debrief should include what felt difficult or easy, what sort of things it was comfortable to become aware of, what it felt like to concentrate on something so simple. . .

'The revolutionary struggle in China; how your digestion is doing; the income tax; what kind of bird just flew past the window; there is so much to be aware of, or to tune out. . .

'This exercise is partly diagnostic, to give you a chance to notice if you form vivid awarenesses, and to see if they all tend to be of a particular character. It can also be an opportunity to enhance your own perception, your taking in and appreciating what is inside and around you.

'*If you are an uneven number, form yourself into threesomes, as well as, or instead of, pairs. Give your pair or three a bit of space, and sit a little apart from the others. Now take turns saying a couple of sentences which begin "Now I am aware of . . ." At first, experiment with focusing for one of your sentences on something that goes on inside you, and for the next, on something going on outside you.*

'*Awareness is of this moment. Notice if you want to rehearse. If you do, rather than chastise yourself, just report that as the awareness. Then see if you trust yourself next time to wait until the moment when you speak, and simply say whatever is in the foreground of your noticing. Unless you are asleep or unconscious or in a catatonic stupor or dead, none of which states is suitable for doing this exercise, then there is always something, in every second, for you to be aware of, even if it seems to be no more than the blank feeling that you have somehow stopped or blocked yourself.*

'After some minutes, extend the time you take to report, to perhaps three minutes each. . .

'Stay with the exercise long enough for each of you to have two or three of these longer turns.'

Tip: Keep it light.

Guided Visualisation

Due care and attention must be paid to the use of guided visualisation, and some straightforward guidelines (Box 10.5) will help make these a useful practice. Visualisations are stories in their own right, with an outline supplied by the facilitator and the plot lines and details supplied by each individual. In this way, the facilitator and participant co-create a story, with an outcome known only to the participant.

Box 10.6 gives a short example of visualisation.

BOX 10.5   Guided Visualisation Guidelines

1. In a group setting, make it very clear that everybody has the choice of whether to participate or not. Support the decision of non-participants if they are the minority group (they generally are).

2. Be clear about the remit of the exercise. For example, 'We have been speaking about engaging the five senses and using imagination. For those who want to try it, I'm going to spend five minutes talking you through a journey of the imagination that includes attending to the senses. It's entirely voluntary and if you'd rather not do this exercise then it's fine to just sit quietly instead. Afterwards we'll talk about what the experience was like, and you can say as much or as little as you want to.'

3. Unless you have specific training, this is not a therapy or interpretation opportunity.

---

4. Choose words that are likely to create a comfortable experience, and if a location is needed then allow participants to
choose individually where that will be. For example, 'This
involves an imaginary walk, and you can make up a place or
bring to mind a place that you like, as long as it's somewhere
you are going to enjoy visiting.'

There is a story of a psychotherapy trainee who entered into
quite a long visualisation to discover, part-way through, that
she was being asked to get in a boat to cross a lake. She started
to vividly recall an incident when she was six years old, of
falling out of a rubber dinghy at the seaside, where the waves
pushed her down and down again until she thought she was
going to drown. One of the authors knows somebody who was
asked to walk through a beautiful forest; the facilitator didn't
know that this person's brother was found dead in one.

5. The visualisation is the property of the individual. For a group
debrief, questions should be about process rather than content.
For example, 'What was doing that exercise like?' rather than,
'What did you choose to eat?' or 'What did you see in your
view?' If people volunteer content, that is fine, however refer to
(3) above, which applies equally to group participants who
should be steered away from interpreting the images.

BOX 10.6   A Journey of the Imagination

We're going to take a short journey of the imagination and
include our five senses. It takes the form of a short walk to look at
the view. The place is somewhere you like being, whether that's a
real place or an imaginary one.

Sometimes people prefer to have their eyes closed; sometimes
open. You can do whichever suits you. But it's best to make sure
that you are sitting comfortably, that you can feel where the chair
is supporting you, and that you are relaxed. Use your breathing to
help make you comfortable, taking a deep breath in through the
nose . . . and out through your mouth. And again . . . and now
breathing as it suits you.

Now, in your imagination, in this nice place you have chosen,
notice what is around you. Notice colours . . . the temperature . . .
the quality of the light. Notice that you will be taking a short

walk, and see where the starting place will be. Maybe you are already there, and if not then you can go there now. Notice whether there is a gateway of any kind and how you will open it if you need to. Notice what sort of noise you make on your walk . . . the texture of the ground . . .

You go through any gateway and start your walk. What time of year is it? What do you see around you? What sort of scent is in the air? What can you hear?

Up ahead, there's some food or drink that you can have. It's just exactly what you would like. As you reach the food or drink you pause to taste some. Make it the best of its sort that you have ever had. Notice its colour and texture. That it smells good. And its flavour. How good it tastes. The amount you've had is all you need, and you continue on your way.

You are reaching the viewpoint. It's going to be an interesting and welcome view. And now, as you arrive, have a really good look at what you can see. Look to the left. And to the right. Look at what is farthest away. And nearest. Notice what you like most about it.

And now it's time to go back to where you started. You turn away from the view and head back past where you had your food or drink. Notice any changes in the temperature . . . in the ground under your feet . . . in the sounds you can hear.

You go back through any gateway needed to complete your walk, and as you reach your starting point, your imaginary journey is coming to an end.

You can bring back with you any good memories from the journey. And as you leave the imaginary world you become aware of the feeling of the chair you are sitting in, in this room. And you hear the sounds around you in this room. And if your eyes are not already open then you can open them now and become aware of all the things around you here in this room.

Tip: This is good for both individuals and groups, and a useful skill to provide a few moments of meditative calm in a busy day. As well as a debrief, it may be useful to engage in a short physical activity afterwards as part of ensuring that people are re-engaged with the present and ready to continue.

Encouraging Emergence

In Chapter 4, on peer development, individual emergent stories started each Themis day, as well as being continued in some sense throughout the day. They helped sensemaking and the creation of community as well as knowledge-sharing and creation.

It is possible to support the emergence of stories by developing attentive listening, open questioning and dialogic practice. Dialogue can be used as the format for any discussion or debrief, simply by first discussing and then leaving visible, the guidelines in Box 10.7 from Nancy Dixon's excellent text (1998). This practice was found valuable by M4 in Chapter 2.

Tip: A circle supports this practice a lot more effectively than sitting in rows. In early sessions you may need to remind participants to speak only for themselves.

BOX 10.7   Dialogue Guidelines

From *Dialogue at Work* by Nancy Dixon (1998), supplied by Doris Adams at Trinity College.

- Speak from your own experience (use 'I', not 'we' or 'you' or 'people').
- Practice generative listening (i.e. listening to learn from the other).
- Suspend judgement when listening to the other.
- Avoid 'cross-talk' – talk to the whole group rather than another member of the group.
- Give up advice-giving and problem-solving.
- Let silence create spaces for reflection between each person's speaking.

Developing Your Own Skills

Tips from Jeanenne LaMarsh and Joan Levey

Joan Levey, founder of the Chicago company Phone Joan!, has worked alongside Jeanenne LaMarsh to support a story-telling approach. In Chapter 3, AutoCorp – Learning, we told the tale of how Leonora had used this approach.

Joan says, 'Jeanenne uses stories in two designs, called EAT and CPR. EAT is Experience, become Aware, reveal the Theory. The stories come through role play as individuals are invited to "become" a character relevant to their workplace and become quite engrossed with this.

'As the story unfolds they become aware of certain principles, feelings and conflicts. When Jeanenne reveals the logic behind the exercise, that awareness component solidifies – and the participants can relay the story to others.

'CPR is Content, Presentation and Review. The stories are of individual experiences. For example, in looking at change processes, Jeanenne may offer a brief explanation of the stages Kubler-Ross created from her research about loss and grieving. Groups then share stories about work-related or personal losses and try to identify what they did to move from one stage to another. After a brief presentation by the groups, Jeanenne draws out parallels with Kubler-Ross' conclusions.

'Both these methodologies are modern ways of perpetuating story-telling – a tradition of oral verse that helps us learn from those who came before us – and gaining insight to the contemporary experience.'

Elisabeth Kubler-Ross is the author of the very influential text *On Death and Dying*, her first book, published in the early 60s. Her work on a cycle of grieving is very well known and is one of the main ways of understanding bereavement taught in counselling and other related courses.

Box 10.8 contains some story-telling tips from Phone Joan!, and Box 10.9 includes tips from Jeanenne LaMarsh.

BOX 10.8   Facilitator's Story-telling Tips for Facilitators from Phone Joan!

1. Facilitators must see themselves as performers. You need to explain and entertain, and create/maintain momentum.
2. Learn how to deliver the punchline. Acting lessons and improvisation techniques can help you create engrossing stories and field questions and comments from your audience.
3. Allow yourself to be videotaped so that you can see yourself as others see you. Capitalise on the movements (eye, body, etc.) that work best, what props are best and what to eliminate.
4. Take a course on appreciative inquiry. This approach to organisational and individual development concentrates on seeking out and building on those things that are going well. Using this approach will help you to ask positive open-ended questions about other people's stories.

5. Audiotape your voice, or take voice/drama lessons so you can use your voice for certain effects (urgency, humour, thoughtfulness and so on).
6. Be joyful! And make it contagious. Create a positive, safe, and humour-filled environment. Make your audience want to be there!
7. Read! Read! Read! Find stories that elicit your emotions – then examine the story's structure and how you can use it to structure your own.
8. Learn to really listen. (This is the hardest skill for performers!) You never learn anything when you are speaking . . . so learn how to listen when others tell their stories, ask a question, etc. It's when we share common memories that we create a platform for explanation of the new, the mysterious, the unknown.

BOX 10.9   **Story-telling Tips from Jeanenne LaMarsh**

- Make it real.
- Make it connectable to the lives of your audience.
- Make it exciting.

In content
- Don't assume anything: tell all that is required.
- Give enough small details to paint a picture.
- Build the suspense but let the listener work to figure out the ending before you give it to him.
- Introduce several threads and weave them together.*

In delivery
- Exaggerate voice and body movements: this is acting.

* This skill takes a little developing and is useful in certain circumstances even though very simple tales can be very effective. To explore weaving more complex stories, you may like to look at the work of Garrison Keillor (1989, 1993) who tells stories on the radio about his mythical hometown in Minnesota: Lake Woebegone. He starts with one thread, then seems to be distracted by some point he has just made, elaborates on that point, goes off on another tangent, then another and, just when you have no idea what is going on, pulls the whole thing back together to the first point he made and ties it all up in a tight and powerful ending. This makes *you*, the listener, work hard to try to stay ahead of him and ensures that you 'own' the story.

Collecting Tales

Collection is the key. To be a good teller of tales, you need to be a good listener in order to discover them. In Chapter 3, Leonora remembered and borrowed tales heard elsewhere.

Instructions
Try collecting a story a week? Easy? Then try collecting a story a day. Don't collect them as word-for-word perfectly preserved stories. Collect their themes and characters, collect them because they amuse or entertain, and collect them because they have captured your attention or stuck in your memory. Collect them from books, collect them from newspapers, and collect them from other people. And then spread them about.

The way in is really simple, and you can tell your tale as a shorthand two-sentence reference or as a longer fully-developed story.

Here's the way in. . .

'That reminds me of the time when . . .'
'Well, did you hear about the . . ?'
'Talking of . . .'
'It's interesting you say that because . . .'
'Isn't that a bit like . . .'
'Well, I heard something quite different . . .'

Tip: If you want to make a start, then collect a couple of tales you think are interesting, and find a place to tell one of them some time this week. It's the same deal as getting to Carnegie Hall (practise, practise, practise). The Further Reading and Resources section could start you off.

Unpacking Anecdotes

Mac McCarthy, a consultant and associate lecturer at the universities of Central Lancashire and Salford in the UK, as well as the Open University, uses the stories people tell in group learning situations to help identify underlying themes and concerns. He finds that such spontaneous recollections of anecdotes and incidents are rich in ideas and learning opportunities, but only sometimes are they told for the first time in a way that brings out their full value.

Instructions

In debriefing emergent stories, or in helping people clarify the important points of stories they want to tell, it may be helpful to work
through some of the questions in Box 10.10.

Tip: Remember that all questions are voluntary, and individuals are in
sole charge of what they wish to share of their stories. You may find it
useful to have the questions as a handout for people to use at their own
pace and in their own way.

BOX 10.10	Unpacking Anecdotes
Self	What was your role in the situation?
	What were your thoughts during the incident?
	What were you trying to do?
	How well were you listened to?
Protagonist(s)	Who else was involved?
	What was their perspective?
	What were they trying to do?
	How powerful were they in the situation?
	What were the pros and cons of their approach?
Key incident	What happened?
	What decision needed to be taken?
	What were the different perspectives on this?
	What key factors were operating?
	What was hidden beneath the surface here?
	What other factors were important?
	Where were the conflicts?
	Where were the compatibilities?
Issues and concepts involved	What were the key issues?
	What principles needed to guide the actions?
	What other principles were involved?
	How compatible were these?
Action/decision	What was decided?
	How?
	Who was involved and listened to?
	What was the decision taken?

Personal response	How did you feel about the way the incident was dealt with? What was satisfactory about it? What was unsatisfactory about it? What would you change and why?
Outcomes and consequences	What has been the result of the decision? How helpful has it been? What consequences occurred? How helpful are these now?
Reflection	What did you learn from the incident? What did you learn about yourself? How did it challenge you? How did you change or reinforce your beliefs? Are you right?

Creating Individual Tales

This is an exercise that can be used in a workshop, giving people time to create an individual version of a group story that has been created and explored. However you might also like to consider it for your own development as a story-teller. The keys are: memorable and meaningful. You should put emphasis on: getting the bare bones of the story in place – this way the sequence will always come out correctly so the message won't be lost, and it can be told in two minutes or ten, according to the situation.

Instructions
Here is a short story to illustrate the process.

John, who was in a leadership role in a charitable organisation, wanted a story that was about going through change and getting a new view, but which was very 'human'. The group story in the session saw an initiate successfully collect five cups made of gold, silver, bronze, wood and ice [leadership skills] but sometimes fail to find them when the pressure was on.
Here's what he came up with:
'Well, it's like moving house isn't it? When did you last move? [Pause to hear story]. Yes, well, we've all been there. Ours was last May. End-

less rows about what was in the loft; much of which had been there for about ten years. I mean, why keep it? Anyway, we did ditch a lot – charity or the rubbish tip, depending on what it was. But there's always two things that happen, aren't there? One thing comes along that you thought had been left behind, and another thing turns up that you never knew you had. It was just the same for me.

'First thing was, somehow or other, a teapot with a broken spout and cracked handle, in the shape of the pub from The Archers, somehow walked back from the tip where I thought I'd taken it and into the kitchen of the new place. Marvellous. Must have been the wife. Second thing – a thank-you letter fell out of a book while we were unpacking them some weeks after the move, and it was from somebody whose mother I'd helped with her garden when I was a teenager. Do you know, I'd forgotten I did that. Mrs O'Rourke, she was called. And she loved The Archers.

'So now, I can't say I like the teapot but at least it's balanced out by a good memory. Mrs O'Rourke was not only a very chatty old lady, but very interesting because her parents had been involved in music hall, and this seemed slightly scandalous – at least it did the way she told it.

'And maybe this is stretching a point, but I really do think this . . . When I'm trying to make changes in the organisation, and some of the habits or practices that I think are chipped and useless come along, I do three things. First, I realise they're important to somebody or else they wouldn't still be around. Second, I look for what's good about them. And third, I think to myself, "If I really feel I have to make some unpopular decisions, would I be able to explain them to Mrs O'Rourke?" If I can, then I know I've made the best decision I can, and I've explained it the best way I know how.'

Here are some of the factors that make this a good story for John to tell:

- it is personal
- it includes common experience
- it's interactive
- there's a sense of journey, with various 'cue' points
- there's an interesting character
- a situation is set up, with a surprise to follow
- there's a resolution (a lesson in this case)
- it suits his informal style (and can be adapted as a more formal anecdote).

The bare bones he remembers are:

- house move
- teapot you try to throw away
- things you rediscover (Mrs O'Rourke's garden)
- important to somebody; look for the good; explain to Mrs O'Rourke.

The lessons for story creation from this example are:

- make stories your own – personalise them
- make them interactive or inviting of response and empathy in the audience
- have a sense of journey, which includes:
  - a starting point
  - a precipitating incident or factor
  - a surprise or unforeseen occurrence
  - a redress to this, which produces a new state (rather than re-balancing to the previous state).

Tip: the story addresses in some way each of Lahad's questions (see p. 236) and also contains some of the components of what are known as 'quest' stories. You may like to try constructing a quest story. In such stories, a journey is undertaken, challenges are met, and the traveller achieves a new 'stasis' point as a result of his wisdom and achievement. In quest stories we may expect more arduous challenges and more spectacular reversals of fortune, but not every story has to be a showy one – the cycle of stasis, precipitating factor, journey, surprise/obstacle, reversal of fortune/insight and outcome/new stasis can serve in a low-key way.

The Artist's Date

In her book *The Artist's Way* (1995), Julia Cameron includes a concept she calls the artist's date. She regards this as one of the basic 'tools' available to support creativity, through providing time dedicated specifically to feeding that creativity. Not specifically written for story writers or tellers, Cameron's twelve-week plan was developed through use with people in like professions, and Cameron herself is an award-winning writer whose work includes poetry, plays and films as well as newspaper articles.

Instructions
In practice, the date could constitute a weekly excursion of a couple of hours that you find fun, interesting and enjoyable. Cameron explains:

> 'in its most primary form, the artist date is an excursion, a playdate that you preplan and defend against all interlopers. You do not take anyone on this artist date but you and your inner artist, a.k.a. your creative child. That means no lovers, friends, spouses, children – no taggers-on of any stripe.' (p. 18)

Morning Pages

Instructions
A second main tool offered in this text is to take up the writing of 'morning pages'. These are a number of pages of writing, done first thing every day, without fail, and containing whatever comes into your head. They don't have to be great fiction, or true, or neat. They just have to be done. One purpose is to free the mind up for later creative endeavours.

Writing for Professional Development

 In her 2001 work *Reflective Practice: Writing and Professional Development*, Gillie Bolton forwards the view that such writing creates bridges and promotes learning, especially in borderlands and boundary areas where people are at the stretch of their capability and confidence.

In Chapter 4, writing was one of the story practices used by Themis.

Instructions
Here is Gillie Bolton's six-minute starter exercise extracted from her book. It has some similarity with the 'morning pages' practice and can pave the way to more detailed story creation.

1. Write whatever is in your head, uncensored.
2. Time yourself to write without stopping for about six minutes.
3. Don't think about what you are writing; it will probably be disconnected and might seem to be rubbish – but don't stop to think or be critical.

4. Allow it to flow with no reference to spelling, grammar or proper form.
5. Give yourself permission to say anything, whatever it is. You don't even have to re-read it. Whatever you write, it can't be the wrong thing – because no one will read your writing in this form.

Gillie Bolton recommends following this with a longer period of writing – say twenty to forty minutes – again, with the censor switched off and no intention to follow any particular 'proper' story form, but this time with a specific focus on an occasion that you consider vital in some way. It should be the first such occasion that comes to mind, you should stay true to what you recall happening rather than changing things to some preferred outcome, but otherwise regard it as a work of fiction, and allow space for reactions, emotion and details.

These straightforward beginnings can then be used as the base material on which to build. In Bolton's work the emphasis is on drawing out further details, curiosities and the heart of the matter. Plot lines, narratives, turning points, characterisations, different viewpoints, and emotion can come later, using some of the approaches discussed elsewhere in this chapter.

A Note on Story-Telling and Organisational Research

It is outside the scope of this book to detail, or even to review, the large and growing literature on qualitative research of all types. However, its relevance to story-telling practice in organisations cannot be ignored. The processes being used to gather and create stories in organisations are often, knowingly or not, taken from the field of qualitative research. The first of Kleiner's imperatives (see Chapter 9) is Research – the rest of the story comes later.

There are many basic tools, techniques and approaches used in qualitative research. They may include some or all of: interviewing (generally semi-structured or unstructured), either written, audio or visual; questionnaires with open questions; diary-keeping; critical incident techniques; participant observation and projective or arts-based techniques, among many others. These will be housed within approaches such as action research, grounded theory or learning histories, for example, and within disciplines such as psychology (organisational, social or counselling, among others) and anthropology.

These research methods are being used in the service of storytelling, to provide (or reveal, depending on your viewpoint) the landscape, themes, plots and turning points of individual and organisational life. However, story-telling is also being used in the service of research, in a chicken-and-egg kind of a way, since it is often the stories of individuals that are being elicited and collected. Furthermore, narrative psychology, among other approaches, says that we don't just tell and use stories, but we *are* the stories we tell. To quote Mair (1990), 'As we tell, so we come to know . . . the words and sentences we speak are speakers of us, as much, if not more, as we of them' (p. 123).

All this activity is part of the debate concerning changing views of what constitutes knowledge, moving towards a view of knowledge, culture and so on as being continually created through interaction rather than being 'out there', waiting to be passed on. In this debate, knowledge is evolved through relationship, and is not a fixed commodity to be extracted from an individual and distributed. Such a viewpoint supported the use by Allan and Ward (1999) of a story-telling approach to examining collaborative working. Each author independently wrote the short story of their meeting and first collaboration, which was subsequently annotated by them to consider similarities and differences in personal style, professional 'language' and so on. A short extract may be found in Box 10.11.

In order to support what might emerge as 'best practice' story-telling in organisations, if such a term can be used, we believe it would benefit practitioners to acquaint themselves with the history and practice, across disciplines, of research approaches and ontology. Such study is complementary to the more general study of psychology, philosophy, entertainment and the traditions of story-telling.

The Handbook of Ethnography (Atkinson *et al.* 2001) is a comprehensive review of the history, practices and issues in a wide range of settings, while Boje's *Narrative Methods for Organizational and Communications Research* (2001) concentrates on eight ways of using narratives in organisational research. There are many specialised and overview texts available from which to choose, and Symon and Cassell's *Qualitative Methods and Analysis in Organizational Research: A Practical Guide* (1999) includes a variety of story-related approaches including

BOX 10.11   Story and Collaborative Working

Our mutual friendship	Labels and Signposts		A traveller's tale
. . . What happened next was nothing until about six months later when two things happened.	Dormant assets	*Negotiated meaning*	Is it better to translate, to attempt a new language, or to seek new negotiated meanings? And what does it take to be skilful?
A university contracted us to develop part of an MBA programme. This seemed a perfect opportunity to involve J., combining complexity with knowledge and transition.	*Triggers*	Multiple narratives	I mention *I Am Phoenix* – a poetry book in which all the poems are for two voices. Sometimes the voices share a line, and sometimes they speak different lines
The second thing happened by chance. We were delivering a workshop at a conference and had a free place. We offered it to J. She accepted.	Serendipity		simultaneously. I want to find out where we will speak together and where separately.
So J., Sue and I ended up in Buxton one very rainy November. The plan was that J. would observe a workshop being run by Sue and me on the future role of librarians. What actually happened was quite different. J. played the role of workshop jester, challenging us all to rethink the language. In one perfect small moment she picked her way through a whole welter of words and created 'Nice Assertive Freedom Fighters' as the defining self-description of librarians. We have called it Nice Assertive Freedom Fighters ever since.	Twos and threes

Pivots

Language and labels

Librarians | Embedding *fractals*

Unfolding meaning

History Timelines Place

Person–person connections | I also want to find out if this story will have the whole Spark–Julie enterprise patterned within it. Fractals have a certain charm: each small iterative part unfolds the pattern for the whole, a little like a hologram. Of course, fractal patterns iterate the same formula, whereas V. and I may change ours.

There was a previous cup of tea, this time at the Charing Cross Hotel, where the waiters have splendid coat-tails. And I was talking with Claudine, who I'd met at a London School of |
| We decided to try to run future events as a trio, incorporating a free agent who would make the space safer, or challenge it. Word spread that Freedom Fighters had been fun. We were invited to do another workshop about story-telling for librarians. . . | Observers

Story-telling | | Economics Complexity seminar. She told me about a new business venture she was involved with, called Spark, and we shared our interests in change, story-telling, complexity, networking and so on. You really should meet Victoria, she said. . . |

Extracted from Allan and Ward (1999)

critical incident technique, conversation analysis and a chapter by Yiannis Gabriel. In his chapter, which is titled 'The Use of Stories', Gabriel states:

> Researchers who want to use stories as a research instrument . . . must rid themselves of the assumption that quality data are objective, reliable, accurate etc. and must be prepared to engage with the emotions and the meanings . . . the very recognition that a narrative constitutes or is moving towards becoming a story rather than a factual account depends on such an emotional engagement. (p. 136)

Conclusion

This chapter has built on the stories told in the rest of the book to offer a range of practical tips, exercises and ingredients that relate to different facets of story-telling in organisational settings. There are many, many more available than we could make room for here.

In the Further Reading and Resources section you will find some starting points from which to expand on what we have included.

Sometimes, looking at the workings or underpinnings of something can detract from its wonder. We hope instead to encourage interest in story-telling and speculation about the story-teller you may become. It will never be possible to reduce such a complex whole to component mechanics, and it is not our intention to do so.

Surprises will always occur because, in the world of story-telling, the trickster (or coyote) is never far away.

11

The Future of Story-Telling in Organisations

A story is like water
that you heat for your bath.

It takes messages between the fire
and your skin. It lets them meet,
and it cleans you!

From Rumi's 'Story Water'

This chapter looks to the future and suggests some ways in which story-telling in organisations might evolve. The future of story-telling in organisations depends on, and will itself influence, the future of organisations. Organisations and story-telling will co-evolve.

This chapter looks to the future in the following ways:

- We pick up key points from the seven histories we told in Chapters 2 to 8.
- We tell the story of an intellectual and emotional journey – the journey made by us, the three authors of this book, while writing it together.

- Once again, we look at a constant theme of the second half of the book – the link between story-telling and complexity – and at where this might lead us in future.
- We take up another theme – the link between story-telling and proper respect for human beings – also from a future-related perspective.
- We explore the effects of a wider practice of the art of story-telling on the emotional life of organisations.
- We look at possible negative effects of story-telling if there were to be a trend towards extreme behaviour in future organisations.
- Finally, we speculate about the interaction between story-telling and sustainability in a complex future world.

Key Points from the Seven Histories

In Chapter 2, the history of M4 Technology suggests one future direction for organisations: they will become more inclusive. To succeed in a knowledge economy, organisations must use the talents of all their people. This is a familiar cry, but we hope the tales we have told in this book have made it more than just a slogan. Inclusion means understanding the diverse talents of individuals and finding ways to use them well. It means finding constructive ways to cope with people's stress, doubts, fears and individual hang-ups. At M4 story-telling allowed people's personal characteristics to be appreciated by their colleagues, as well as binding everyone closer together. Inclusion would not have happened if there had not been a sincere respect for other people on the part of the founders of M4. That respect was there is illustrated by the story of the company's system for choosing its projects. Separately from the M4 history, the story about the Quaker meeting illustrates the same point: respect for others gives an organisation, religious or business, access to those people's knowledge and capabilities.

Stories showing leaders as human can be traditional (Alfred and the cakes; see page 30), emergent (Melissa gets egg on her face; page 22), or planned (Ethel the 'tea-lady', who is actually an actor; page 45). Melissa Thorpe was a strong personality and she was confident enough to be able to admit her mistakes, although this was hard for her to do. This suggests another future direction for organisations: towards servant leadership. The stories we told about Melissa and the sales people's bonuses (page 22) (and separately the story about Hatim and the Honda; page 24) illustrate this kind of leadership, where the common objective is more important than the dignity of the leader.

Servant leadership and inclusion do not remove the dangers of 'groupthink' – they might even make it worse. The stories of Abilene (page 39) and of Fred and the Police Camera (page 41) are examples of ways to question too easy a consensus without disrupting the group's cohesion.

The history of AutoCorp's learning, told in Chapter 3 (and continued in Chapter 6), includes several stories about senior people abusing their power and shows what a fear-ridden atmosphere such abuse can engender. Other stories in this history, like Sponsors and Targets (page 60) and F. Breather (page 66), demonstrated that brave people can successfully stand up to corporate bullies. And the tale of the Dragon Who Lived on the Edge of the World (page 135) showed how people with ability can blunder into fire-breathing mode without really meaning to. A natural, but unhelpful, response to bullying is to view yourself as a victim – the story of the Three Dogs (page 72) is about talented people becoming victims. Tommy Spriggett's decision to stop telling that story suggested that his section of AutoCorp is ready to assume an autonomous, not a victimised, role and to evolve towards self-organisation. Using everybody's talents will mean that organisations will, on a regular basis, have to learn to see situations from several viewpoints. The stories of the Two Frogs (page 73) and of the two cancer patients, Adele and Betty (page 71), remind us how different viewpoints can be – and how constructive the difference is in some situations, and how unrewarding in others.

Themis is an example of a completely non-hierarchical organisation. Some might say it is not an organisation at all. However, it has a clear function, which it performs effectively, with minimal resources. Themis helps busy people, many of them freelance, who need emotional support in their stressful lives and intellectual support for their continuing professional learning. They get these mostly by listening to others' stories and telling their own. The group also evolved a story-like form for their own meetings. Perhaps more formal organisations might, in future, benefit from setting up some Themis-like groups for their staff or adopting some of Themis's practice.

Chapter 5 included both a nice collection of stories from the NHS and another history – that of Gilbert Sammler and his Oncology Outcomes unit (page 112). It also introduced the ideas of Charles Hampden-Turner on the resolution of dilemmas. The first step in dilemma resolution is to get them into the open. This is not as easy as it might seem, since the distress caused by an active dilemma makes people find scapegoats or blame 'the system' rather than looking at what is really happening. To find out what is happening in an organisation, story-telling is the best diagnostic tool. Collect, analyse and feed back the stories that are being told around the organisation, and its dilemmas will start to emerge quite clearly, as they did from the stories about the doctors who ate pizza on the job, and the junior nurse who took it upon herself to tell the truth about a patient's condition. Once a dilemma is in the open, telling stories has another function: to provoke constructive resolution. Hampden-Turner writes: 'By helping the group reinterpret its history, myths and stories, you can give these new force, new meaning and new direction . . . only corporate cultures with a thirst for discovery can survive' (p. 205).

A further theme in Chapter 5 was complexity thinking, which we will take up again shortly. Chapter 6 – AutoCorp – Evolving – discussed uncertainty, ambiguity and self-organisation. The Chirpy story is an example of the creative capability that everyone can call on. It also emphasises the importance of relationships. Reframing is one way to tackle uncertainty and this was illustrated by the story of Sisyphus. Story-tellers like to keep their listeners or readers guessing – ambiguity is a natural device for them. Ambiguity can be so productive of creativity because it engages sensemaking abilities. The sports analogies story that Chuck Mascone liked to tell (page 144) was good for getting people to think about self-organisation. All the sports needed teamwork, but with very different ways of co-operating in each case.

The history of LIFT was told in Chapter 7, and it showed that innovation need not flag as an organisation matures. Perhaps this striking example of sustained innovation comes from its contact with very creative people – artists from all over the world. Perhaps it comes from the two-year cycle of renewal that has been its style for twenty years. Perhaps it has been aided by clear rules and strong values and by the occasional strategic review to which LIFT has subjected itself.

The stories told about LIFT, alongside stories about innovation in science, technology and business, suggest that the processes of innovation in these varied spheres are rather similar. Imagination, risk-taking, dedication to a vision, plus lots of hard grind are some of the common ingredients. The story of the Blue Tits and the Red Robins (page 160) carries a general lesson: birds that flock are birds that learn. Innovation is as much about generating a culture of trust and openness as it is about individual creativity. 'Flocking' in humans spreads knowledge and produces new songs.

The last of our histories was of the Kenya scenarios project. A wider range of mental models, shared by many people, is often the most significant result of a successful scenario project. It certainly was in the Kenya and South Africa cases, and this is also so for organisations. Scenarios produce multiple, alternative views of the future, so the process is more about adding new mental models than changing old ones. The process also encourages people to hold conflicting models in their minds as a means for dealing with uncertainty. Sharing models promotes dialogue about an unfolding future.

Story-telling was useful in the Kenya project in several ways. It helped in choosing subjects for research, and then in getting researchers to present their data in a form that would grab the attention of non-experts. It unlocked the imagination of workshop participants by bringing up emotionally charged memories and in seeing things about their country that were hard to articulate. (*Titanic* is an example; see page 193.) It helped people to understand the new mental models the scenario process created. Finally, story-telling skills were needed to write the scenarios themselves. As the scenarios spread around Kenya, they helped to create a more open political climate.

What We Learned While Writing This Book

One advantage of a multi-authored book is that the authors can learn from each other. The three of us decided to write *The Power of the Tale* because we'd all had good experiences of story-telling in organisations of different kinds, and we knew it worked. Two of us had been advisers to the LIFT Business/Arts Forum since its inception and had seen how practicing managers had gained new insights and learned new skills from the theatre. A different pair had devised a game as part of a short course on complexity thinking. This game connected abstract thinking with practical reality. One of us was a trained user of stories in organisation development. Two of us had worked in journalism or publishing. All of us had used story-telling to good effect in encouraging creative problem-solving and innovation.

What we learned while writing the book was the sheer range of situations in which story-telling works. We learned it could be used in many more places than we'd imagined. Here are some reasons for this:

- The better stories are, the more impact they have. This is obvious for writers or speakers who earn their living that way. But it is so even with people who have never thought of themselves as professional story-tellers. We asked ourselves this question: should story-tellers in organisations be mainly those with some native talent for story-telling? Our answer was no. Of course, those with special talents should develop them and use them. But organisations don't need an elite group who tell the tales while others sit and listen. Nearly everyone can be, and should be, a story-teller because of the variety this gives. This should be possible since story-telling talents are diverse.

- As we read and talked and gathered examples, we came to realise how pervasive story-telling already was in organisations and how under-rated was its influence. Because it is such a natural skill, we don't always notice it. This made us confident we weren't exaggerating the importance of our subject.

- We saw how nearly everyone's story-telling skills could be developed by example and by training. Creating apposite new stories, telling old ones in new ways, finding the right time and place to tell a story were all skills that could be learned or fine-tuned. There are certain skill sets, like financial analysis, negotiation or presentation, that are generally recognised as valuable for many people in organisations. You don't have to be a professional analyst or negotiator to benefit from greater skill in these areas. We came to see that it was the same for story-telling – nearly everyone can benefit by improving their story-telling skills.

- We came to appreciate how daunting story-telling might seem to the average uninitiated person. The standard seems to be set by Scheherazade, or by Chaucer's Canterbury pilgrims, and many of us, knowing we'll never reach that standard, decide not to try. But modest improvements are perfectly possible and very useful. We don't say that because we'll never be a J.P. Morgan, we therefore needn't try to learn anything about finance. We don't think because we'll never be a Jung, we can't benefit from some understanding of psychology. So we shouldn't give up practising story-telling or on improving our story-telling skills because we can't be world masters in the art.

- However, we learned that when the task is straightforward, story-telling may not be needed. 'Just do it', should then be the rule.
- Because story-telling is such a natural human activity, we realised it is easier for people to learn than, say, molecular biology or computer graphics or charity law. And for many people, it is more enjoyable. We saw how the narrative skills used every day in pubs or around coffee tables could be brought into the office or the conference room.
- We learned how story-telling can get us through tough moments in organisational life – when problems seem insoluble, conflicting groups seem irreconcilable, when situations are totally baffling. Then story-telling enables us to tap our own knowledge and experience in surprising ways, as happened when people in the Kenya workshop told stories about their earliest political memories. When a group is 'stuck' or cynical, its energy can often be revived by a few stories.
- We understood better why storying is the right response to complexity. The human brain has a narrative style and going along with that style gives greater capability.
- We remembered how exciting it was when a story engages a particular audience.
- As discussed in Chapter 9, we found that stories could be both supportive and subversive of authority in organisations. However, for people who have previously had little or no voice in their organisation, story-telling gives a particular opportunity to develop that voice.
- We already knew that story-telling had close connections with drama and visual art, and we learned that this was also the case in organisations.
- We were reminded of Laurel Richardson's views on writing (1998, quoted in Bolton 2001):

  I consider writing as a *method of inquiry*, a way of finding out about yourself and your topic. Although we usually think about writing as a mode of 'telling' about the social world, writing is not just a mopping-up activity . . . Writing is a way of 'knowing' – a method of discovery and analysis. By writing in different ways, we discover new aspects of our topic and our relationship to it. Form and content are inseparable. (p. 345)

- And it was brought home to us that, like birds that flock, story-tellers learn from each other and borrow from each other. Rudyard Kipling, without doubt a superb story-teller whatever you might feel about his politics, wrote this on mutual borrowing among story-tellers:

> When 'Omer smote 'is blooming lyre,
> He'd 'eard men sing by land an' sea,
> An' what he thought 'e might require,
> 'E went an' took – the same as me.
>
> The market-girls an' fishermen,
> The shepherds an' the sailors too,
> They 'eard old songs turn up again,
> But kep' it quiet – same as you!
>
> They knew 'e stole; 'e knowed they knowed.
> They didn't tell, nor make a fuss,
> But winked at 'Omer down the road,
> An' 'e winked back – the same as us.
>
> Wavell 1994, p. 362.

- We realised that our book itself is a story – a story about stories.

Story-Telling and Complexity

 Kevin Kelly's hyperbolic, but always interesting, book *New Rules for the New Economy* (1998) argues that the information economy works very differently from the old, material-based economy. He argues that the new economy is about relationships, about connectedness. He says that 'if you are in doubt about what technology to purchase, get the stuff that will connect the most widely, the most often, and in the most ways' (p. 139). He tells us to start with technological connections but then go on to build relationships built on trust. Complexity theory has many aspects, and for organisations its emphasis on relationships is one of the most important. The nerd from the story we told in Chapter 7, who picked up the talking frog (page 164), won't succeed in the new economy until he decides that a human relationship would be a good idea after all.

Story-telling's first big advantage for today's world is in strengthening interpersonal relationships, the bonds between humans. Story-telling in the form of gossip had survival value for hunter-gatherer tribes, because of the relationships it established in a tribe, and the deep understanding of other people's characters and motivations that it developed. Stories, together with other forms of knowledge, are easily replicable. I share an apple with you, and we each have half an apple. Share a story, and we each have a whole story, which we can in turn share with others. Stories spread like the networks of relationships they sustain.

Another advantage is its contribution to pattern recognition. The work of Damasio and of Bruner (see Chapters 5 and 9) suggests that human consciousness is closely linked to narrative, particularly autobiographical narrative. Thus, the computational power of the brain while using narrative may be far greater than when using a linear or deductive approach. Stories may be dismissed with a sneer. If factual, they are 'only anecdotal evidence'; if not, they are 'just fiction'. But people who are active in an organisation, or who are immersed in a process like the Kenya scenarios project, will be aware of a huge amount of data. The problem is to make sense of it all. Stories may be the only way to get to the heart of really complex situations. If you tell stories about something you have noticed but cannot explain, you will probably enjoy the benefit of this built-in pattern-recognition facility.

The connection of story-telling with self-organisation may be less direct than its connection with relationship building and pattern recognition. Self-organisation is clearly dependent on the strength of the interpersonal relationships involved. Pattern recognition has much in common with re-framing or re-conceptualisation, which we discussed in Chapter 5, and with innovation, discussed in Chapter 7. The processes of re-framing and innovation are aided by the use of narrative. Looking to the future, we can forecast a co-evolutionary growth of self-organisation and story-telling.

The future of story-telling may include widespread agreement on the value of narratives and clearer distinction between different narrative types. Remarks, fables, myths and tales may come to have their separate places in organisational life. At present these distinctions do not, to us, seem particularly important. This is why we have used the terms 'story' or 'tale' in most places in this book. However, this might change in the future.

Respect for Other People

In Chapter 10 we noted that story-tellers have to consider the ethics of what they are doing. There are certain rules, such as leaving theapy to the professionals. But respect for others is the main guideline. Respect and care for others doesn't mean you can meet their every need. Likewise, respect doesn't mean going along with everything others say or do. The concept of 'tough love' and the distinction between assertion and aggression tell us that true care for others isn't always soft. Nevertheless, we must be on our guard against unwitting hardness. In his *Contingency, Irony and Solidarity*, Richard Rorty (1989) writes that the centre of personal morality is constant learning to be less cruel to others. He says that this learning comes not from moral analysis but from stories.

The stories Rorty wants us to read are mainly great novels. He says these can be divided into two kinds: those that help us to see the potentially cruel effects of social practices and institutions and those that help us to see similar effects from our own private idiosyncrasies. The first kind includes novels like *Les Misérables.* The second kind includes novels like *Lolita.* Rorty writes that in *Animal Farm*, Orwell made his point by 'retelling the political history of his century in terms suitable for children'. By leaving political analysis on one side, and telling a simple tale, the horror of the betrayal of the other animals by the pigs becomes clear.

Some of the stories we have told in this book work in the same way. For instance, the Dragon who Lived on the Edge of the World (page 135) did lots of damage, but in the end he was able to control his fire-breathing. By reading about Humbert Humbert's callous lust, about Napoleon's manipulation of his fellow pigs and Sam the Dragon's clumsy behaviour we notice things about ourselves, and others, that are actually, if unthinkingly, cruel. This is why story-telling tends to make the world a better place, whether the tales are told by writers like Victor Hugo, Vladimir Nabokov or George Orwell, or by any one of us in an organisation.

We will end this section on respect for others with a story about two elderly ladies.

They had been friends for decades, sharing all kinds of activities and adventures. Lately they had only been able to meet to play cards a few times a week. One day, one of the ladies looked at the other and said, 'Now don't be cross with me. I know we've been friends for a long time, but I just can't think of your name. I've thought and thought but I can't remember it. Please tell me what your name is.' Her friend glared at her. For several minutes she just stared. Finally she asked, 'How soon do you need to know?'

Art and Emotion

If story-telling becomes regular practice in many organisational settings; if, through widespread use, story-telling skills proliferate in organisations of every kind; and if more and more people take care to learn the art of the story, then there could be a big shift in organisational culture. Command-and-control organisational models inevitably suppress emotions. This is logical. We all know from personal experience how uncontrollable emotions can be. But self-organising models of organisation will have to find an open and prominent place for emotion. For instance, the personal pain of being fired, or of doing the firing, or of seeing your friends and colleagues being fired while you survive, would not be denied, or covered up by descriptions like 'a necessary exercise in downsizing'. Even the occasional sadistic delight in others' misery might need to be recognised.

A 'community of practice' that regularly and transparently surfaces emotions will be more robust than one that tries to suppress them. Constantly recognising the (minor) emotional content of minor issues, bringing it out and giving it its due, prepares the community for rarer major issues. And if skills for doing this spread throughout an organisation, it will be able to accept that around every issue, minor or major, there is a tangle of facts, values and feelings. The communicative competence that can cope with this tangle provides the organisation with emotional intelligence and robustness.

Chris Mellor, CEO of AWG PLC (formerly Anglian Water PLC) has a passion for learning and an appreciation of the role of emotion in business. When asked, he has his own story to tell of the part of the organisational transition process that meant he had to tell senior and valued people that they no longer had a position in the organisation.

People, whose emotional as well as financial lives were tied in with the organisation, didn't want to leave. He thought that nobody would want to speak to him afterwards, but he was advised to have a leaving event for all the people who had been made redundant, and he did so. 'One by one,' he says, 'each person was able to stand up and say how sorry they were to go, and to explain their sadness with great dignity. It wasn't planned in that way, it's just what they did. And I cried. I was deeply sad too. But it was the right thing to do. To give a proper place for all those emotions. It was important for me, and people told me on that evening, and have told me since, how important it was for them too.'

This isn't a story that Chris trots out as a party piece. But if the subject comes up, and he's asked, that's the personal story he tells.

At the start of William Thackeray's novel *Vanity Fair*, two teenage girls are saying goodbye for ever to Miss Pinkerton's Academy for Young Ladies. One girl, Amelia Sedley, is the daughter of a rich merchant. As she goes, she carries with her Miss Pinkerton's flowery letter to Mrs Sedley and a copy of Dr Johnson's Dictionary. The other girl, Becky Sharp, is poor and kept her place at the school through drudgery of all kinds. Miss Pinkerton thinks Becky does not deserve a dictionary, but her more kindly sister slips her a copy. However, just as the coach drives off, Becky flings the book back into the garden. Amelia taxes Becky: how could you do that? 'I hate the whole house,' is Becky's reply. 'For two years I have only had insults and outrage . . .'. Becky Sharp is clever, unscrupulous and determined to make her way in the world. As painted by Thackeray, it is a world as ruthless, greedy and boot-licking as the worst Wall Street brokerage. If Becky actually was as coolly calculating as she planned always to be, she would have kept the dictionary. It might have been of some use, or she could have given it away. She upset Amelia, whom she needed as a friend. And insulting Miss Pinkerton and her kind sister could do Becky no good in the world. But the horror of her servitude at the Academy and the joy of her release aroused strong emotions in her. At that moment her caution went out of the window with the dictionary. This incident shows us Becky's heart, making us like her in spite of her grave faults, and foreshadowing the other much more serious lapses from calculating behaviour that happen later in the novel. It is an example of how art can give us insight into emotion; and of why *Vanity Fair* continues to be read and made into films long after it was written.

Negative Possibilities

The power of the tale could, like other forms of power, be used for bad ends. Stories connect with emotions, such as anger and hate, and can easily be used to whip up intolerance and antagonism towards a minority. The Nazi myth of racial superiority is one example of a terrible use of a story; and a rumour that leads to a lynching is another.

Elias Canetti in *Crowds and Power* (1973) writes that one of the most striking traits of a crowd is the feeling of being persecuted, 'a peculiar angry sensitiveness and irritability directed against those it has once and forever nominated as enemies' (p. 24). Tabloid journalists and unscrupulous politicians can play on this paranoid tendency, as they do in many European countries, making immigrants the enemy.

In organisations, as well as crowds, carefully placed stories may unsettle a rival in a battle for power, or disrupt a coalition that is pressing for particular policies. Whether such tactics are practised by the organisation's leadership, or by dissident groups, they usually involve telling different stories to different people. It is much harder to play these games in a culture of openness, and an organisation which respects people and promotes autonomy of action is less likely to be infected by paranoia. Alertness to stories being told in the organisation will help to spot sources of infection.

However, if the future of organisations were to fall back towards secretive, hierarchical modes, then story-telling would in some ways aid the fall. But as the story of Radio Trottoir in Chapter 1 suggests (page 5), stories would also undermine these modes of management or politics. As we have said, story-telling and organisation style will co-evolve, whether the direction of evolution is desirable or undesirable.

Story-Telling and Sustainability

In the twenty-first century, humankind may face less danger of eliminating itself through the use of weapons of mass destruction than it did in the last century, but the threat from environmental degradation – conversely, is growing and may eventually prove to be an even more serious danger. In this final section of our book, we look briefly at story-telling as a way of reducing environmental threat – or in other words, how the power of the tale might help to create a sustainable world.

Lynton Keith Caldwell's article (1999) in the journal *Politics and the Life Sciences* had the title: 'Is humanity destined to self-destruct?' and speculated that there might be no further future for humanity because 'the ingenuity of humans may impel them to their own demise' (p. 3). Sardonically, one could say that this would be the ultimate in self-organisation. In the next issue of the same journal (Caldwell and others, 1999), a number of writers responded to Caldwell's question, including Donald Michael (p. 247) who wrote that 'whatever happens to the human race, in the large, is too complex, too interconnected, too dynamic to comprehend'. Michael is saying that analysis alone will not be enough for us to achieve sustainability. If so, we should apply, on a grand scale, the lesson that when we have noticed something we cannot explain, we should tell stories about it. This colossal problem will need many, many stories.

One of us once heard a story told by a young Dutch development worker.

This young man was asked to join a meeting in Cameroon. The local ruler, called the Fon, and his elders were adjudicating in a dispute between a husband and wife. First one of the elders told a story about a similar dispute in the past, about the judgement that was reached in that case and about the outcome following the judgement. Silence followed as the Fon and the elders pondered that story's implications. Then another elder told another story that also had a bearing on the case. More silence. Then another story, followed by more silence. Finally, an elder recalled a story the others had forgotten. When they heard this one, all the elders said 'Aaah. Aaah.' The Fon said, 'That is the story. It is the one which tells us what to do about this man and this wife.'

To reach a judgement in the hugely important, hugely difficult, case of sustainability, it is essential that the human race listens to many stories. We must hope that all stories get a wide hearing. We must hope that among these stories some will turn out to be reasonable candidates for guiding us to a sustainable future. And we must hope that people will carefully ponder their implications, preferably in periods of silence; although silence is not much evident in today's media or politics.

What would happen then? Would it be desirable to narrow down the choice to a single story? Or should we hope that multiple stories might live alongside each other? For a complex situation a single story is unlikely to give us the guidance we need.

The characteristic of stories, as illustrated by the practice of scenario-building, is that the human mind can easily hold them together as alternatives. Humans do not necessarily seek to tell a single tale. Post-modern thought suggests that there need not be a single story about anything. Post-modernism has a slogan: no meta-narrative, meaning no single narrative that trumps all other narratives. So we would advocate lots of story-telling about the possible human reaction to the problems of the environment, not just one story.

Multiple stories should be told, re-told, and adapted to the understanding of various audiences. Each story should give birth to novels, plays, films, music and visual art, as well as to rituals, ceremonies, temples and symbols. Philosophy, history, the social and natural sciences should all interact with the central stories. Each central story should be strengthened as much as possible, not by rubbishing its rivals, but by making it as coherent, plausible and entertaining as possible. Story-telling, that natural human activity, might then ensure that humanity does not destroy itself.

References

Adler P. S. and Borys, B. (1996) Two types of bureaucracy: enabling and coercive. *Administrative Science Quarterly* **41**, 61–89.

Allan, J. and Ward, V. (1999) Creating the future: a narrative enquiry into collaborative working. From a workshop presentation, 'Stories of the Future: a live case study and participative enquiry'. In Proceedings of the AMED (Association for Management Development) Frontiers Conference, 1999. London: AMED.

Anderson, B. (1991) *Imagined Communities*, second edition. London: Verso.

Anderson, J. R. *Cognitive Psychology and its Implications*, second edition. New York: WH Freeman and Co.

Arendt, H. (1973) *On Revolution*. London: Pelican. (First published 1963.)

Argyris, C. (1992) *On Organizational Learning*. Oxford: Blackwell.

Argyris, C., Putnam, R. and Smith, D. M. (1985) *Action Science*. San Francisco: Jossey Bass.

Atkinson, P., Coffey, A., Delamont, S., Lofland, J. and Lofland, L. (2001) *Handbook of Ethnography*. London: Sage.

Baddeley, A. (1976) *The Psychology of Memory*. New York: Basic Books.

Bandura, A. (1977) Self-efficacy: Toward a Unifying Theory of Behavioural Change. *Psych. Rev.* **84**, 191–215.

Bandura, A. (1977) *Social Learning Theory*. Englewood Cliffs, NJ: Prentice-Hall.

Barber, B. (1984) *Strong Democracy: Participatory Politics for a New Age*. Berkeley: University of California Press.

Bateson, G. (2000) *Steps to an Ecology of Mind*. Chicago: University of Chicago Press. (Originally published in 1972.)

Berne, E. (1975) *What Do You Say After You Say Hello?* London: Corgi/Transworld.

Bettelheim, B. (1991) *The Uses of Enchantment*. London: Penguin. (First published in Great Britain by Thames and Hudson, 1976.)

Bohm, D. (1983) *Wholeness and the Implicate Order*. New York: Harper & Rowe.

Boisot, M. H. (1999) *Knowledge Assets: Securing Competitive Advantage in the Information Economy*. Oxford: Oxford University Press.

Boje, D. M. (1991) The storytelling organization: a study of story performance in an office supply firm. *Administrative Science Quarterly* **36**, 106–126.

Boje, D. M. (2001) *Narrative Methods for Organizational and Communications Research*. London: Sage.

Bolton, G. (1999) Stories at work: reflective writing for practitioners. *The Lancet* **354**, 241–243.

Bolton, G. (2001) *Reflective Practice: Writing and Professional Development*. London: Paul Chapman.

Bruner, J. (1990) *Acts of Meaning*. London: Harvard University Press.

Buber, M. (1958) *I and Thou*. Edinburgh: T and T Clark.

Burgoyne, J., Pedler, M. and Boydell, T. (1994) *Towards the Learning Company: Concepts and Practices*. Maidenhead, Berkshire: McGraw-Hill.

Caldwell, L. K. (1999) Is humanity destined to self-destruct? *Politics and the Life Sciences* **18**(1), 3–14.

Caldwell, L. K. and others (1999) Symposium: humanity and self-destruction. *Politics and the Life Sciences* **18**(2), 201–283.

Calman, K. C. (2000) *A Study of Story Telling Humour and Learning in Medicine*. London: The Nuffield Trust.

Cameron, J. (1995) *The Artist's Way*. London: Pan.

Canetti, E. (1960) *Crowds and Power*, translated by Carol Stewart. London: Penguin.

Clarkson, P. (1991) *Gestalt Counselling in Action*. London: Sage.

Clarkson, P. (1996) *The Bystander: An End to Innocence in Human Relationships?* London: Whurr.

Cohen, T. (1999) *Jokes: Philosophical Thoughts on Joking Matters*. Chicago: University of Chicago Press.

Csikszentmihalyi, M. (1997) *Creativity: Flow and the Psychology of Discovery and Invention*. New York: HarperPerennial.

Damasio, A. (2000) *The Feeling for What Happens: Body and Emotion in the Making of Consciousness*. London: Heinemann.

De Geus, A. (1997) *The Living Company*. Boston: Harvard Business School Press.

Denning, S. (2000) *The Springboard: How Storytelling Ignites Action in Knowledge-Era Organisations*. London: Butterworth-Heinemann.

Dixon, N. M. (1994) *The Organizational Learning Cycle: How we can learn collectively*. Maidenhead, Berkshire: McGraw-Hill.

Dixon, N. M. (1998) *Dialogue at Work*. London: Lemos and Crane.

Dunbar, R. (1996) *Grooming, Gossip and the Evolution of Language*. London: Faber & Faber.

Edmondson, A. (1999) Psychological safety and learning behavior in work teams. *Administrative Science Quarterly* **44**, 350–383.

Empson, W. (1961) *Seven Types of Ambiguity*. Harmondsworth: Penguin (First published 1930).

Estes, C. P. (1992) *Women Who Run with the Wolves*. London: Rider.

Fairtlough, G. (1994) *Creative Compartments: A Design for Future Organisation*. London: Adamantine Press.

Fineman, S. and Gabriel, Y. (1996) *Experiencing Organizations*. London: Sage.

Flecker, J. E. (1960) *The Golden Journey to Samarkand*, in *The Penguin Dictionary of Quotations*. London: Penguin.

Fordham, F. (1991) *An Introduction to Jung's Psychology*. London: Penguin. (First published by Pelican Books in 1953; reprinted with revisions 1957.)

Gabriel, Y. (1998) The use of stories. In G. Symon and C. Cassell (eds) (1999) *Qualitative Methods and Analysis in Organizational Research: A Practical Guide*. London: Sage.

Gabriel, Y. (2000) *Storytelling in Organizations: Facts, Fictions and Fantasies*. Oxford: Oxford University Press.

Gardner, H. (1997) *Leading Minds*. London: HarperCollins.

Gardner, R. A. (1993) *Storytelling in Psychotherapy with Children*. Northvale, NJ/London: Jason Aronson.

Gendlin, E. (1991) Thinking beyond patterns: body, language and situations. Reprinted from B. den Ouden and M. Moen (eds) *The Presence of Feeling in Thought*. New York: Peter Lange.

Glaser, B. and Strauss, A. (1967) *The Discovery of Grounded Theory*. Chicago: Aldine.

Greenhalgh, T. (2000) *Telling the Story of Diabetes*. In Wellcome News.

Habermas, J. (1984) *The Theory of Communicative Action*, translated by Thomas McCarthy. London: Heinemann.

Hampden-Turner, C. (1990) *Corporate Culture: From Vicious to Virtuous Circles*. London: Hutchinson.

Harris, P. (2000) *The Work of the Imagination*. Oxford: Blackwell.

Harvey, J. B. (1996) *The Abilene Paradox and Other Meditations on Management*. San Francisco: Jossey-Bass.

Heath, S. B. and Smythe, L. (1999) *ArtShow: Youth and Community Development*. Partners for Livable Communities, Washington DC.

van der Heijden, K. (1996) *Scenarios: The Art of Strategic Conversation*. Chichester: Wiley.

Heinzen, B. (1994) Political Experiments of the 1990s. In *The Deeper News*, Vol. 5, No. 3. Global Business Network, Emeryville, CA.

Hobsbawm, E. and Ranger, T. (1992) *The Invention of Tradition*. Cambridge: Canto.

Honey, P. and Mumford, A. (1982) *The Learning Styles Questionnaire*. Maidenhead, Berkshire: Peter Honey. (New edition (2002) published by Peter Honey Publications Ltd.)

Houston, G. (1990) *The Little Red Book of Gestalt*. London: The Rochester Foundation.

Jung, C. G. (1995) *Memories, Dreams, Reflections*. London: Fontana Press/ HarperCollins.

Kahane, A. (1996) *Learning from Mont Fleur: Scenarios as a Tool for Discovering Common Ground*. Hamilton, MA: Centre for Generative Leadership.

Karpman, S. (1968) Fairy-Tales and Script Drama Analysis. *Transactional Analysis Bulletin* (1976): *Selected Articles from Vols 1 through 9, 51–56.* San Francisco: TA Press.

Keillor, G. (1989) Lake Wobegon Days. BBC Radio Collection Audio Cassette. London: BBC Audio.

Keillor, G. (1993) Lake Wobegon Days. London: Faber & Faber.

Kelly, G. A. (1955) *The Psychology of Personal Constructs*, vols 1 and 2. New York: WW Norton.

Kelly, K. (1998) *New Rules for the New Economy: Ten Radical Strategies for a Connected World*. New York: Penguin Putnam.

Kipling, R. (1992) When 'Omer Struck 'is Blooming Lyre. In A.P. Wavell (ed.) *Other Men's Flowers*. London: Pimlico.

Kleiner, A. (2001) The three imperatives: a design for creative awareness in putting a story together. In *Journal of Storytelling and Business Excellence*, Jonesborough, TN: Storytelling Foundation International. See also `www.storytelling.net/articles`.

Kleiner, A. and Roth, G. (1997) Learning Histories: A New Tool For Turning Organizational Experience Into Action. Working Paper, MIT 21st Century Corporation Project. See `www.learninghistories.com`.

Kleiner, A. and Roth, G. (1999) *Car Launch: The Human Side of Management Change*. New York: Oxford University Press.

Kolb, D. A. (1976) *The Learning Style Inventory: Technical Manual*. Boston: McBer.

Kolb, D. A. (1984) *Experiential Learning: Experience as the Source of Learning and Development*. Englewood Cliffs, NJ: Prentice Hall.

Kolb, D. A. and Fry, R. E. (1975) Toward an applied theory of experiential learning. In C. Cooper (ed.) *Theories of Group Processes*. Chichester: Wiley.

Kraiger, K., Ford, J. K. and Salas, E. (1993). Application of cognitive, skill-based, and affective theories of learning outcomes to new methods of training evaluation. *Journal of Applied Psychology*, **78**, 311–328.

Lahad, M. (2000) *Creative Supervision*. London: Jessica Kingsley.

Lakoff, G. and Johnson, M. (1980) *Metaphors We Live By*. Chicago: University of Chicago Press.

LaMarsh, J. (1995) *Changing the Way We Change: Gaining Control of Major Operational Change*. Reading, MA: Addison-Wesley.

Lang, A. (1951) The two frogs. In M. L. Shedlock, *The Art of the Story-Teller*. London: Constable and Company.

Lave, J. and Wenger, E. (1999) *Situated Learning: Legitimate peripheral participation*. Cambridge: Cambridge University Press.

Lewin, R. and Regine, B. (1999) *The Soul at Work: Unleashing the Power of Complexity Science for Business Success*. London: Orion Business.

Luria, A. R. (1976) Cognitive development: its cultural and social foundations. In W. J. Ong *Orality and Literacy: The technologizing of the word*. London: Routledge.

Maina, B. and Muliro, A. (2000). *Kenya at the Crossroads: Scenarios for Our Future*. Nairobi: Institute for Economic Affairs.

Mair (1990). Telling psychological tales. *International Journal of Personal Construct Psychology*, **3**, 121–135.

Malby, R. and Pattison, S. (1999) Living Values in the NHS: Stories from the NHS's 50th Year. London: The King's Fund.

McKelvey, M. (1996) *Evolutionary Innovation: The Business of Biotechnology*. Oxford: Oxford University Press.

Michael, D. N. (1985) The futurist tells stories. *Futures*, 17 April.

Michael, D. N. (1997) *Learning to Plan – and Planning to Learn*, second edition. Miles River Press. (First edition published by Jossey-Bass in 1973.)

Michael, D. N. and Anderson, W. T. (1987) Norms in conflict and confusion: six stories in search of an author. *Technological Forecasting & Social Change*, **31**, 2 April 1987, pp. 107–116.

Milburn, M. and Conrad, S. (1996) *The Politics of Denial*. Massachusetts: MIT Press.

Nonaka, I. and Takeuchi, H. (1995) *The Knowledge-Creating Company: How Japanese Companies Create the Dynamics of Innovation*. New York: Oxford University Press.

Ong, W. J. (1982) *Orality and Literacy: The technologizing of the word*. London: Routledge.

Ostrom, E. (1990) *Governing the Commons: The Evolution of Institutions for Collective Action*. Cambridge: Cambridge University Press .

Perls, F., Hefferline, R. F. and Goodman, P. (1994) *Gestalt Therapy: Excitement and Growth in the Human Personality*. London: Souvenir Press.

Pirandello, L. (1954) *Six Characters in Search of an Author*, translated by Frederick May. London: Heinemann Drama Library.

Polanyi, M. (1967). *The Tacit Dimension*. Garden City, New York: Anchor Books.

Putnam, L. L., Phillips, N. and Chapman, P. (1996) Metaphors of communication and organization. In S. R. Clegg, C. Hardy and W. R. Nord (eds) *Handbook of Organization Studies*. London: Sage.

Raymond, E. S. (1999) *The Cathedral and the Bazaar: Musings on Linux and Open Source by an Accidental Revolutionary*. Sebastopol, CA: O'Reilly.

Richardson, L. (1999) Writing: a method of inquiry. In N.K. Denzin and Y.S. Lincoln (eds) *Collecting and Interpreting Qualitative Materials*. London: Sage.

Rogers, C. R. (1951) *Client-centred Therapy: Its Current Practice, Implications and Theory*. Boston: Houghton-Mifflin.

Rorty, R. (1989) *Contingency, Irony and Solidarity*. Cambridge: Cambridge University Press.

Rumi, (1988) Be with those who help your being. In *These Branching Moments*, translated by Coleman Barks.

Rumi, (1998) Story water. In *Lion Of the Heart*, translated by Coleman Barks with John Moyne. London: Penguin Arkana. (First published in the USA in *The Essential Rumi*, HarperCollins, 1995.)

Rushdie, S. (1990) *Haroun and the Sea of Stories*. London: Faber & Faber.

Schein, E. H. (1992) *Organizational Culture and Leadership*. San Francisco: Jossey-Bass.

Schein, E. H. (1993) How can organizations learn faster? The challenge of entering the green room. *Sloan Management Review*, Winter, 85–92.

Seely-Brown, J. and Duguid, P. (2000) *The Social Life of Information*. Boston, MA: Harvard Business School Press.

Shields, C. (1995) *Small Ceremonies*. London: Fourth Estate. (Originally published in 1976.)

Snowden, D. (2001) Presentation at 'Linkage' conference on 'Knowledge Management and Organizational Learning', London, March.

Sparkteam and Ward, V. (2001) *Corporania (The Treasure Map)*. London: Sparkpress.

Sunderland, M. (1993) *Draw On Your Emotions* (illustrated by P. Engleheart). Bicester: Speechmark Publishing.

Symon, G. and Cassell, C. (eds) (1999) *Qualitative Methods and Analysis in Organizational Research: A Practical Guide*. London: Sage.

Tannenbaum, S. and Yukl, G. (1992) Training and development in work organisations. *Annual Review of Psychology*, **43**, 400–434.

Vickers, G. (1985) *The Art of Judgement: A Study of Policy Making*. London: Harper and Row (First published in 1965).

Wack, P. (1985) Scenarios: uncharted waters ahead. *Harvard Business Review*, Sep–Oct, 73–89.

Wack, P. (1985) Scenarios: shooting the rapids. *Harvard Business Review*, Nov–Dec, 39–149.

Wahl, B. (publication forthcoming) The body in counselling psychology. In W. Dryden, R. Woolfe and S. Strawbridge (eds) *Handbook of Counselling Psychology*, second edition. London: Sage.

Watson, J. D. (1968) *The Double Helix: A Personal Account of the Discovery of DNA*. London: Weidenfeld and Nicholson.

Wavell, A. P. (1992) *Other Men's Flowers. An anthology of poetry*. London: Pimlico. (First published 1944.)

Weick, K. E. (1995) *Sensemaking in Organizations*. London: Sage.

Wenger, E. (1998) *Communities of Practice: Learning, Meaning and Identity*. Cambridge: Cambridge University Press.

Wenger, E. (2001) Review of 'The Social Life of Information' by J. Seely-Brown and P. Duguid. *Reflections: The SoL Journal* **2**(3), 68.

West, M. A. (2000) State of the art: Creativity and innovation at work. *Psychologist* **13**(9), 460–464.

Yontef, G. M. (1980) Gestalt therapy: a dialogic method. In Clarkson P. (1999) *Gestalt Counselling in Action*. London: Sage.

Further Reading and Resources

Further Reading

Aesop (1998) *The Complete Fables*. Translated by Robert and Olivia Temple, London: Penguin.

Andersen, H. C. (1993) *Andersen's Fairy Tales* (complete and unabridged). Ware, Herts: Wordsworth Editions Ltd.

Arendt, H. (1958) *The Human Condition*. Chicago: University of Chicago Press.

Aristotle (1996) *Poetics*. Translated by Malcolm Heath, London: Penguin. An account of the components of Greek tragedy.

Benjamin, W. (1999) *Illuminations*. Translated by H. Zorn, London: Pimlico. Particularly for the chapter on The Story-teller.

Berman, M. and Brown, D. (2000) *The Power of Metaphor*. Story Telling and Guided Journeys for Teachers, Trainers and Therapists. Carmarthen: Crown House.

Boal, A. (1992) *Games for Actors and Non-Actors*. London: Routledge.

Boal, A. (1995) *The Rainbow of Desire*. London: Routledge.
Creator of Forum Theatre – giving voice to people in circumstances of oppression, through telling and re-telling their stories.

Bulfinch, T. (1977) *The Age of Fable*. First published in 1855 as The Illustrated Bulfinch's Mythology. New York: Macmillan.
Wide-ranging illustrated journey through legend, myth and fable, including Greek, Roman, Celtic, Nordic and Eastern characters.

Campbell, J. with Moyers, B. (1989) *The Power of Myth*. London: Doubleday/ Transworld Publishers.
Illustrated text of a conversation between Bill Moyers and Joseph Campbell, also filmed for a Public Broadcasting Service series, ranging widely across myths and spirituality.

Carter, A. (1984) *The Bloody Chamber and Other Stories*. Harmondsworth, Middlesex: Penguin.
Grown-up versions of well-known fairy-tales, one of which was turned into the film *The Company of Wolves*.

DeMello, A. (1990) *Taking Flight*. New York: Doubleday.

Edwards, B. (1988) *Drawing on the Right Side of the Brain*. Glasgow: William Collins.
Fun and interesting have-a-go book for encouraging creativity.

Egudu, R. (1973) *The Calabash of Wisdom and Other Igbo Stories*. Enugu: Nok Publishers.

Gendlin, E. T. (1981). *Focusing*, revised edition. New York: Bantam.

Goldratt, E. M. and Cox, J. (1998) *The Goal: A Process of Ongoing Improvement*, second edition. Aldershot: Gower.
A novel about a hard-pressed manufacturing manager, written to illustrate the theory of constraints.

Graves, R. (1965) *Greek Gods and Heroes*. New York: Random House.
Small paperback containing tales of ancient Greece re-told by Robert Graves.

Graves, R. (1984) *Greek Myths* (illustrated edition). London: Penguin.
A comprehensive and attractive text.

Green, R. L. (1970) *Tales of Ancient Egypt*. Harmondsworth: Puffin.

Greenhalgh, T. and Hurwitz, B. (eds) (1998). *Narrative-based Medicine: Dialogue and Discourse in Clinical Practice*. London: BMJ Publications.

The Brothers Grimm (1974) *The Complete Grimm's Fairy Tales*. New York: Pantheon Books. (Originally published in 1944 by Pantheon.)
One of the Pantheon range of books, with an introduction by Padraic Colum and commentary by Joseph Campbell. Text based on a translation by Margaret Hunt, revised, corrected and completed by James Stern.

James, M. and Jongeward, D. (1992) *Born to Win: Transactional Analysis with Gestalt Experiments*. Wokingham: Addison-Wesley.
Theoretically and practically interesting self-development book looking at scripts and stories.

Juraver, J. (1995) *Contes Creoles*. Dakar: Editions Presence Africaine.

Kipling, R. (1994) *Just So Stories*. London: Penguin.

Kleiner, A. (1996) *The Age of Heretics: Heroes, Outlaws, and the Forerunners of Corporate Change*. New York: Doubleday.

Lakoff, G. (1987) *Women, Fire and Dangerous Things*. Chicago: University of Chicago Press.

Lang, A. (1965) *The Blue Fairy Book*. New York: Dover.
The first in the series of fairy books (also including the Brown, Crimson, Green, Grey, Lilac, Olive, Orange, Pink, Red, Violet and Yellow fairy books) edited by Andrew Lang and reprinted as unabridged and unaltered versions of works published by Longmans, Green and Co. circa 1889. Tale of the two frogs reprinted in *The Art of the Storyteller*, Marie L. Shedlock.

Lehrer, W. (1995) *Brother Blue*. Seattle: Bay Press.
Extraordinary book of tales from and about Brother Blue (aka Dr Hugh Morgan Hill), a story-teller from the USA who is much travelled and can be found at story-telling events in the UK. The typeface tries to follow his vocal style. An audio cassette is also available.

Lightman, A. (1994) *Einstein's Dreams*. London: Sceptre.
Engage your imagination with this fictional work exploring what would happen if time didn't run as it usually does . . .

Lipman, D. (1995) *The Storytelling Coach*. Little Rock, Arkansas: August House.
Doug Lipman is an American story-teller and coach of story-tellers. His book explains his view on coaching. However, because story-telling is his focus, it contains many anecdotes and insights of help to budding story-tellers. See also Website listings.

McAdams, D. P. (1997) *The Stories We Live By*: Personal Myths and the Making of the Self. New York: Guilford Press.
Excellent review concerning the viewpoint that life is a story.

McLeod, J. (1997) *Narrative and Psychotherapy*. London: Sage.
Explains the therapeutic process in terms of it being a story-telling process.

Megginson, D. and Clutterbuck, D. (1999) *Mentoring in Action*. London: Kogan Page.

Mellon, N. (1993) *Storytelling and The Art of Imagination*. Shaftesbury, Dorset: Element Books.
A host of story 'ingredients' are explored in this book, with short practical exercises.

Michael, D. N. (1992) *Governing by Learning*. In S. A. Rosell et al *Governing in an Information Age*. Montreal: Institute for Research on Public Policy.

Parkin, M. (1998) *Tales for Trainers: Using Stories and Metaphors to Facilitate Learning*. London: Kogan Page.

Patrick, J. (1992) *Training: Research and Practice*. London: Academic Press.

Patten, B. (1999) *Beowulf and the Monster* (illustrated by Chris Riddell). London: Scholastic.

Shah, I. (1993) *The Subtleties of the Inimitable Mulla Nasrudin*. London: Octagon Press.

Sherlock, P. (1978) *West Indian Folk Tales*. Oxford: Oxford University Press.

Varela, F. J., Thompson, E. and Rosch, E. (1993) *The Embodied Mind, Cognitive Science and Human Experience*. Cambridge: MIT Press.

Whyte, D. (1994) *The Heart Aroused: Poetry and the Presentation of the Soul in Corporate America*. New York: Currency Doubleday.

Pantheon Press also publish collections of fairy-tales from a range of different countries including Russia, Norway and India.

Web Addresses

The Internet is an ever-changing virtual space and Website addresses change all the time. These sites were current at the time this book went to press.

`www.aradford.co.uk` – Newsletter, books/resources, events and international contacts concerning appreciative inquiry as a developmental approach. Comprehensive introductory site.

`http://cbae.nmsu.edu/~dboje/` – David Boje's 'The Story-telling Organisation' game. Links to information on a wide variety of related topics and Boje's work.

`www.ccweb.co.uk/home1.html` – A graphical storyscape about stories.

`www.davidwhyte.com` – Including the use of poetry in/about organisational life (poetry@work).

`www.emerson.org.uk/storytelling.htm` – Courses in story-telling. Links to a range of other story-telling and creative writing sites.

`www.focusing.org` – This site concerns specific instructions for direct access to implicit experiencing. It also has a fully developed philosophy on the articulation of implicit knowledge, concept-formation from non-representational 'responsive order', generating logical terms from newly emergent factors, bodily knowing, thinking beyond conceptual patterns, Wittgenstein and a 'process model' for generating new concepts.

www.folklore-society.com/ – London-based registered charity dating back to the 1800s. All aspects of folklore, including story-telling. Library resources etc. available for scholars and the generally interested.

www.home.aone.net.au/stories – An Australian site with lots of resources, including interviews with story-tellers.

www.ilhawaii.net/~stony/loreindx.html – Native American tales.

www.leadertalk.com/Pages/Communication.html – The LeaderTalk™ network. Video clips and links to other sites concerning story-telling and narrative in leadership.

www.learninghistories.com – Art Kleiner and George Roth's company, Reflection Learning Associates Inc. Contains lots of information on learning histories and related publications.

www.lilliput.co.uk/faq.html – Contains a huge range of information and frequently asked questions (FAQs) about story-telling, story-tellers, books to read, places to go, etc. Based in the UK.

www.newsgate.co.uk/uk/uk.culture.arts.storytelling/ – This is an unmoderated Usenet newsgroup with a mixed bag of discussions. The charter statement for uk.culture.arts.storytelling reads: 'For discussion of the oral tradition of story-telling in and out of the UK and Ireland, by story-tellers and those interested in story-telling alike.'

Discussion can include topics about performance issues, venues, historical roots of story-telling, reviews (including international visiting story-tellers and UK story-tellers overseas (although not of international story-telling *per se*), events, workshops, organisations (such as the Society for Story-telling) and services relevant to it.

http://www.pitt.edu/~dash/folktexts.html – D.L. Ashliman of the University of Pittsburg has compiled and/or translated a large electronic collection of folk tales and fairy-tales. Links to comprehensive information, including about the Brothers Grimm.

www.sfs.org.uk/ – The Society for Storytelling Website. Has information, networking, publications, events and so on for all those interested in story-telling. The Society produces a newsletter, (*Storylines*) and organises events.

www.storydynamics.com – Doug Lipman's Website (see Further Reading section) with hints, tips, stories and links to his Hasidic stories Website (as well as the sale of his goods and services).

www.storytellingfoundation.net/ – Storytelling Foundation International's Website, affiliated to the Smithsonian Institute. Has links to a variety of articles by well-known (American) names such as Steven Denning, Art Kleiner and Richard Stone of the StoryWork Institute via the *Journal of Storytelling and Business Excellence*.

`tech-head.com/dstory.htm` – A site for digital story-telling. Contains lots of additional resources for this specialised area, including, if you look far enough down, links to 'Story Resources Online', which is far more general.

`www.tiac.net/users/papajoe/ring/ring.htm` – A ring of connected sites offering stories, information, bibliographies and so on, mainly concerning the spoken tradition of story-telling.

`www.rider.edu/users/suler/zenstory/zenstory.html` – John Suler of Rider University's (Lawrenceville, New Jersey, USA) collection of short Zen stories.

`www.vcu.edu/hasweb/for/grimm/grimm_menu.html` – Web edition of stories by the Brothers Grimm, in English and German, from Virginia Commonwealth University's Department of Languages.

People

Gillie Bolton (Chapters 4 and 10) may be contacted about her use of writing and reflexive practice in medical and other settings, via her position as lecturer in medical humanities at: University College London School of London, Joint Department of Primary Care and Population Sciences, Whittington Hospital, London N19 5NF or e-mail `g.bolton@sheffield.ac.uk`.

Professor Petruska Clarkson (Chapter 4) D Litt et Phil, Ph.D, C Psychol, MIMC, Fellow of the British Association for Counselling and Psychotherapy, and Fellow of the British Psychological Society, can be contacted at petruska.c@dial.pipex.com or www.physis.co.uk.

Sue Hollingsworth, Ashley Ramsden and Bernard Kelly/Storytelling in Organisations (Chapters 9 and 10) can be contacted at Berrington House, Southview Road, Crowborough, East Sussex TN6 1HG. Tel: 01892 663536; `storyorg@btinternet.com`. The Emerson college Website is listed in the Web addresses section. Emerson College, Forest Row, East Sussex RH18 5JX, or e-mail `mail@emerson.org.uk`.

Art Kleiner (Chapter 9) can be contacted at 535 1st Ave, Pelham, NY 10803, USA or via his company Website (see above).

Jeanenne LaMarsh (Chapters 3 and 10), CEO of LaMarsh and Associates, Inc. may be contacted at www.lamarsh.com , 505 N. Lake Shore Drive, Suite 1210, Chicago, IL 60611.

Joan K. Levey (Chapter 10), President of Phone Joan!, may be contacted at www.phonejoan.com or 401 E. Ontario, Apt. 2102, Chicago, Illinois 60611.

Mac McCarthy (Chapter 10) can be contacted about his approaches to using metaphorical story-telling in action research and other organisational contexts at macmccarthy@yahoo.co.uk.

Sparknow/Sparkteam/Victoria Ward (Chapter 9) can be contacted at 2 Dufferin Avenue, London EC1Y 8PQ, at
sparkteam@sparknow.net or by visiting www.sparknow.net.

Index of Stories

Subject and Author Index